A Constitution for the Living

A
CONSTITUTION
FOR
THE LIVING

Imagining How Five Generations
of Americans Would Rewrite the Nation's
Fundamental Law

BEAU BRESLIN

STANFORD UNIVERSITY PRESS
Stanford, California

STANFORD UNIVERSITY PRESS
Stanford, California

Printed in the United States of America on acid-free, archival-quality paper
Library of Congress Cataloging-in-Publication Data
Names: Breslin, Beau, 1966– author.
Title: A constitution for the living : imagining how five generations of
    Americans would rewrite the nation's fundamental law / Beau Breslin.
Description: Stanford, California : Stanford University Press, 2021. |
    Includes bibliographical references and index.
Identifiers: LCCN 2020035299 (print) | LCCN 2020035300 (ebook) |
    ISBN 9780804776707 (cloth) | ISBN 9781503627543 (epub)
Subjects: LCSH: Constitutional history—United States. | Constitutional law—
    United States. | Imaginary histories. | LCGFT: Counterfactual histories.
Classification: LCC KF4541 .B74 2021 (print) | LCC KF4541 (ebook) |
    DDC 342.7302/9—dc23
LC record available at https://lccn.loc.gov/2020035299
LC ebook record available at https://lccn.loc.gov/2020035300

Cover design: Rob Ehle & Kevin Barrett Kane

Cover image: First page of the US Constitution, via Wikimedia Commons

Text design: Kevin Barrett Kane

Typeset at Stanford University Press in 11/14.4 New Baskerville

To Martha and Molly, with *enduring* love.

Contents

It is no small thing to build a new world.
BENJAMIN FRANKLIN

The people themselves must be the ultimate
makers of their own Constitution.
THEODORE ROOSEVELT

Preface

There comes a point in the self-guided tour of the National Constitution Center, America's first (and only) museum devoted entirely to the U.S. Constitution, where the hairs of every American citizen ought to stand up. This point, which arrives at the end of an outing to the Philadelphia museum, should stir the emotions. To put it mildly, there is real wonder in the moment. It marks a potentially transcendent experience, one that in the most literal sense does not come along every day. It taps into the intellectual in all of us, and it forces us to contemplate one of the most critical challenges we face as citizens of this nation. Yet most Americans have absolutely no idea what they are experiencing.

The moment occurs when one enters Signers' Hall, the room at the end of the tour, which is filled with life-sized bronze statues of all the delegates to the federal Constitutional Convention. One enters the room and is literally confronted by the "Founding Fathers." Benjamin Franklin is there, sitting at a table, cane in hand. So is James Madison, who stands behind a second table, seemingly watching over all the proceedings. George Washington, at six foot three, towers over the other constitutional signers and, indeed, most of the museum's visitors as well. Alexander

Hamilton (whose radical ideas were about as popular as he was) stands, fittingly, alone in the center of the room. Gouverneur Morris, James Wilson, John Dickinson, and all the rest of those who framed America's fundamental law are positioned throughout the space. Even the three delegates who refused to sign the constitutional text—George Mason and Edmund Randolph of Virginia and Elbridge Gerry of Massachusetts—are present in the room, though they are decidedly on the periphery. The room itself is also a fitting shrine to America's most important constitution-makers. Its dimensions are identical to the original space used for the drafting and signing of the Constitution—the Assembly Room in Independence Hall that stands just two blocks down the road. The ceiling is high in Signers' Hall; the walls are adorned with stately bookshelves, and the lighting is such that the atmosphere is both somber and celebratory.

Yet it isn't the objects in the room or the room itself that should stir the soul. The private emotion one feels in Signers' Hall is not necessarily about reverence for the Constitution and what it has come to represent or for the individuals who drafted the text over 230 years ago. Rather, the sensation citizens experience in that room should come from the *active* role they are asked to play in that moment. Each visitor to that room is invited to either endorse or renounce the Constitution—to either ratify or reject the country's most important public document. Think about that. Visitors to the museum are being asked to consider whether they, like the figures in the room, would sign the Constitution. We are constitutional Founders at that particular moment.[1]

Although some would argue that the stakes for us as visitors in Signers' Hall are much lower than the ones confronting the founding generation, I disagree. We are in essence replicating the actions of the first Federalists and the anti-Federalists through the self-conscious act of placing our names on "paper." We are figurative members of the 1787 Constitutional Convention, or at least of the state Ratifying Conventions, when we decide whether we still believe in the promises and the power of our governing constitutional charter. In that instant, we can pretend to be the eighteenth-century merchant who endorsed the Constitution because he believed increased economic stability would come from a greater concentration of power in the federal government, or instead, we can imagine ourselves as the early American farmer who rejected the Constitution because he believed in the small-scale republicanism that characterized political society under the Articles of Confederation. We can pretend to be those early American citizens at the same time that we remain twenty-first-century citizens wrestling with our own perspectives on the continued worth of the constitutional document. While thinking about the narrative of America's constitutional experience through the ebbs and flows of history, we can simultaneously be the contemporary craftsperson, or nurse, or mechanic, or lawyer who is convinced that the Constitution no longer reflects the true complexities of a modern American state and the current teacher who does. We can be the supporter who insists the Constitution is the greatest political invention in history and the member of a minority or marginalized group whose experience of living under the Constitution has not been so positive. The point is, our active involvement in the ratification or rejection of the Constitution demands our focused attention and our most contemplative skills. It asks us to decide what we truly think of the Constitution—whether we are prepared to ratify the text or not—and then to seal that decision with our signature. The moment is pregnant with imagination and significance.

Today, the process is entirely electronic. One signs (or refuses to sign) a computer tablet, and the signature temporarily appears in the on-screen replica of the Constitution, alongside the original Framers' signatures. It's a neat and technologically sophisticated process. More importantly, one is making a political commitment, much like taking an oath in that it requires an assertive act: "(re)affirming one's fidelity to the original constitutional instrument by [in effect] placing pen to paper (parchment?), and *publicly* acknowledging acceptance."[2] Sanford Levinson probably says it best: "Presumably, adding one's signature would serve to transform the experience from a mere remembrance of times past to a renewed dedication to—a continuing ordination of, as it were—the Constitution as an ever-living presence encouraging the establishment of a more perfect Union committed above all to the realization of justice and the blessings of liberty."[3] Of course, visitors are not without a choice at this moment. Though the museum's preference is clearly that visitors will endorse the Constitution—in fact, the statue of Abraham Baldwin of Georgia, complete with quill pen in hand, has been cast in such a way that he is pointing directly to the place to sign the Constitution— guests can walk away from ratification.

For a citizenry wrestling with weighty principles such as patriotism, liberty, equality, sovereignty—a citizenry that absorbs hysteria and hyperbole from both sides of the political aisle—Signers' Hall presents a significant opportunity. If taken seriously, there is perhaps no greater symbolic moment for an American. Indeed, it is a powerful act of patriotism to contemplate the authority of the Constitution and then to decide whether or not to lend one's signature to the document. Unfortunately, the magnitude of the experience at Signers' Hall is often lost on the museum's many visitors. According to officials at the National Constitution Center, Signers' Hall has not yet lived up to the lofty expectations of the museum's architects, who deliberately designed the space to compel individuals to confront the choices inherent in the act of ratification. They wanted the public to ponder the seriousness of a commitment to democratic self-rule, to take part in a personal referendum on the continuing importance of America's Constitution, and to deliberately choose whether to ratify. In one sense, the museum designers are almost certainly being too hard on themselves. It is probably fair to assume that most citizens who self-consciously decide to *reject* the Constitution are doing so for some specific reason and are not acting casually. Sadly, we can't always say the same for the majority of those who approve the Constitution. Blind faith probably rears its unthinking head for many Americans, those who instinctually gravitate toward endorsement because they think they should.

Many Americans, I suspect, don't give the opportunity more than a moment's thought. They sign the tablet in favor of ratification and proceed directly to the gift shop.

It's a missed opportunity. Each of us should make time to reflect on the practice of contemporary ratification; in fact, we have a profound responsibility to consider what exactly we are doing when we stand in Signers' Hall with pen in hand. As American citizens, we should continually engage in that personal referendum that asks us to determine the Constitution's enduring value. In short, we should contemplate the authority of the Constitution on our lives, and we should do it regularly. Signers' Hall gives us a concrete assignment to get us thinking about the worth of the Constitution, but the exercise it represents—reflecting on America's experiment in constitutional government—could and should be a more important part of our daily lives.

Don't get me wrong. I do not mean to suggest that we should ponder the Constitution in a shallow or superficial way. Often politicians and pundits will seize the opportunity to celebrate or condemn the Constitution because doing so will advance their particular partisan objectives. I may appear overly cynical, but I suspect many public officials wave the Constitution in front of our faces in nothing more than a ceremonial attempt to convince us of their commitment to some broad and vague notion of patriotism, just as the leaders of the 112th Congress (both Republican and Democrat) appeared to do when they read the Constitution out loud on the floor of the House on January 6, 2011, their first full day in power for that session, or as former Speaker of the House John Boehner did by announcing at a rally that he was "going to stand here with the Founding Fathers, who wrote in the Preamble, 'We hold these truths to be self-evident, that all men are created equal, that they are endowed by their Creator with certain unalienable Rights, that among these are Life, Liberty and the pursuit of Happiness.'"[4] Never mind that it was the Declaration of Independence and not the Constitution he was quoting; the moment struck many as shallow and phony—political theater at its finest.

Such displays are not what I am talking about here. Contemporary ratification of the Constitution requires something deeper, something far more significant than just reading the words of the document on the floor of the House of Representatives or being vaguely familiar with a few of its provisions. The decision to ratify is, simultaneously, infinitely private and immensely public. It represents a personal choice about one's fidelity to a written Constitution, and it becomes part of a collective dialogue about the extent to which the Constitution still resonates with the public.

Doubtless modern Federalists outnumber contemporary anti-Federalists. That fact says something about America's fidelity to its Constitution, to be sure. We are at least comfortable with the Constitution, as it exists today. But the sizeable number of constitutional critics also says something. It reminds us of those eighteenth-century opponents of the Constitution—men like Patrick Henry, Richard Henry Lee, George Clinton, and Robert Yates—who contested ratification precisely because they believed the Constitution was flawed. "The Constitution is a racist document because it protected slavery in its original incarnation," some of today's critics argue; "it is sexist," say others, "because it took almost a century and a half to amend it to include suffrage for women"; "it does not speak to the modern American," remarks a third group, "because it does not adequately account for contemporary problems like the lack of health care, immigration concerns, or the rising budget deficit."

Make no mistake: there is measurable dissatisfaction with our governmental systems and with the politicians who occupy our local, state, and national political offices. A good portion of the public would likely choose to replace parts or the whole of the Constitution if given the chance. Our veneration for the Constitution protects the document in the abstract, but the individual provisions, clauses, and rules embedded in the Constitution are not immune from serious attack. With the right questions, the results of a nationwide referendum on the enduring relevance of the Constitution would indeed be interesting.[5]

I suspect any referendum would support my untested hypothesis that Americans often think casually about the broad contours of their Constitution—they sign the text because they think they should—but that they are not similarly relaxed when pressed about the implications of the document's failures. Yes, we love the Constitution and don't think a new one is necessary; but we sure are discouraged about how the document has helped foster a hopelessly broken government. We eagerly ratify the text in Signers' Hall, but then we criticize the political systems and institutions that the Constitution spawns practically as soon as we exit the museum. Members of both major political parties lambast government officials while calling for a restoration of the Constitution's basic principles, not quite putting together the possibility that the Constitution itself may be partly to blame. Conservatives claim that we need greater fidelity to the text as it was originally written, but they can't escape the irony that neither the document nor the Framers identify a favored interpretive approach. It seems the Constitution is taking a beating even as we claim to venerate it.

We can't have it both ways. Or, I should say, having it both ways promotes an uneasy relationship between America's citizens and their Constitution. All of this begs a simple question: If there is measurable discontent with the Constitution and the political institutions it has created, is it time to return to Philadelphia and convene a new federal constitutional convention? Perhaps the 88 percent of Americans who reported that the Constitution still works today might approach the question differently if there were something more at stake in Signers' Hall, if that moment captured the gravitas it deserves. Is now the time to try again? Has the Constitution outlived its usefulness? What if we knew that there were millions of visitors to Signers' Hall who self-consciously rejected the Constitution? Would that trouble us? Would that be enough contemporary anti-Federalist opposition to get our attention? What about tens of millions? Does the number of ratifiers even matter if most Americans can't even recall much about the specifics of our current constitutional text?[6] Are the constitutional naysayers criticizing the text because they don't support particular items found within its pages (think Electoral College), or are they genuinely focused on a comprehensive constitutional overhaul?

These questions (and so many more) spring from the exercise in Signers' Hall, and they inform the entirety of this book. The *answers* to the questions are important, and were I a more capable political scientist I might endeavor to design certain experiments and instruments to uncover them. But I am more interested in the questions themselves, in the idea and consequence of revisiting the constitutional text from time to time and contemplating a complete overhaul. This book is about constitutional renewal, about imagining comprehensive constitutional change. I am not focused on the collective intelligence of the American people—what we might call America's citizenship quotient—when it comes to issues related to the constitutional text. Certainly, I am made somewhat uneasy by the ignorance of the American public on basic constitutional questions, but others are more capable of evaluating the particulars of that phenomenon than I am. Nor am I focused on the ways in which institutions interpret and misinterpret our constitutional document, leading to understandable frustration among some pockets of the population. Those too are concerns that are better left to a different book. Instead, my central focus is on the process, and possibility, of constitutional renewal.

History is a powerful tool for the student of America's constitutional experiment, and we will examine it through the lens of one of the founding generation's most intriguing, and important, disagreements: the debate between Jefferson and Madison on the value and legitimacy of an enduring constitutional document. Jefferson was clearly of the mind that each generation should write its own constitution—that one generation should not control another—whereas Madison argued that a constitution must endure across many generations—across long stretches of time—in order to amass the credibility and legitimacy it needs to successfully order a political regime. They fiercely debated this exact question throughout their long lives. Crucially, this debate is alive and well in the symbolic moment of ratification. The individual choice we make in Signers' Hall is precisely an exercise in choosing between the Madisonian view of enduring constitutions and the Jeffersonian position favoring generational Constitutions. When we decide to ratify or reject the Constitution, we become participants in this debate.

Ultimately, then, my goal in this volume is twofold: first, to imagine what the U.S. Constitutions would have looked like throughout America's history if Jefferson had won that debate, and second, to take up the ultimate present-day question: should we return to Philadelphia to draft a new Constitution? That's the main reason I am especially curious about why visitors to Signers' Hall choose to ratify or to reject the Constitution. Reflecting on the meaning and importance of the Constitution, and then taking the active step to signal acceptance or rejection of the text, is but one step removed from a broader and more important conversation about whether now is the time to scrap the constitutional experiment and start all over. I hope this book in some way contributes to that conversation.

But let's not get ahead of ourselves. First, a story. We begin the task of imagining constitutions exactly two years after the American Constitution was proposed to the public: September 17th, 1789. On that date, Thomas Jefferson hosted a secret, and important, dinner gathering. The topic of conversation that night was constitutions.

A Constitution for the Living

1787

An Introduction

THOMAS JEFFERSON LOVED everything about Paris, though
the circumstances of his appointment as minister to France might
suggest otherwise. He arrived in August 1784, still grieving the
death of his beloved wife, Martha, who had succumbed to massive bleeding two years earlier while giving birth to their sixth
child, Lucy Elizabeth. Jefferson's friends and confidants, seeing
that the stately Virginian probably needed a change of scenery,
encouraged him to take the post as America's principal diplomat
in France. Jefferson jumped at the opportunity.

Jefferson was also delighted by his appointment, though his
new job was anything but easy. Probably the most important diplomatic assignment for an American overseas, the minister to
France was constantly observed and scrutinized. He was expected
to participate in the conversations of the day and to represent
the United States with the utmost decorum. Of course, Jefferson's task was made all the more difficult because he was sent
to Paris to replace an ailing Benjamin Franklin and an ornery
John Adams. It was the replacement of Franklin that unnerved
Jefferson. As everyone knew at the time, Franklin was a tough act
to follow. Though charming in his own right, Jefferson did not

possess the same public charisma and allure that made Franklin so popular. But he shared at least some things with Franklin: a deep intellect and a passion for politics and, more specifically, for the importance of transitions in political order that must occur from time to time. He famously quipped, "a little rebellion now and then is a good thing."[1]

Jefferson held those same passions and beliefs on the evening of September 17th, 1789. September 17th, of course, marked an important anniversary in his mind, as it was on this day two years earlier that the delegates to the American Constitutional Convention had completed their work and signed the unratified Constitution. Now, two years later, September 17th would again prove to be an important day in the development of modern constitutionalism. On this day Jefferson called a secret dinner meeting in his Paris residence—on the Rue de Barry—and the topic of conversation was the future of constitutional government.[2] The guest list was small. Fellow American Gouverneur Morris, who was in France to try his hand at international business, was invited. So was the Marquis de Lafayette, George Washington's confidant and strategist during much of the Revolutionary War. Lafayette had recently been appointed Commander in Chief of the French National Guard, and he would play a key role in the brewing French rebellion. Lafayette had caught Jefferson's eye because he had helped to draft the French Declaration of the Rights of Man and of the Citizen, a document that promoted some of the same basic themes found in the U.S. Declaration of Independence, Constitution, and Bill of Rights and in the Virginia Declaration of Rights.

The Duc de La Rochefoucauld was also expected that evening, a nobleman who, like the others, was deeply sympathetic to the American Revolution and the principles of universal liberty and expansive equality. He endeared himself to the Americans living in Paris during the founding period—including Franklin, Adams, and Jefferson—by translating the American state constitutions and publishing them anonymously in a volume that was widely read by European elites.

The final guest that night was the Marquis de Condorcet, perhaps the most famous of the French invitees. He, too, had much in common with Jefferson. A shy and potentially volatile man, Condorcet's intellect placed him way ahead of his time. He was, for example, a vocal supporter of equality for women, as well as for an unregulated economy and a free public education for his country's citizenry. He was also an innovative and creative mathematician (which further endeared him to Jefferson). The Frenchman would come to be known as the father of social choice theory and the inventor of various electoral systems. Condorcet's invitation to the dinner party, though, was extended because he was well respected as an expert on written constitutionalism. Much of that expertise came from looking over the Atlantic to the experiment in constitutionalism that was unfolding in the newly independent United States. He was quick to praise the language of the Declaration of Independence and he admired the U.S. Constitution so much that he believed it was bound to change the future of ordered government. He called the Virginia Declaration of Rights "the first Bill of Rights to merit the name." And he wanted those same things for France.

In all, five gentlemen sat around the dinner table talking politics that night. The dinner was early by contemporary standards; Lafayette arrived last, at four o'clock. The menu was extravagant, with food and wine befitting the stature of the guests. It would be the final time Jefferson dined with this group, as he would set sail for the United States just three weeks later. On everyone's mind was the rapid development of the French Revolution. The guests were no doubt on high alert, worried at least in part about how their public comments over the past months might be used by revolutionaries to stir further unrest. In July, rebels had stormed the Bastille, releasing only a handful of prisoners but signaling to the nobles (and the world) that the *ancien regime* was in real jeopardy. By mid-September, around the time of Jefferson's secret dinner, things in France were unraveling in ways almost no one could predict.

The time was ripe, Jefferson thought, for a conversation about constitutions. The Virginian believed that the American Revolution and the French Revolution shared many of the same basic characteristics—a commitment to natural rights, an abhorrence of tyranny, a longing for self-determination and popular sovereignty—and that the circumstances in Paris were beginning to resemble the circumstances in the United States during the decade preceding the drafting of the U.S. Constitution.

Most American and French Founders believed that a key to stable government was to establish the (political) rules of the game prior to the (political) game's starting, and then to write those rules down in some fundamental law. That is, embed the specifics about governmental rule in a form that makes political leaders accountable for their actions and that the citizens could point to if they felt abused. The British Constitution, though admired around the table and around the world, did not quite get at what the dinner guests were after: it was not a single, codified constitutional document that stood apart from the policies and rules passed by the British Parliament. Instead, the British Constitution was (and still is) a series of parliamentary enactments, policies, judicial decisions, customs, and the like that, taken together, form the basis of British political rule.

Jefferson and others of his generation wanted to try something altogether new: a single written constitution for an expansive republic. These late eighteenth-century Founders insisted that the people could ensure political accountability, making leaders answerable to the general principles of the revolution and to the public at large, if they could textualize constitutional rules in a single document.

The major political theorists of the eighteenth century, including Madison, Hamilton, and the diners at Jefferson's residence that night, were true constitutionalists. To be a proponent of modern constitutionalism requires a certain, not always flattering, outlook on the human condition. For the most part, these men distrusted individuals, especially those in power. Madison famously wrote, in *Federalist* 51: "If men were angels, no government would be necessary."[3] But men were (and are) not angels, and so he and other constitutionalists structured modern politics in such a way as to prevent the concentration of power in the hands of one individual or one branch of government. They understood that constitutions were one piece of a complex set of structures and mechanisms—structures that included popular sovereignty, representative government, divisions of power, bills of rights, and so on—that, if all worked well together, might prevent the possible rise of tyranny.[4]

Jefferson, of course, was not present at the American Constitutional Convention, but he was intimately familiar with the process of constitution-making, having partnered with George Mason, James Madison, and others on the drafting of the original Virginia Constitution in 1776. He was also an impressive student of constitutional foundings. He had studied with great acuity the proposed American Constitution, commenting to Madison a few months after the drafting of the Constitution on all the virtues, as well as the vices, of the document.

Jefferson was also a man of opportunity. Doubtless he held some regret about missing the Constitutional Convention in Philadelphia, but he saw his opportunity to contribute to the making of a constitution in France. He and his dinner guests were convinced that the French National Assembly would act both as a representative body and a constitutional drafting convention. A new constitution for France, they thought, was inevitable. The events in France immediately preceding the dinner bolstered their confidence. One in particular was prescient: when King Louis XVI barred the door to the chambers of the Estates-General, France's primary representative body, the members of the Third Estate—all 577 of them—convened on an indoor tennis court and managed to sign the "Tennis Court Oath," a pledge "not to separate, and to reassemble wherever circumstances require, until the constitution of the kingdom was established." The members of the now barred Third Estate renamed their body the "National Assembly" and identified themselves as the true sovereign power in France.

This event appealed to Jefferson's revolutionary affections, as well as to his constitutional sensibilities. It stirred his emotions and fired his spirit. It reminded him of the intellectual fortification that the oppressed so often feel when they are threatened. In the United States, the results of that shared urgency were the Declaration of Independence and eventually a series of written constitutions. Unsurprisingly, Jefferson saw similarities in the comments of members of the new National Assembly in France and of his rebellious friends in the United States. The primary message that emerged from that famous tennis court on June 20th, 1789, was that France needed a new, and more importantly, *written*, Constitution.

All periods of human history are marked by some major innovation, and the period of the late eighteenth century is well-known for its invention of new political systems and ideas, the greatest of which was the fully written constitutional text. Empowering institutions, controlling political authority, setting aspiring goals for a polity, resolving conflict among governmental branches—these are the ingredients of a comprehensive and effective modern constitutional text. Beginning with state constitutions in the United States and extending to America's 1787 Constitution and to France's 1791 Constitution, countries around the world began to embrace the idea of written constitutionalism.[5] Now, all but three nations—Great Britain, New Zealand, and Israel—rely on a textual constitution as the primary (though not exclusive) means to order political authority.[6]

It was a risky endeavor. To put faith in the concept that political leaders would somehow abide by constitutional passages—no more than mere words on a page—is breathtakingly bold. What would give Madison, Hamilton, and Jefferson, as well as their French colleagues, any confidence that the sovereign might tolerate predetermined limitations on its power when prior experience suggested that monarchs were willing to go to almost any length to maintain power? And yet it *did* work.

Perhaps the fact that the birth of modern constitutionalism happened to coincide with the Enlightenment-inspired wave of shifting power from the few to the many—that is, with the emergence of popular sovereignty as the preferred form of governance—had something to do with the success of the experiment. No doubt a citizenry, rather than a single monarch, would find it difficult to circumvent agreed-upon rules. Perhaps the belief, spawned by many Enlightenment thinkers, that politics could be reduced to scientific analysis made it more palatable to put faith in the written word. Hamilton famously referred to the new science of politics and insisted that it, "like most other sciences, has received great improvement,"[7] including the introduction of the written constitutional instrument. Still, to build a polity on the concept of ideas transcribed on a piece of parchment is certainly audacious.

Americans have tried this audacious experiment at the national level only twice.[8] To put that number into context, consider what has gone on in the rest of the world. The Comparative Constitutions Project notes that over 2,200 constitutions have been written or substantially revised since 1789. That's an average of more than fifteen constitutions per nation over the past two centuries, or roughly one new constitution for each country every fifteen years. Project experts say "that most constitutions die young, and only a handful last longer than fifty years."[9] When contemplating these data one cannot help but think that constitutions are fragile, that most will flame out fairly quickly, and that only a tiny handful will have the staying power to endure beyond a generation or two.

We have examples of both here in the United States. The lifespan of America's first constitution—the Articles of Confederation and Perpetual Union—was a mere eleven years, if we calculate constitutional life-spans from the moment of drafting to the moment the next one is written. The current U.S. Constitution, however, is a good bit older than the country's initial experiment in written constitutionalism. It has lasted 230-plus years, and it seems unlikely to fold anytime soon. Both environmental and design factors contribute to the failure of most modern constitutions. Some fail because the design of the institutions was not adequate to properly order the polity and provide the necessary liberty and security a modern people expect. Others have an admirable institutional design but fail because the political, economic, and social environment is not conducive to sustaining the important purpose of the constitution.[10] Most fail because of the challenging interplay between design and environmental features. Of course, design features and environmental factors can also ensure the survival of a constitutional instrument, just as they can promote the longevity of some of the world's fundamental laws.

America's first constitution was born out of necessity. The situation at the time of America's split with Great Britain forced leaders to create a fresh political world largely out of ether. America's early Founders had never constructed a political constitution—a written plan for political organization—that united the various states.[11] And yet becoming a new, loosely united country literally overnight forced constitutional drafters into quick action.

Thankfully, by the late 1770s, the framers of the Articles of Confederation and Perpetual Union were quite familiar with the task of constitution-making if not union-making. In fact, the political landscape during the Revolutionary War was as fertile as any in modern history for drafting constitutional texts. Newly independent states were eager to announce to each other, and to the world, that they were sovereign entities. They did so by writing and then ratifying constitutional texts. These states wanted to counter the idea of arbitrary and capricious rule by placing their guidelines for governance on paper, where they could be seen and (roughly) understood by all. Most state legislators undertook the task of hammering out a formal text for their state shortly before or just after the Union declared independence on July 4th, 1776. By the winter of 1776, eight states had drafted and ratified constitutions: Delaware, Maryland, New Hampshire, New Jersey, North Carolina, Pennsylvania, South Carolina, and Virginia. Less than a year later, New York and Georgia joined that group. In

1780, Massachusetts would finally get around to drafting its own constitutional text. Even the Vermont Republic, not yet a formal state, convened legislators in 1777 to draft its own constitution.

A few states undertook the process of drafting a constitution more than once during this stretch. From the thirteen former colonies plus Vermont, fifteen constitutions emerged in the four-year span between 1776 and 1780; nine were written by drafting committees made up of state legislators or by the entire state legislature acting as one big drafting committee, while six originated in separate bodies called constitutional conventions, a novel idea at the time. What is equally noteworthy is that two states—Connecticut and Rhode Island—chose to remain under the authority of their original colonial charters. It was not until well into the nineteenth century that they finally put pen to parchment and constructed constitutional documents.

Ratification of these constitutions was a different story. Few states considered whether to seek popular ratification, and only one, Massachusetts, would formally present its proposed text to the people (mainly through its town hall meetings). State legislators worried that their proposed constitutions would not be ratified and they would be left having to revise or redo them in their entirety. There was not yet the understanding that ratification itself could be a positive force for constitutional and regime stability. In contrast to the experience of the states, the power "the people" held over ratification of the U.S. Constitution a decade later, and the legitimacy ratification lent to the ultimate adoption of that governmental instrument, would be among the important design features and environmental factors that guaranteed the text's success.

That second constitution—the 1787 Constitution that remains in place today—was also born out of necessity and experience. Thus, the constitutional Framers in 1787 were familiar, perhaps even comfortable, with the task of drafting a fundamental law. We've been down this road before, many thought, and so we can surely do it again. These newly selected Framers also felt a sense of urgency in the moment. The Articles of Confederation were perceived at the state level as only moderately effective, whatever success they had was probably due to their light touch in local affairs. Most leaders at the time favored a governing structure in which the bulk of power resided in the states, and that is what the Articles promised. But strip off the veneer, and it was pretty clear that a change had to be made. Nationalists like James Madison, Alexander Hamilton, and James Wilson argued that, at a minimum, alterations to the existing Articles were required. What is more likely is that these Founding Fathers secretly hoped they might commence the constitution-making process anew.

Those Framers who advocated for constitutional renewal leading up to the federal Constitutional Convention of 1787 were fighting a different revolution from the one just a decade earlier. But it was no less a revolution. They too imagined a distinctive political world, one that their extant Constitution and governing bodies could not deliver. It is true that blood was not widely shed in order to change from the Articles of Confederation to the Constitution of the United States of America, and yet in a sense, comparing the ways in which the newly independent states fought to rid themselves of British rule and the ways in which the 1787 Founders battled to rid themselves of a largely impotent political system suggests at least a few similarities. Both the American Revolution and the revolutionary act of constitution-making in Philadelphia represent decisive efforts to introduce political structures that would guarantee liberty and moderation. The 1787 Constitution is no less an attempt to promote "life, liberty, and the pursuit of happiness" than is the Declaration of Independence. Consider Hamilton's words in *Federalist* 1: "Yes, my countrymen, I own to you that, after giving [the proposed constitution] an attentive consideration, I am clearly of opinion it is your interest to adopt it. I am convinced that this is the safest course for your liberty, your dignity, and your happiness."

The Framers of the 1787 Constitution chose the words of the entire text carefully, and the particulars of the Preamble were a response to the recently concluded colonial experience. Consider the Framers' concern over a just society. It is no coincidence that they used the word *establish* to provide context for that aspiration. To them, the narrative of the previous twenty years was one of injustice and abuse of power—embargoes, illegal taxes, tyrannical public officers, and so on. The Declaration of Independence itself identifies dozens of complaints against England's King George III. Hence, the Framers of the U.S. Constitution believed that they had to start from scratch and *establish* a culture of justice, not just preserve or continue one. They needed to identify the very conditions required to alter the political environment and achieve a just polity. And then they had to design and build the institutions (including the Constitution itself!) to realize that goal. At the most basic level, then, the battle for independence was forged over the sense of personal and political freedom that accompanies genuine self-determination. Patriots recognized that as long as they lived under the wing of British rule, the very aspirations that generated the Revolutionary War in the first place, and that eventually characterized the Constitution's Preamble, would remain elusive.

The formal process of drafting America's first national constitution began one month before the country's literal birth on July 4th, 1776. The exact date was June 7th and the place was a sweltering and uncomfortably humid Philadelphia. Richard Henry Lee, a highly respected statesman and lawyer from Virginia, sat in the Philadelphia Statehouse (now known as Independence Hall) along with more than fifty other delegates to the Second Continental Congress. He rose that afternoon to propose a radical resolution. It was, in fact, a resolution in three parts. The first part called for immediate independence from Great Britain. Of course, the Continental Congress had been debating the wisdom of declaring independence for some time, but Lee's resolution essentially called the question. The time for debate was closing: the delegates would have to vote up or down on whether to formally adopt a statement of divorce from the British Empire. The second part of Lee's resolution called for the states to form "foreign alliances," connections with countries across the ocean. Yet it was the third part of the resolution that most intrigued the constitution-makers in the room. Let a "plan of confederation be prepared and transmitted to the respective Colonies for their consideration and approbation," Lee declared. Let us consider the type of government we want and commend that design to parchment. In short, let us draft a national constitution.

Others quickly lined up with the Virginian. John Adams stood to second the proposal and several delegates around the room nodded in agreement. The entire delegation was not ready to approve the three-part resolution just yet, but votes in favor of each proposal would come in the weeks and months ahead. On that day, the wheels were set in motion to fundamentally alter the colonies and the world. The nation would officially file for divorce from the only national government it knew, and in the process, it would begin the task of imagining an entirely new vision for its political future. The Lee resolution is rightly remembered for starting the formal procedure of drafting the Declaration of Independence, but it should also be celebrated for commencing the process of national constitution-making in this country. The resolution, at eighty total words, may be, pound for pound—or rather word for word—second only to the Gettysburg Address in importance to the American polity.

The Continental Congress determined that the first order of business was to form a drafting committee and to select a leader to manage the writing process. Unsurprisingly, the responsibility for creating a constitutional document would remain with the legislative body. On June 12th, 1776, a committee was fashioned to draw up a version of a constitution, and John Dickinson was chosen to head the group. Dickinson knew that another committee, which included Thomas Jefferson, John Adams, Benjamin Franklin, Roger Sherman, and Robert Livingston, had been charged with constructing a declaration of independence. He worried about the outcome of that committee's work—he ultimately refused to sign the Declaration of Independence—but he also recognized that his document, which represented the logical outgrowth of birthing a new nation, required his full attention. He thus took on the assignment and, along with twelve other delegates to the Continental Congress (one from each state), set out to draft a constitutional text.

His task was arduous, but it was not without a few guideposts. First, there were the previously mentioned state constitutions that were beginning to pop up. Then, there was already an outline of the eventual Articles of Confederation floating around the legislative chamber that Dickinson and his colleagues occupied. Just a year earlier, Benjamin Franklin had outlined a plan for union that he called a "sketch of Articles of Confederation." That was presented to the Second Continental Congress in July 1775, and though never adopted, it would form the basis of Dickinson's draft a year later. Dickinson copied the structure of Franklin's proposal—each text had exactly 13 articles—as well as much of the substance. Seeing what amounted to a preliminary version of the Articles of Confederation and Perpetual Union comforted Dickinson and the drafting committee, producing a sense of familiarity. Exactly one month after initiating the writing, Dickinson laid the committee's draft of the Articles of Confederation and Perpetual Union before the Continental Congress' famous President, John Hancock; their task now complete.

Congressional debate ensued. Dickinson of course was not present through it all, having been dismissed as a member of the Continental Congress by virtue of his opposition to independence. For the next seventeen months, a committee of the whole—the entire Continental Congress—discussed the particulars of the draft constitution. Article I was innocuous enough; it identified the country's name: "the United States of America," which represented the first official pronouncement of that title. Article II, which clearly and unequivocally announced the impenetrability of the states' individual "sovereignty, freedom, and independence," was also comparatively well received. Subsequent articles were fiercely debated, however, including those defining representation in Congress and the percentage of funds each state should pony up to keep the federal government running (it was eventually agreed that states would contribute based on geographical size).

Finally, in November 1777, the Second Continental Congress adopted the Articles of Confederation and Perpetual Union. All that remained was ratification by the states; no easy task to be sure. The message to the state Ratifying Conventions that accompanied the newly drafted Articles hinted at the delicacy of the enterprise. It came in the form of a letter. The business of writing America's first constitution, the letter began, in order "[t]o form a permanent union, accommodated to the opinion and wishes of the delegates of so many states, differing in habits, produce, commerce, and internal police, was found to be a work which nothing but time and reflection, conspiring with a disposition to conciliate, could mature and accomplish." It continued: "Hardly is it to be expected that any plan, in the variety of provisions essential to our union, should exactly correspond with the maxims and political views of every particular state."[12]

The letter, in many ways, was an admission of the difficulties of finding common ground among delegates from the various states. Though most states would ratify the text in 1778, America's first constitutional document, the Articles of Confederation and Perpetual Union, would not become official until Maryland voted in favor of ratification on March 1st, 1781. In all, the process of bringing America's first constitution into existence took almost half a decade.

The 1787 U.S. Constitution was hardly swifter in coming. The Articles of Confederation have received a bad rap in the two-plus centuries since they were adopted, and much of the criticism is certainly warranted. The Articles failed to remedy problems associated with a war-torn economy, an underdeveloped foreign commerce stream, and an aggressive expansionist agenda, all the things a fledgling country desperately wants to manage. No doubt they were also part of the reason for the rise of rebellious activity in the various states. By 1786, nationalists such as James Madison and Alexander Hamilton were deeply skeptical about the long-term utility of the nation's inaugural constitution.

Ideas for constitutional repair would be discussed in statehouses, taverns, homes—almost everywhere across the country[13]—such was the politically electric environment. But the real plan for revision and renewal would be hatched in Annapolis, Maryland. There, a group of twelve statesmen from five states met between September 11th and September 14th, 1786, to consider structural ways in which they might buoy the listing national government. The formal title for the assembly says it all: "Meeting of Commissioners to Remedy Defects of the Federal Government."

John Dickinson would again lead the proceedings, but it was a young, diminutive Virginian who provided the intellectual energy for the occasion. James Madison was eager to get at the Articles of Confederation. He wrote, "every word decides a question between power and liberty."[14] He believed that a more capable and powerful national government was necessary for the country to succeed, and that the Articles were insufficient to get Americans to the promised land. He was not alone in his opinion. The entire Annapolis group acknowledged the severe shortcomings of the Articles and proposed that a "deliberate and candid discussion, in some mode, which will unite the Sentiments and Councils of all the States," was needed. It was subsequently decided to invite representatives from all states to a constitutional convention the following summer. "Deeply impressed with the magnitude and importance of the object confided to them," the Annapolis participants concluded that they could not "forbear to indulge an expression of their earnest and unanimous wish, that speedy measures be taken, to effect a general meeting, of the States, in a future Convention."[15] All eyes would thus shift to Philadelphia.

To assemble in convention had not been the traditional approach to constitution-making up to that point. Around the time of the Articles, state *legislators* were primarily tasked with writing state constitutions, often as part of their regular legislative business. The Second Continental Congress itself was the body that drafted the Articles of Confederation. Over time, however, the preferred venue for constitution-making shifted from legislatures to separate (though probably no more independent) drafting conventions. Oliver Ellsworth of Connecticut noticed the shift:

"A new set of ideas," he remarked, "seemed to have crept in since the Articles of Confederation were established. Conventions of the people, or with power derived expressly from the people, were not then thought of."[16]

This shift from legislatures to drafting conventions spoke to John Dickinson. He supported the idea of a constitutional convention in 1787 and was proud to represent Delaware at the proceedings. He wanted to be there for many reasons, not the least of which was a sense of duty and humility. He knew that he brought constitution-making skills to the table and, even more, a passion for popular sovereignty. The people, he insisted, should retain the ultimate power to adopt an amended (or even new) Constitution. He would not let fellow delegates forget that fundamental principle.

Because of illness, Dickinson arrived in Philadelphia a few days late and left several weeks early. And yet he played a very significant role in shaping the new Constitution that summer. Ever the moderate, he proposed several ideas that were eventually adopted by the delegation, including the election of Senators by state legislators and the use of an Electoral College to select the President. Noted historian Forrest McDonald insists that Dickinson's moderating voice during the convention deliberations paved the way for the eventual ratification of the Constitution. He tempered the nationalists in Philadelphia, McDonald argues, who wanted to vest more authority in the central government.[17] Dickinson helped to craft some of the most important design features of America's current Constitution, features that include bicameralism, an independent judiciary, the delegation of powers, the process of constitutional amendment, and the importance of constitutional ratification. All of these features, and the other major components of the text, were in some ways a consequence of the perceived failures of the Articles of Confederation. The political environment forced certain choices.

Once finished with the drafting process, Dickinson immediately saw it as his civic responsibility to defend the product that emerged from the 1787 Constitutional Convention. He took up the pen to try to convince his fellow citizens of the virtues of the proposed constitutional text. Like so many others of his time, he chose to do this by writing letters under a pseudonym and sending them to a newspaper. For Dickinson, that meant the *Delaware Gazette*. In April 1788, Dickinson published a series of letters in his home-state newspaper, and he did so under the name "Fabius," a Roman statesman and military general most famous for inventing the tactics that would later be known as guerilla warfare.

What is most interesting is that there is no hint from Dickinson that the proceedings of the Constitutional Convention were in any way illegal or illegitimate. Quite the contrary; Fabius believed in the authority of that body and the legitimacy of the text it produced. He did so because all power ultimately rested with "the people." What emerged from the drafting convention was a proposal. Nothing more. The power to ratify or reject the proposed Constitution was not left to the fifty-five delegates in Philadelphia—*that* would have been illegal, Dickinson thought— but rather to the farmers in Pennsylvania and the merchants in Massachusetts, the landed gentry in Georgia and the small property owners in South Carolina. In short, the citizenry. And, yes, that included the anti-Federalists around the country, who were skeptical of the new text and concerned that they might surrender their way of life. They, too, were citizens of these newly independent United States, and they, too, must have a say. Ratification, to Dickinson, was the key. Much as he had done a decade earlier when he relinquished the decision to declare independence to more progressive characters, he would leave the ratification decision to the whim and will of others. Dickinson's wisdom and patience would eventually be rewarded.

Many in the founding generation believed that the Constitution would go the way of the Articles of Confederation. Patrick Henry was one who was not shy about his expectation, or at least his hope, that the Constitution would not survive very long. Speaking to the Virginia Ratifying Convention on June 25th, 1788, Henry admitted temporary defeat. Still, he exhibited a quiet confidence that he would be right back in that same place soon enough, debating another, very different constitutional plan:

> If I shall be in the minority, I shall have those painful sensa-tions which arise from a conviction of *being overpowered in a good cause*. Yet I will be a peaceable citizen. My head, my hand, and my heart, shall be at liberty to retrieve the loss of liberty, and remove the defects of that system in a constitutional way. I wish not to go to violence, but will wait with hopes that the spirit which predominated in the revolution is not yet gone, nor the cause of those who are attached to the revolution yet lost. I shall therefore patiently wait in expectation of seeing that govern-ment changed, so as to be compatible with the safety, liberty, and happiness, of the people.[18]

This history, and the theories, ideas, and dreams of a constitution-making populace, were floating around in Jefferson's head as he and his guests dined on September 17th, 1789. Like Henry, he certainly had quibbles with parts of the U.S. Constitution. He specifically identified two principal problems: the absence of a Bill of Rights and the tenuous rotation of Presidents (Jefferson thought Presidents would not likely leave office after four years simply because they had been voted out).[19] Yet despite these two flaws, Jefferson's overall opinion of the text was cautiously posi-tive. He believed it would foster a virtuous government, and he hoped it would encourage a simple, agrarian lifestyle for most of the population. Shortly after expressing these concerns, he concluded that the Constitution was "a good canvas on which some strokes only want retouching."

Yet something still nagged him, something about the broader place of a constitution in a modern polity: the problem of consti-tutional longevity. A constitution that endures over time, he said, preferences the thoughts of the generation that drafted it. And that's a problem. It is unjust in that it constrains the actions of *future* generations. He was troubled by the assumption, as he saw it, that a constitution written in one time period and reflective of one generation's priorities and preferences would influence and limit the priorities and preferences of future generations. It made no sense to him that a single document should hamstring the aspirations of individuals who had not yet been born. He famously quipped, in a letter to John Adams, "I like the dreams of the future better than the history of the past."[20]

Jefferson, in fact, viewed an enduring constitution in the same way he viewed the problem of colonialism. What's the difference, he wondered, between a group of thirteen states trying to break the bonds of an unjust colonial despot and a future people trying to break the chains imposed by constitutional Founders of the past? Little, he insisted; both are tyrannical.

Though he did not use this exact terminology, Jefferson was concerned about the "problem of precommitment," the concept that a *current* group of democratic people are limited in what they can do by some original compact written by a group of people who are, not to put too delicate a label on it, deceased.[21] Constitutions—or I should say, *enduring* constitutions—represent the epitome of the problem of precommitment. A critical responsibility of a liberal constitution in the modern age is to balance popular rule with the rule of law and to occasionally limit the power of the democratic sovereign. That applies equally to the sovereign at the moment of the constitution's drafting and all future sovereigns that fall under the constitution's authority. But why? In a democratic polity, shouldn't the majority get its way? And isn't it even more unsettling to think that a democratic majority cannot get its way because of a constitutional compact that was written in a different era and by a completely different generation of people?

Jefferson was troubled over the fact that the framers of a regime's constitution are afforded a certain exclusivity in defining the regime's identity both at the moment of drafting and as long as the constitution remains authoritative. He puzzled over it, asking himself a simple question: if one purpose of a constitution is to limit the power of the sovereign—to protect minority interests by constraining what majorities can do—why shouldn't the *origi-nal* drafters of the text also be constrained? They, too, represent the views of a particular majority. He struggled with the broader question that relates to the hold the founding generation has on future generations: Is a constitution itself untouchable because it ranks as fundamental law? Can't a constitution become uncon-stitutional, Jefferson wondered, especially if some of the clauses become outdated (think, for example, about the Three-Fifths Clause that was once authorized by the U.S. Constitution)?

One role constitutions play is to bind a community, to iden-tify certain things that a group of citizens—usually a majority—*cannot* do.[22] Put differently, constitutions are drafted to constrain a population that may choose, for example, to abuse the minority or to pass laws that aim to keep itself perpetually in power. A constitution does this by identifying what powers the majority retains (those that are enumerated in the text) and what powers it has no control over (those that are not enumerated). Jefferson, for example, recognized that the U.S. Constitution granted Con-gress the "Power to Lay and Collect Taxes, Duties, Imposts and Excises . . . ; The power to Borrow Money on the Credit of the United States; The power to Regulate Commerce with foreign nations, and among the several States, and with the Indian Tribes; and so on," by virtue of spelling out these powers in Article I, Section 8. In contrast, though, Jefferson insisted that Congress did *not* retain the power to charter a federal bank, because there was no expressed constitutional grant of that specific authority. If the Constitution did not explicitly authorize a specific power to one or more institutions of government, Jefferson thought, those institutions could not seize it.

Jefferson's constitutional vision is best described in the con-temporary vernacular as strict-constructionist, but at the time, he had a far more practical view of the document. The U.S. Constitution served important functions, to be sure, but it was not sacred. Many years after the ratification of the document, Jefferson famously complained: "Some men look at constitutions with sanctimonious reverence, and deem them like the ark of the covenant, too sacred to be touched. They ascribe to the men of the preceding age a wisdom more than human, and suppose what they did to be beyond amendment."[23] Constitutions ran their course, he insisted. They should never endure in perpetuity.

Jefferson laid out his famous argument in a letter dated September 6th, 1789, and addressed to his friend and fellow Virginian James Madison. The two Virginians had a lot in common, including a sense of what ideas count as basic features of good constitutional government. Both prominent political minds and students of the Enlightenment, they were teammates on many of the policies and practices that emerged in early America. And yet they most assuredly differed on this one salient issue. Jefferson's letter gets right to the point. After a few sentences of pleasantries, he states the purpose of his correspondence: "The question Whether one generation of men has a right to bind another," he states, "seems never to have been started either on this or our side of the water." He intends to start it. "I set out on this ground, which I suppose to be self-evident," Jefferson continues, "*that the earth belongs in usufruct to the living*: that the dead have neither powers nor rights over it." So as to emphasize the point, he repeats himself later in the same letter: "the earth belongs to each generation," he insists, "during its course, fully, and in their own right."[24]

Jefferson was largely concerned with the issue of authority. He is quite intentional when using the metaphor of the "living" and the "dead" to describe the distinction between different generations. Constitutions could be seen in the same way. Some live, namely those that constitute a people whose vision of the world is reflected in the document; and some (all?) die when they no longer represent the current generation. More to the point, Jefferson thought constitutions that endure beyond the years of a particular generation cannot be authoritative within a community of living souls who enjoy every right to shape their own collective destinies. Jefferson's letter to Madison states unequivocally that "the dead have neither powers nor rights over [the living]."

As he moves toward the end of his letter, Jefferson seems to be setting Madison up for a bombshell. He claims, "by the laws of nature, one generation is to another as one independent nation is to another." Generations are distinct. They have beginnings and ends—borders, continuing the global metaphor—and for Jefferson, this is an important characteristic of modern society. Surely, general knowledge in science, politics, agriculture, architecture, and other areas that Jefferson was passionate about does not stagnate when new generations emerge. Neither do constitutions. "No society," he argues, "could make a perpetual constitution. . . . The earth belongs always to the living generation. . . . The constitution and the laws of their predecessors are extinguished then in their natural course with those who gave them being." Jefferson maintained that constitutions have natural sunset clauses. Given the fundamental principle of self-governance, they should (and will) expire when a new generation takes its rightful place in a polity. He then concludes his letter: "Every constitution then, and every law, naturally expires at the end of 19 years. If it be enforced longer, it is an act of force, and not of right—It may be said that the succeeding generation exercising in fact the power to repeal, this leaves them as free as if the constitution or law has been expressly limited to 19 years only."[25]

There it was. Jeffersonian constitutionalism laid out in correspondence with the "father of the Constitution." There is, of course, more subtlety and nuance to Jefferson's constitutional vision, but much of it ties back to his core argument about generational constitutional renewal. The question of rights, for example, was crucial to Jefferson, especially as it related to the specific authority of a constitutional text. He was not speaking of the innate rights individuals possess as a consequence of being human—those universal natural rights he defended so passionately in the famous words of the Declaration of Independence—but rather the rights that one individual or group retains over another. For Jefferson, here, the distinction between powers and rights was one of degree, not of kind. People retain rights only insofar as they deserve them. The powers and rights of a given generation expired, Jefferson said, at a fixed moment in time. They did not endure, just as a constitution for an identifiable generation should not endure beyond the life-span of the generation itself.[26]

Jefferson maintained this belief his entire life. Indeed, when he wrote to Samuel Kercheval almost three decades after he expressed his original concerns to Madison, his words were remarkably similar. The letter to Kercheval is largely about proposed amendments to the Virginia Constitution, on which Kercheval (who was once Jefferson's teacher) was seeking Jefferson's advice. The now former U.S. President is reluctant to reveal his honest thoughts about the amendments, but he jumps at the chance to offer additional insight into his views on constitutional renewal. Jefferson reminds his tutor that he is a member of the preceding age and that the men who penned both the state constitutions and the federal text warrant acclaim. But constitutions, he insists, must go "hand in hand with the progress of the human mind. As that becomes more developed, more enlightened, as new discoveries are made, new truths disclosed, and manners and opinions change with the change of circumstances, institutions must also advance, and keep pace with the times."[27] Here he strikes a familiar chord. As knowledge is advanced, so should be political forms. Constitutions are not so sacred as to be untouchable. They, too, require regular upgrades as our understanding of political institutions and procedures matures.

Jefferson then introduces a useful metaphor. Relying on constitutions that have not progressed with the human mind is like relegating an adult to wear a child's coat in winter. Such a coat might provide some warmth, and it is most assuredly still a piece of necessary clothing; but it is far from ideal, and it does not account for the improvements the apparel industry has made since the wearer was a mere tyke. We would think it quite odd for an adult to choose a familiar, though no longer effective coat when others are readily available for wearing. The same is true for constitutions. Thus, the Virginian implores Kercheval to "provide in our constitution for its revision at stated periods. What these periods should be, nature herself indicates. By the

European tables of mortality, of the adults living at any one moment of time, a majority will be dead in about nineteen years. At
the end of that period, then, a new majority is come into place;
or in other words, a new generation." "Each generation," he concludes, "is as independent as the one preceding, as that was of all
which has gone before. It has then, like them, a right to choose
for itself the form of government it believes most promotive of its
own happiness." Though Jefferson was referring to the Virginia
Constitution in his letter to Kercheval, his suspicion surrounding
all enduring constitutions remained evident. He insisted that
the text of a constitution should include the mechanism for significant alteration so that "it may be handed on, with periodic
repairs, to the end of time."[28]

Jefferson's support for periodic constitutional renewal received
mixed reviews during his lifetime. Perhaps coincidentally, the
division of support for the idea broke mainly along geographical
lines. The Frenchmen at Jefferson's secret dinner were generally
enthusiastic. Their eagerness for regular constitutional conventions assembled to revise the instrument and/or for constitutional
structures that mandate the literal expiration of the text was genuine. In fact, the principle of generational constitutional renewal
was broadly debated in the months immediately following Jefferson's dinner. Condorcet, in particular, was fond of the idea, and
he, along with Emmanuel Joseph Sieyés (Abbé Sieyés), urged the
French National Assembly to introduce a provision mandating a
new constitutional document every thirty years. Both Condorcet
and Sieyés even used the same Enlightenment language that Jefferson admired. They, too, claimed that new constitutional forms
should reflect the progress of the human mind.[29] Though, like
Jefferson, they were unsuccessful in convincing their contemporaries to adopt the thirty-year plan, Condorcet and Sieyés pushed
the idea whenever possible.

So did Thomas Paine, the author of two of the most famous
pamphlets ever penned, *Common Sense* and *Rights of Man*. He,
too, advocated for generational ownership of the constitutional
form, because he so feared the rise of tyranny. Nadia Urbinati, in

her work *Representative Democracy: Principles and Genealogy*, writes that Jefferson, Condorcet, and Paine all "explained [the right of constitutional revision] with the argument of antityranny . . . and the argument of fallibility."[30] In fact, Paine maintained that insisting on periodic constitutional conventions was essential, not just as a preventative measure but also because it is illogical and immoral for one generation to maintain any control over another. He wrote, "every age and generation must be as free to act for itself, in all cases, as the ages and generations which preceded it."[31] Unsurprisingly, Paine's argument about generational precommitment mirrors his position on the succession of thrones. He is perhaps most famous for arguing against the practice of passing the crown based simply on heredity. To him, that principle violates both the natural order of things and, to use his phrase, any notion of common sense. Passing a constitution from one generation to the next simply because it was effective in constituting a people at a given time, Paine thought, made about as much sense as empowering a young man because he shares the same blood as the monarch.

It was a very different story across the Atlantic. Neither Madison nor Kercheval was convinced of the need for periodic constitutional conventions. As was Madison's custom, he rebutted Jefferson's argument with a systematic and calculated response. For Madison, the distinction between the people and separate generations was neither meaningful nor significant. Stable, lasting, and enduring constitutions, he said, were critical to the success of a nation. A constitution should persist over a long period of time so as to build up the necessary respect and solemnity that a revered document deserves. Any constitution, he thought, is more effective if it spans many generations and encourages deep and continuing veneration. In fact, he worried so much about a natural reverence for the Constitution that he warned about frivolous and repeated amendments to the text.[32] Like fine wine, constitutions get better—or at least more commanding—with age. Madison's position on the authority of the Constitution over time could not have been further from Jefferson's.[33]

Madison placed the constitutional form within the first class of "acts of a political society" and questioned the efficacy of Jefferson's idea. "However applicable in theory [Jefferson's] doctrine may be to a Constitution, it seems liable in practice to some very powerful objections. Would not a government so often revised become too mutable to retain those prejudices in its favor which antiquity inspires, and which are perhaps a salutary aid to the most rational Government in the most enlightened age?"[34]

Perhaps too polite to confront Jefferson directly, Madison probably also thought that the master of Monticello was seeing in the newly forged U.S. Constitution only what he wanted to see. For Madison never points out that there is, in fact, a mechanism for constitutional reform built into the Constitution's text. Article V reads: "The Congress, whenever two thirds of both Houses shall deem it necessary, shall propose Amendments to this Constitution, or, *on the Application of the Legislatures of two thirds of the several States, shall call a Convention for proposing Amendments*, which, in either Case, shall be valid to all Intents and Purposes, as part of this Constitution . . ." (emphasis added). Madison might have closed the debate by reminding Jefferson that the method of using conventions to amend the Constitution was precisely the justification used by the fifty-five delegates in 1787 to replace the ineffective Articles of Confederation.

Of course, Madison's general position was the one adopted by the founding generation; a large percentage of the 1787 Framers ultimately believed in the power of an *enduring* constitutional text. One hint is provided in *Federalist* 49. Here, Madison cautions that regularly asking the people to comment on (and critique) the particulars of institutional policy will erode the necessary reverence for government that is required for regime strength. He writes, "it may be considered as an objection inherent in the principle, that as every appeal to the people would carry an implication of some defect in the government, frequent appeals would, in a great measure, deprive the government of that veneration which time bestows on every thing, and without which perhaps the wisest and freest governments would not possess the requisite stability." The same is true, Madison said, for constitutions.[35] They require a degree of endurance in order to cultivate reverence for the fundamental law and, ultimately, in the governmental institutions that are created by that law.[36]

Prominent voices in the anti-Federalist camp also echoed Madison and rebuffed Jefferson. An anti-Federalist employing the pen name Brutus was perhaps the most vocal. Though he was firmly against ratification of the proposed instrument, he did recognize the importance of an enduring constitutional text (just not this one). He wrote: "when a building is to be erected which is intended to stand for ages, the foundation should be firmly laid. The Constitution proposed for your acceptance, is designed not for yourself alone, but for generations yet unborn."[37] His point was that the stakes of the ratification process were extremely high. If adopted, Brutus said, this Constitution would endure beyond the lifetime of his readers and that fact should enter into the deliberations in the state Ratifying Conventions. Those conventions were not just agreeing to a constitution that would impose rules over the living, but also over future generations. Brutus wanted the ratifiers to be forward thinking.

In the end, most in the founding era acknowledged that constitutions reflect the priorities and preferences of the drafting generation and that the trick was to design constitutions with the right balance of specificity and ambiguity to ensure that they would last longer than France's first charter. These important documents differ in critical ways from ordinary law. A constitution is often referred to as a nation's "higher" or "fundamental" law precisely because it is distinct from the stuff of everyday politics. It is the tangible manifestation of the rule of law in a political society enamored with the idea of popular sovereignty. It is the single legal code that governs the many routine legal codes that make up a complex federal union such as that found in the United States. As Publius noted in *Federalist* 78, "there is no position which depends on clearer principles, than that every act of a delegated authority, contrary to the tenor of the commission under which it is exercised, is void. . . . To deny this, would be to affirm, that the deputy is greater than his principal; that the servant is above his master; that the representatives of the people are superior to the people themselves." Routine laws could be changed regularly, but the meta-law—the higher law—had to last. The longevity of a written constitution, Madison insisted, was directly related to a country's political strength.

The idea of the enduring constitution frightened Jefferson. In so many ways it did not square with his fundamental political vision. Many accepted that Jefferson was considered the most committed advocate of popular sovereignty among the founding generation; the political vision of the chief architect of the Declaration of Independence had at its core the idea that a people should control its own collective destiny. And thus he thought constitutions ought to be written so as to promote rather than stifle a living people's collective wishes. A present, living citizenry, he said, has the right to decide for itself how it governs and what policy decisions are necessary for its shared progress.

Of course, we know that Jefferson ultimately lost the debate about generational constitutions; indeed, his critics prevailed. The United States is now recognized as the undisputed leader in enduring constitutions. The document that emerged from Philadelphia on September 17th, 1787, and that was scrutinized by Jefferson and his dinner guests two years later, is now more than 230 years old. By Jefferson's own calculations, more than twelve generations have now suffered from what he described as a constitutional "act of force." For more than two centuries, the constitutional ground has belonged not to the living, but to the dead.

But imagine if Jefferson had been more persuasive. What if his idea of convening a periodic constitutional convention every nineteen years had been realized? What might the various generational constitutions of the nineteenth century have looked like? Or the ones drafted for each generation during the twentieth century? And the twenty-first? All would have been different, for sure. But these constitutions might share some basic features too. Exploring what these texts would have included, and *not* included, is a deeply interesting experiment in constitutional imagination, and one we will conduct here. At the foundation of this book is a simple question: What would America's Constitution have looked like in each major era if Jefferson had convinced Madison, Kercheval, and all the rest in the founding period that each generation ought to draft its own text? In this book, then, we will take on the important role of constitutional framer. We will put ourselves in the position of those who have to craft a constitutional text that represents a particular generation. In so doing, we will join a long and illustrious line of American constitutional renegades.

Jefferson was not the only American constitutional rebel of his time. John Dickinson, James Madison, Patrick Henry, John Adams, Benjamin Franklin, and many others of the founding generation were individuals wishing to dismantle the existing power structures and replace them with an alternative vision. We like to think of them as heroes, and they were. But they were also dissidents. Whether exercised by those individuals who defied the King of Great Britain in 1776 or by those, like Dickinson and Madison, who defamed the Articles, dissent has always been part of America's constitutional composition. The anti-Federalists are perhaps the most celebrated members of this company. Their protesting of the new fundamental law set the standard for all future opposition. But the founding-era dissenters are far from the only critics that have walked these lands. Skepticism of the U.S. Constitution has surfaced in almost every era of American history. Even now, after 230-plus years, critics—modern anti-Federalists, if you will—continue to voice serious concerns about the inadequacies of the American constitutional text.

It's actually hard to find even a small window of time in American history when the country was constitutionally content. Beginning with the anti-Federalists and continuing through the work of contemporary organizations like the Friends of the Article V

Convention,[38] thousands of doubters have surfaced to condemn parts or the whole of the constitutional instrument. Frederick Douglass described the Constitution as a "cunningly-devised and wicked compact, demanding the most constant and earnest efforts of the friends of righteous freedom for its complete overthrow."[39] Others have been less piercing in their language, but still no less committed to voicing disapproval of the constitutional document. Many agree with the sentiments of Sanford Levinson, who asserts it is time for Americans to recognize that a "substantial responsibility for the defects of our polity *lies in the Constitution itself.*"[40]

A good portion of criticism surrounding America's Constitution derives from the blind faith of many American citizens. Ponder the sobering data we receive when we ask questions about the text's imprint on our lives. Teachers regularly report that students often confuse the Declaration of Independence with the Constitution: a National Constitution Center survey reveals that a whopping 84 percent of Americans believe that the Constitution includes the phrase "all men are created equal."[41] In another survey, the National Constitution Center asked teenagers to identify the famous words that begin the Constitution's Preamble. Only one in three could recall "We the People."[42] Moreover, in the first poll mentioned, only 25 percent of those surveyed could name any of the freedoms guaranteed by the First Amendment. Three-quarters said "the Constitution is important to them, makes them proud and is relevant to their lives." But 83 percent admitted they know very little about what is written in the text.[43]

Contemporary criticism of the Constitution also lies right under the surface of some of the most compelling and fiercely contested political debates of the twenty-first century. For instance, the debate between advocates of a "living" U.S. Constitution, on the one hand, and an "originalist" U.S. Constitution, on the other, relates directly to the call for constitutional renewal. Those who view the Constitution as living believe the document is flexible enough to adapt to changing circumstances and contemporary realities, thus requiring little or no formal constitutional reform. Whereas an originalist Constitution is perceived to have been written for an altogether different and unrecognizable generation in the past. Advocates of this latter view, such as the late Justice Antonin Scalia and the current Supreme Court Justice Clarence Thomas, insist that the Constitution must be read with the understanding that it was written at a distinct moment in history and that its central meaning has not changed in the years since it was ratified.

Justice Scalia argued that an originalist view is compatible with an enduring constitution, but opponents are not so convinced. If we are to agree that our Constitution's meaning is fixed, supporters of the living version insist, the need for dramatic (and probably regular) constitutional reform is more urgent. Critics of the originalist position maintain that it is impossible to understand the Constitution as it was written and, moreover, that it is troubling and even harmful to try to do so. Their solution to the prolonged tenure of the American Constitution is to interpret the document as if it were written yesterday. Such a solution suggests that an altogether new constitutional document would be preferable to an interpretive approach that resembles originalism.

The contemporary debate over the budget deficit has also spurred loud cries for constitutional change, the latest controversy, in February 2011, involving Kentucky. That state's Senate passed a resolution calling on the U.S. Congress to convene an Article V constitutional convention to fix the nation's budget crisis. Though the prospects for a successful groundswell of state support in favor of a federal convention are at best slim, Kentucky, for a time, managed to move the issue to the front burner.

In similar fashion, the controversies surrounding the 2000 and 2016 presidential elections continue to inspire advocates of constitutional reform who seek a transformation of the Electoral College. Most of us are at least moderately familiar with the circumstances that enabled George W. Bush to succeed Bill Clinton as the forty-third President of the United States in 2001, but some context may still be in order. You may recall that the entire election hinged on the contested electoral votes in

Florida—twenty-five votes in all. After much legal wrangling, including a controversial decision by the U.S. Supreme Court in the case of *Bush v. Gore*, those votes, and the election itself, went to Bush. The problem was that the popular vote favored Al Gore. Cries for constitutional amendment, and even constitutional renewal, followed. Practically the first proposal made by Hillary Clinton, at the time the newly elected junior Senator from New York, was to revamp the Constitution to do away with the Electoral College. It seems oddly prescient that, sixteen years later, Hillary Clinton would suffer the same electoral indignity when she lost the presidency to Donald Trump despite winning the popular vote.

Almost any significant debate in American politics can be traced in some way back to the supposed shortcomings of the constitutional document. And that is not just an American phenomenon. Indeed, fundamental constitutional change across the globe does not happen in a vacuum. There is a distinct pattern by which constitutions are drafted, live out a certain existence, and then begin to fail. In every instance around the world, the drafting of a new constitution is a direct response to the failures of the old constitution.

In the 1980s and '90s, there was an explosion of constitutional conventions around the world as a result of nations turning to constitutional reform in an effort to achieve much-needed regime stability. Nowhere was this more evident than in the former Soviet bloc countries. When the Berlin Wall fell and many Eastern European countries gained a greater degree of independence, officials in those countries immediately called for constitutional renewal. The region became the most fruitful laboratory for constitution-making in the history of the world. Political leaders in Poland, Hungary, Romania, and Ukraine (among others) set out to draft constitutional texts that would reflect the area's shift toward democracy, popular sovereignty, and capitalism. Along with an army of consultants from the United States and other Western countries, constitutional framers in Eastern Europe were keenly aware of the particular flaws of previous Soviet-based constitutions, as well as the region's significant cultural, political, and economic traditions.

What is interesting is that despite differences in the characteristics of constitutional failure, the *circumstances* in which constitutions are discarded and new ones adopted are remarkably similar. Framers don't sit down to prepare a new constitution when things are going well. As pointed out earlier, sometimes it is the environment that causes constitutions to break down and sometimes it is constitutional design features. Often it is both. Political theorist Carl Friedrich famously commented that new constitutions "flow from the negative distaste for a dismal past."[44] Constitutions are almost always written during periods of turbulence and disorder.

Calls for constitutional renewal are common, and yet those same calls often neglect the complexities that emerge when a nation undergoes such monumental change. Americans are lucky. We have occasionally experienced the instability and disruption that accompanies a fundamental constitutional shift, most notably during the American Civil War.[45] And yet those moments are rare in our history. The irony should not be lost on us at this moment. We have the luxury to contemplate discarding our current Constitution and, invoking Article V, to return to Philadelphia to draft a new charter precisely because of the very stability the Constitution affords. In other words, it is partly due to the Constitution that we can seriously contemplate getting rid of it. Without the constancy provided by our political institutions, we would be in a very different place right now, and our conversations about constitutional renewal would take on a far more urgent tone.

Has America's current constitutional text outlived its usefulness? Perhaps. Should we at least consider minor adjustments to the existing charter? Definitely. This may be the time to pounce on Jon Elster's historical exception: "Being written for the indefinite future," he writes, "constitutions ought to be adopted in maximally calm and undisturbed conditions."[46] Despite America's weakening political, economic, and moral credibility across the globe, its troubling partisanship at home, the continued plague of racism and other domestic discrimination, withering criticism about leadership in the White House and Congress, and the unprecedented disaster of the COVID-19 pandemic, *political* stability still reigns. Protests are not calling for the complete overhaul of the government, as they are in places like Venezuela. America's social, financial, religious, and political institutions still command the attention of the country's citizens. The frustrating and critical messages from many corners of the country notwithstanding, now is precisely the moment to think rationally and carefully about constitutional change.

This book provides a fresh perspective on the call for constitutional renewal. It is a book that entertains the possibility of *future* constitutional reform primarily by imagining *past* constitutional texts. One means by which we can measure the credibility of any argument in favor of constitutional change, as well as what a redrafted U.S. Constitution might look like if we returned to Philadelphia for a new constitutional convention, is to imagine what past constitutions might have looked like if America's Founders had endorsed the principle of periodic constitutional renewal—if they had embraced Jefferson's position on generational constitutions.

This is a counterfactual book, one that takes the simple historical debate between Jefferson and Madison over the virtues and weaknesses of an enduring constitutional text and reconsiders American constitutional development from the perspective of the loser. It is, therefore, a work of fiction.[47] But even fiction can teach us a lot. In the words of Gary J. Kornblith, "historians can run experiments only in their heads, where they imagine what would have happened if a given factor were absent, or, alternatively, if a factor not actually present had been added to the historical mix."[48]

This is a book about imagination, about *constitutional* imagination to be more precise. Jeffersonian constitutionalism is all about imagination. Together, we'll enter unfamiliar territory and construct mental images of constitutional texts. We'll be constitutional framers. Indeed, framers participate in the act of imagining every time they sit down to design new constitutions. They find themselves in strange territory, with nothing but the broad contours of a plan for a new polity in their heads. They must conjure up deeply complex pictures of a yet to be seen political world and then they must translate those pictures into words—into the powers, rights, and responsibilities that are the stuff of modern constitutional regimes. You give it a try: imagine that you are sitting in front of a blank piece of parchment and you have been given the responsibility to construct a new political system, one that you believe is best for the community in which you live. You've been empowered to visualize a new political order for the citizens of your particular society, to attempt, in Alexander Hamilton's words, to establish good government from "reflection and choice" rather than "accident and force." How thrilling would that be?

If you imagine yourself in that position for a very long time, with many eyes fixed on your every move, you might get a glimpse of what it must be like for a constitutional framer to do her work. Everything about the making of constitutions—from the dissenters who call for revolution to the drafters who actually pen new constitutions, even to the citizens who must endorse the new constitutional text—is grounded somehow in imagination.

Arguably, the most important moments of the 1787 Constitutional Convention were spent before any delegates arrived in Pennsylvania's capital, when the august group of convention leaders engaged in the same imaginative project I just asked of you. James Madison spent months at Montpelier, his stately home in the foothills of Virginia's Blue Ridge Mountains, ruminating and reflecting on the failures of past political regimes and imagining a structure of government that would work for a newly independent collection of states. We are told that he sat in his second-floor library, surrounded by political treatises and classic works of political thought, and pondered what it would take to usher in the particular world he envisioned.

The eighteenth-century Framers were an imaginative lot; so too were they speculators. They wrestled with questions whose answers were based on projections and hope: What institutions *should* be built that *might* secure the blessings of liberty? What political systems and mechanisms *should* be implemented that *could* provide the best chance of establishing justice and ensuring domestic tranquility? What public ingredients *should* be combined that *could perhaps* promote the general welfare? None of these ingredients were immediately available, or at least none were yet positioned to deliver on the promises. The constitutional Framers had to trust that what they envisioned and enumerated on sheets of parchment would eventually mature into a working government that, among other things, protected the safety and secured the rights of American citizens.

The character of imagination that is so crucial to all constitutional framers is also a requirement because of the moment in which they are asked to do their job. It is particularly imperative for framers to imagine new political worlds when things are going south for a regime, when tensions are high and the future stability of the country is in jeopardy. Americans have experienced these moments. The Articles of Confederation were drafted in 1777, just as the former colonies were gearing up to fight a war with a powerful and tyrannical force. The situation wasn't that great when we transitioned from the Articles to the Constitution either. Framers of the U.S. Constitution saw it as their job to respond to the growing discontent felt by political officials and everyday citizens about the inadequacies of the Articles of Confederation. They were reacting to what they perceived as a country in crisis.

And they had evidence. Daniel Shays, the poor, indebted, and infamous farmer from western Massachusetts who barricaded himself in the Springfield arsenal in late January 1787 and scared an entire country, was on everyone's mind. The country was further teetering because of unpaid debts, state and regional squabbles, the recurring fear of mob rule, the currency crisis, and a whole lot more. Citizens up and down the Atlantic seaboard took notice of the actions of another tyrannical group in New England—this time the legislators of Rhode Island's representative assembly, who introduced measures that would forgive private debts all across the state.[49]

These historical episodes provide context for the beginning of our imaginative journey. The lesson learned from Shays' Rebellion, the debt crisis, and similar events in early American history is that in some ways it was probably inevitable that a new constitutional document would emerge from the moment. The difficulties of the time called for constitutional change. We will, however, resist the temptation to construct new constitutions (even imaginary ones) every time there are serious problems in our particular regime. In other words, if we are to remain true to the principles of Jeffersonian constitutionalism, we must identify *fixed* moments in which a deliberative body will meet in convention to hash out a new fundamental law. Jefferson advocated for that body to meet every nineteen years, roughly the moment of generational shift in eighteenth-century America. That seems a tad indulgent; generational shift in twenty-first-century America is surely greater than nineteen years. We'll thus stretch the concept of a "generation" out a bit even as we maintain fidelity to Jefferson's first principle that each generation ought to write its own constitution. Instead, we'll focus on the average life expectancy of the American citizen.

Here's how the periodization will work: in the late eighteenth century and early nineteenth century, the life expectancy for most White males (the demographic with available data) was roughly thirty-eight years. That number held steady for the middle part of the nineteenth century. By the turn of the twentieth century, the life expectancy of the general population had risen modestly to forty years, and by mid-century, the number had grown to fifty years. In 1953, life expectancy was approximately sixty-nine years. Measuring life expectancy is different from measuring generations, of course. Jefferson was rigorously scientific in calculating the precise moment at which more than half of those born at a certain earlier moment would likely be dead, and for him, that moment represented a generational shift. But average life expectancy is also a defensible measure of generational shift. Jefferson could have just as easily used average life expectancy as his threshold.

We will thus use average life expectancy as our generational markers, and that yields some very interesting realizations (or perhaps coincidences). If we plot out the average life expectancy from the founding moment, and assume that each shift represents a separate generation, we find that the first Jeffersonian constitutional convention should have occurred in 1825 (thirty-eight years after the 1787 Convention), the second in 1863 (thirty-eight years after the 1825 Convention), the third in 1903 (forty years from 1863), the fourth in 1953 (fifty years from 1903), and the fifth in 2022 (sixty-nine years after the 1953 Convention). Coincidentally, the average life expectancy for Americans over the last two centuries intersects with some of the most significant periods of American history—the Civil War, for instance—making our imaginary journey through America's generational constitutions all the more fascinating.

The final issue for us to tackle is how we might go about imagining new constitutional texts and the conventions that gave rise to them. What assumptions should we make, and what data should we use, to make credible assertions about conventions and constitutions that are, for all intents and purposes, nothing more than the products of our imagination? The believability of the entire counterfactual project, in fact, depends on the legitimacy of those assumptions and that data. The cynic will doubtless say that my narrative decisions are nothing more than a random coin flip, to which my response is that everything I imagine is (I hope) a *plausible* or *rational* outcome of its time. There is nothing in the following narrative that seems wildly out of character for the development of American constitutional history. Of course, I must also convince the skeptic that the sources I gather, and the smart use of those sources, results in a sincere and compelling story about imaginary constitutional moments. Not an easy task, to be sure, but I will do my best.

Any project of constitutional imagination requires an awareness of the design features and the environmental factors that may solidify or doom a constitutional project. Hence, we are right to ask the following questions as we conceive of invented constitutions: what was happening at the time of the fictional constitutional convention that might influence the thinking of the delegates? What constitutional design characteristics were currently in vogue? How might the environment and design preferences interact with each other to produce a particular constitutional outcome? These are fundamental questions that all constitutional framers consider, and we will as well. These questions influenced America's first two constitutional conventions, and they doubtless would have influenced others had Jefferson won the day.

Let's begin by unpacking a few general assumptions about our fictional constitutional conventions—assumptions that will provide at least a rough image of how these assemblies might look. These assumptions will form the foundation of our exercise in constitution-making. First, let us assume that all constitutional conventions throughout the past two-plus centuries have no formal connection to standing legislative bodies (like Congress) or other elected institutions. In other words, we will follow Jefferson's wishes and imagine that our drafting conventions resemble the 1787 Constitutional Convention in Philadelphia—they will be separate bodies made up of delegates from the states. We will also assume that the process of selecting delegates to our fictitious constitutional conventions will resemble the process in 1787: the delegates to that Constitutional Convention were elected by state legislatures. Next, we will follow the rules of that convention once more and say that the population of each state will determine the number of delegates sent. We could make any number of decisions here—equal representation based on statehood, a small drafting committee that submits its work to a larger convention, representation based on identity or interest group affiliation rather than statehood, and so on—but adhering to the rules of the 1787 Convention in Philadelphia seems every bit as sensible as any other approach. In all, then, our constitutional conventions will be separate bodies; they will be constituted by representatives from the states; and the number of representatives will be based on each state's population.

The size of the convention probably matters. Too many voices and a convention becomes unwieldy; too few and it will not be broadly representative. We know that fifty-five delegates were sent to Philadelphia in 1787, that sum in no small part a product of the total number of states in the Union at the time (13). Pennsylvania sent the largest delegation (8), with Virginia next (7), followed by Delaware, Maryland, New Jersey, and North Carolina (5 each). Georgia, Massachusetts, and South Carolina each sent four representatives. If we discount Rhode Island which refused to send any representatives at all, New Hampshire sent the least number of delegates (2), followed by New York and Connecticut (3). The average delegation was thus a little less than five conveners per state.

Our imaginary constitutional conventions will no doubt comprise more than fifty-five delegates. The number of delegates to the 1825 Constitutional Convention might be twice as many— eleven states, after all, joined the Union between 1791 (Vermont) and 1821 (Missouri), making twenty-four states in all. They will certainly deliver a total of one hundred or more delegates. The aggregate number of delegates at the ensuing conventions will increase as well. Many more states have been added to the Union since 1825, and the country's population has expanded considerably. If we maintain the original *average* of five delegates per state, however, we can cap the total number of delegates at roughly 250 for any given constitutional convention.[50] We'll do that for most of the imaginary conventions.

Continuing the discussion about assumptions, let me posit a few more: first, it is always possible that a constitutional convention will result in deadlock, with no final agreement. Many do. But I'm going to take a chance and assume that our five conventions will end with signed constitutional charters that are then presented to the citizens for ratification. The stories, I think, are more compelling that way. Second, the introduction of new constitutional texts almost always changes the course of history. I understand that events are inevitably altered when a dramatic and impactful shift in constitutional governance occurs. This project, however, assumes that the major historical occurrences of the past two-plus centuries happened much as they actually did, much as they unfolded in real time. It would be pure folly, and well beyond my intellectual capabilities, to imagine the *entire* altered universe of an America that experienced five additional constitutional conventions. My point in writing this book is not to undertake such an endeavor; it is to describe the conventions themselves as if they occurred within the historical environments we know and are familiar with.[51] Third, I will further assume that the products of politics—the laws, orders, enactments, judicial decisions, and so on—introduced under a former constitution will remain largely in place after the ratification of a new fundamental law, unless the new constitution expressly forbids or rejects them. In other words, laws won't simply sunset when a new constitutional text is adopted. Traditionally, renewing existing legislation after constitutional change has been a practice at the state and federal levels, and we will maintain it here; we will assume that the political world won't simply halt when a new convention is assembled.[52]

Perhaps the most critical remaining question is the one about sources. Where will I get the information to make informed choices about what might have gone into a particular generation's constitution? For a variety of reasons, I'll employ a diverse set of sources. Supreme Court opinions; the political, economic, and social events of the time; broad policy initiatives; crises; and much more will inform my decision making. The number of potential sources is considerable, but I will be guided throughout by a simple question: What pressing issues would constitutional framers *most likely* discuss at the particular moment they met in convention, and how might they translate those issues into constitutional language? In the end, my hope is that I can convince the reader that I have imagined rational and reasonable scenarios, based on history, that tell a compelling story of America's constitutional development.

One additional source deserves a bit more explanation. The reader will soon notice that I rely on state constitutions and state constitutional conventions to help tell the various stories. Here, I'm referring specifically to the records from the drafting of state constitutions, including both the original texts states needed to enter the Union and any substantial revisions of those texts. State constitutional conventions satisfy one essential requirement of a project such as this: they explore the same *types* of questions— questions of order, power, function, freedom, and so forth—that would be asked at any national constitutional convention. In all, we can count close to 150 constitutional conventions at the state level.[53] That's a decent amount of data for our use.

State constitutions and state constitutional convention debates are certainly valuable sources of data for imagining new national constitutions.[54] A problem arises, however, when we think about how to apply these state constitutions and state convention debates. We must address the critique that state data will often reflect a state's parochial interests, whereas national constitutional conventions would likely often (though not always) debate broader issues than those found in the states. The trick, then, will be to *nationalize* these state constitutional convention debates, to take what the states are debating and consider the national implications. The way to do so is threefold: first, consider *all* state constitutional convention records around the time of our imaginary federal convention so as to avoid the inclination toward selection bias; second, highlight the development or evolution of state constitutions by considering how they have changed from the earliest to the latest iterations; and third, look for trends among these records and exchanges that hint at commonality or broad-based themes.

At this point, a few observations about the state constitutions are probably in order. We will rely on the 142 state constitutions (and corresponding state constitutional conventions) that have been written and ratified since the country declared independence in July 1776. Some might quibble with that number—it may be as many as 150 or as few as 135—because what counts as a Jeffersonian rewrite is a bit fuzzy. Do we regard a redrafting *by amendment* as representing a new generation's fundamental law, or do we want to limit ourselves to those constitutions that emerged from formal constitutional conventions? For consistency, I have settled on the latter: we will consider only those new texts that were drafted in convention, principally because that is what Jefferson envisioned and preferred. Of course, that means we should add those constitutions that came from state drafting conventions but were not ultimately ratified by the people—those attempts at generational constitutionalism that never got off the ground because of the requirement for ratification. Jefferson would have been satisfied with that overall process. Any generation, he would say, can choose to reject a new constitution, just as long as it is given the opportunity to draft and ratify one. There have been at least seven of those situations in America's history.

Another thing to consider is *when* a convention was called and a new constitution birthed. As a condition for joining the Union, every state had to draft a formal constitution and present it to Congress. Thus, the thirty-seven territories that were granted statehood (after the original thirteen states) all have initial constitutional documents. Many of those are still the governing charter of the state. These constitutions have a special character. They mark the beginning of that state's venture into constitutional governance, and they set up the various institutions, safeguards, and procedures that will inform future constitutional change. Though many did not come straight out of the ether but were able to draw on territorial charters and other fundamental laws, these first state constitutions officially designate a transition to statehood and an important baseline for future revisions of the state's constitutional text.

Further, there is a special character to state constitutions written during the antebellum period, especially those drafted precisely for secessionist reasons. Eighteen of the 142 constitutions—almost one in seven—were drafted between 1850 and 1861 in response to the increasing tensions that ultimately led to the American Civil War. Eight southern states assembled constitutional conventions in 1861 alone. Those constitutions marked the moment in which the southern states declared their independence from the Union. We must be similarly careful when talking about the Reconstruction constitutions. Twenty-seven state constitutions were written between the conclusion of the Civil War in 1865 and the end of Reconstruction in 1877. In the end, I will use all these Civil War constitutions because they (perhaps more so than any other state constitutions) give us a glimpse into the national debate at the time. They are concerned with matters of slavery, sovereignty, freedom, equality, and most of all, power. In fact, there is more "national" material in these forty-five state constitutions than in all the others we will encounter—delegates to those conventions were absorbed with the leading concerns of the time. For that reason, they will be reviewed and considered as part of our data set.[55]

Constitution makers routinely beg, borrow, and steal from other constitutional drafters, so we can draw some conclusions about the issues that might rise to the level of a federal constitutional convention by monitoring the changes that have occurred in state constitutions over time. This is particularly true when considering structural or institutional changes. For example, one theme I've noticed in looking over the various state constitutions and their convention debates is that many state constitutions now emphasize a more democratic (with a small *d*) political system as compared to some of the earlier state constitutions that clearly favored a more republican (small *r*) style of governance. Citizens are more directly involved in policymaking now, especially when we consider the increased use of referenda and ballot initiatives at the state level. The republican style of governance that relied on representatives to carry out the business of governing has lost a bit of its luster in the last century. We might not recognize that shift if we interrogated just the constitutional foundings of a particular moment. Such shifts reveal themselves only when we look at the evolution of state constitutions over a long stretch of time.

That is not to say that scrutinizing state constitutions around the time of each of our imaginary federal conventions has no intellectual value. Quite the contrary. Common themes among many state drafters and ratifiers at a precise moment in American history suggest that an issue—say, the desired method of selecting state judges—has some traction, at least in certain regions of the nation if not across the country. Of course, one cannot necessarily conclude that regional plans and ideas will automatically transfer to a national arena. States might choose to use elections to select their own judges, yet not want to follow suit with federal court jurists. Nonetheless, we can make some reasonable estimates of the types of discussions that might inform federal constitutional conventions by looking at the debates at the state constitutional level.

We'll also need to consider the role of the extant U.S. Constitution's Article V in our analysis. In many ways the most intriguing section of the Constitution, Article V articulates the rules for amending the text. As described earlier, it sets up two mechanisms for change: (1) Congress can propose amendments to the Constitution by securing support from two-thirds of its members in both Houses; and (2) the states themselves can demand a federal constitutional convention to amend the text, provided that two-thirds are in agreement that one is needed. Regardless of which path is chosen, proposed alterations to the Constitution require the endorsement of three-quarters of the states, an extremely high threshold for change. Omitting the Bill of Rights from the equation, it is telling that Americans have altered their fundamental law only seventeen times in the past 230-plus years. Yet that high bar might be less consequential here because we're assuming a complete overhaul. And what is more, we're assuming that the language promising a new constitution to each generation will appear in the Constitution itself.

Had Jefferson persuaded more Founders of the wisdom of his generational approach to constitutional renewal, Article V might look a good bit different than it does today. Jeffersonians likely would have included an additional mechanism for changing the text—this one mandating much more comprehensive transformation. Article V would have been the logical section in which to include a provision for the Constitution to expire at various designated moments. Here, state constitutions provide important insight—it seems Jefferson's idea found more sympathetic champions at the state level. In fact, forty-four state constitutions currently include provisions for constitutional renewal, and most are found in the sections describing the process of amendment.[56] We can thus imagine what a Jeffersonian Article V might look like:

1   The Authority of this Constitution shall remain in force until it naturally expires nineteen Years after its Ratification; It shall be the duty of the Congress at that time, and every nineteen Years thereafter, to call a Convention for the purpose of proposing a new Constitution for the United States of America.

2   The Congress, whenever two thirds of both Houses shall deem it necessary, shall propose Amendments to this Constitution, or, on the Application of the Legislatures of two thirds of the several States, shall call a Convention for proposing Amendments, which, in either Case, shall be valid to all Intents and Purposes, as Part of this Constitution, when ratified by the Legislatures of three fourths of the several States or by Conventions in three fourths thereof, as the one or the other Mode of Ratification may be proposed by the Congress; Provided that no Amendment which may be made prior to the Year One thousand eight hundred and eight shall in any Manner affect the first and fourth Clauses in the Ninth Section of the first Article; and that no State, without its Consent, shall be deprived of its equal Suffrage in the Senate.

Another procedural assumption we should make, then, is that the Jeffersonian version of Article V remains more or less consistent in each of our imaginary constitutional texts. In other words, we will assume an expiration date on each constitution, and we will assume that amendments can be added to each text during the interim period between drafting conventions. This central assumption is somewhat inconsistent with the general purpose and tenor of this book, with the idea that each generation has total liberty to create its own constitutional form, but it will have to do. We'll need at least one rule that encourages consistency in our creative imaginings.

Additionally, we should probably make the assumption that many provisions of the original 1787 Constitution will remain throughout these changing constitutional moments. It seems highly unlikely that constitutional framers throughout American history will completely scrap a prior constitution and draft an entirely new one out of whole cloth. Most will carry on those provisions that still work, while altering those that have run their course. How can we be fairly confident of this? Most state constitutions still maintain the basic form and function of government institutions adopted by the Philadelphia assembly in 1787. They've had plenty of opportunity to try radically different political structures, and still, no state has yet adopted a parliamentary style of government.

With all of those assumptions and caveats in mind, and with the hope that they are viewed by the reader as reasonable and sound, let us now turn to the year 1825 and to a prominent American wrestling with many of the most important issues of the day. Let us follow him as he begins the long journey from Boston to Philadelphia, for he has been selected by the Massachusetts legislature to attend the second federal constitutional convention in America's history.

1825

DANIEL WEBSTER sat at the large mahogany desk in his Marshfield, Massachusetts, office. It was, he thought, his favorite place on earth. Here, he read, wrote, and dictated whenever he had occasion to tend to his law practice. Unfortunately, those occasions were infrequent these days. He was spending much of his time in Washington as a member of the Massachusetts delegation to the United States House of Representatives, and that pulled him away from his first love: the law. Sure, he was making law, but what he cared most about was the wrestling with facts, theories, and strategies that characterized the attorney's craft. He found the occasional argument before the U.S. Supreme Court satisfying, but it felt temporary compared to his former life as a full-time lawyer. He missed his former life. He missed the money. He was, at the time, the highest paid lawyer in the land, but his duties in Washington dramatically cut into that revenue stream. To make matters more challenging, his wife, Grace, and their three children needed him back in Marshfield as often as possible. Webster was, quite literally, pulled in many directions.

The year was 1825. What occupied Daniel Webster's mind as he sat at that desk was a constitutional crisis of sorts. The presidential election of 1824 had resulted in no candidate receiving a majority of the electoral votes, so the House of Representatives—the legislative body in which he served—had been forced to choose the next President. Four candidates—John Quincy Adams, Andrew Jackson, William H. Crawford, and Henry Clay—had campaigned for the presidency in 1824. Everyone understood that 131 electoral votes were needed to secure a majority and win the election. Andrew Jackson, carrying most of the southern states, secured 99 of those votes, while John Quincy Adams, his closest challenger, received 84. Crawford came in third place with 41 electoral votes, and Henry Clay came in fourth with 37. No candidate had mustered the necessary majority, and thus Webster and his fellow congressmen faced the weighty responsibility of deciding between Jackson, Adams, and Crawford.[1] Of course, Webster recognized at the time that the stakes were high and the country was watching. He understood that this would be the first time the Twelfth Amendment to the United States Constitution was truly tested; he was quite concerned.

Webster knew the legislative history and he knew how the country had arrived at this moment. It seemed that political leaders had been tinkering with, or at least criticizing, the machinery of presidential elections practically since the birth of the nation. This would be the second time over the course of the country's first ten presidential elections that the outcome was not neat and tidy. A 20 percent failure rate was troubling. The Twelfth Amendment had been ratified just twenty years earlier, in an attempt to remedy some of the defects of the Constitution's Article II, Section 1, Clause 3. That faulty clause had required each member of the Electoral College to cast *two* ballots for President. The original idea was that the candidate with the most ballots (provided that number was a majority of all electoral votes) would become President, while the individual who received the second most ballots would become Vice President. Simple enough, that process had been viewed by the constitutional Framers in Philadelphia as one that would discourage the type of factional partisanship that inevitably tore a republic apart. It was also a clear nod to the civic republicanism most constitutional Framers favored. Such a mechanism, though, had a fatal flaw: it encouraged ties.

That precise scenario occurred in the election of 1800, with Thomas Jefferson and Aaron Burr each receiving 73 electoral votes. A protracted battle ensued in the House of Representatives, and after 36 ballots in the contingent election, Jefferson emerged as the new President. But not without cost to country and candidates. The entire affair—general election *and* contingent election—came to be known as the "Revolution of 1800" because partisan politics dominated the campaign. The personal insults back and forth (especially between the incumbent President, John Adams, and his Vice President, Thomas Jefferson) are legendary. Jefferson attacked Adams for his small stature and lack of masculine virtues. Adams attacked Jefferson for his promiscuity in fathering a child with an enslaved woman and for his monarch-like aspirations. It was arguably the ugliest presidential election in American history, and in its wake, political leaders in both the federal and state governments set out to calm the partisan waters. They looked to the constitutional amendment process for a solution. The result was the Twelfth Amendment.

This change to the Constitution was simple, but effective. The Twelfth Amendment called for the President and Vice President to be elected *separately*. Permit electors to vote separately and distinctly for one President and one Vice President, and what you get is a process that lowers the likelihood of ties and that encourages presidential and vice presidential running mates, or "tickets," if you will. Despite this important change, some aspects of the original Article II clause remained after the Twelfth Amendment was ratified, specifically the process by which the House of Representatives must, in the event that no candidate receives a majority of the electoral votes, "choose, immediately, by ballot, the President." The Twelfth Amendment further mandates that members of each state delegation to the House vote as a unit. In other words, each state, and not each Member of Congress, can cast a single vote. That was the situation the House faced in 1825. Each state had to decide on the next President. As a member of the Massachusetts delegation, Webster had to caucus with his fellow Bay Staters and decide whom to back. He favored Adams.

He was, thus, initially pleased when John Quincy Adams eventually won the contingent election of 1825, with the Massachusetts delegation joining twelve other states to throw their support behind their friend and neighbor. It was the first time in American political history that the winner of the *electoral* vote failed to also win the *popular* vote. Jackson, from Tennessee, was the clear winner of the popular vote (with 41 percent of that vote), and yet he would not occupy the White House that year. The shenanigans that gave rise to John Quincy Adams' electoral victory were now coming to the surface. Henry Clay, the Speaker of the House of Representatives at the time, had facilitated what came to be known as a "corrupt bargain" to prevent his arch enemy Andrew Jackson from becoming President. He had cut a deal with Adams. In exchange for the electoral votes of his own supporters, Clay insisted upon being appointed Secretary of State, a position he recognized as a stepping-stone to the White House. Adams agreed. The problem was that the "corrupt bargain" was made so brazenly and so willfully that Adams' credibility was practically doomed from the start of his presidency.

Most citizens in 1825 were growing increasingly concerned about the state of American politics. The "Era of Good Feelings" following the War of 1812 and associated with the Monroe presidency—a period characterized by relative harmony, American patriotism, single-party politics, and apparent national unity—appeared to be coming to an abrupt end. To put it a different way, the consequences of the election were profound, and not positive: regional divisions were underscored, the Federalist Party finally made its exit from the national stage, and the Electoral College fell under attack. The 1824 presidential election was casting a long shadow over the progress of the young country.

Moreover, it followed other sobering events: the first collapse of the American economy in 1819, the hand-wringing over the

Missouri Compromise of 1821 and then over the Monroe Doctrine in 1823, and other, smaller concerns. Paul Nagel writes of the debated issues of the time, "men still recalled the Missouri struggles, the abortive Vesey rebellion, the tariff and internal improvement tensions, as well as other public issues which had helped delineate regional interests."[2] These were big issues—important issues!—and ones that dominated the headlines. It was against this backdrop that Webster contemplated his role not only in selecting the President but also in advancing the fundamental interests of the young, and somewhat fragile, United States.

The 1824 presidential election and the 1825 contingent election occurred at a crucial political moment. What troubled Webster shortly after the contingent election was a deeply philosophical problem. The New Englander brooded over the role of the individual citizen in the election of the U.S. President and in American politics more generally. "The America of 1824 was recognizably a republic, in the sense that ultimate sovereignty lay with the people, but much less a democracy, in which the people engage directly in the political process."[3] But now, the political landscape was shifting from one dominated by republican ideals to one far more democratic. The Twelfth Amendment hadn't slowed that shift, and Daniel Webster worried that *nothing* in the 1787 Constitution would prevent the inevitable. As Webster and everyone else in politics knew, political parties in America no longer existed as they once did. James Monroe's sweeping victory in the 1820 presidential election had proved the Federalist Party a relic of the past and the Jeffersonian party the unchallenged victor.[4]

The Federalist Party to which Webster had dedicated his political career lay in ruins, absorbed in pieces by coalitions that sought to challenge the only national political party left: the Democratic-Republicans. The election of 1824 was the first time, in fact, that not a single candidate had run on a Federalist ticket.

All the candidates ran as Democratic-Republicans. Not until the late 1820s would the nation's political environment return to a viable two-party system.

Webster had to face developments he had been seeing and wrestling with for months. A staunch Federalist, proud New Englander, and a well-known "Defender of the Constitution," he yet bore witness to changes in the social fabric and the collective attitude of the American people in recent years. These changes echoed within the walls of the U.S. Capitol, where political factions reverberated. The country was moving rapidly toward industrialization and, Webster contended, haphazardly toward a more democratic society, one in which liberal state constitutions, for example, granted all White males suffrage, no matter how common or how uninformed those citizens were. The increasingly divisive institution of slavery also loomed ahead. Slavery was an issue so fraught with tensions—political, moral, constitutional, economic, and personal—that Webster viewed it as the hammer that would shatter the fragile detente between North and South. This anticipation kept Webster on tenterhooks. He believed the United States had amassed a short but rich history, one with a notable list of achievements built upon the foundation constructed by the forefathers and forged by the leadership of George Washington. The skeleton of that foundation was located in the text of the Constitution, and Webster intended to protect it from fracture.

He had been invited by the Massachusetts state legislature to represent the Commonwealth at the 1825 Constitutional Convention in Philadelphia. He gladly accepted, of course, but he did not know what to expect. The prospect of rehashing and altering the Constitution, a document he considered brilliantly engineered by the likes of James Madison, Alexander Hamilton, and Benjamin Franklin, left him aghast. Indeed, Webster put great stock in the Constitution. He also knew it backward and forward from his years as a preeminent lawyer. Webster felt acutely aware of the social and political changes at work in the country, and sensed that impending change posed a threat to the stability of the Union, of which he had grown fiercely protective over the years. All of this weighed heavily on the New England Federalist as he set off from Marshfield for the long journey to Philadelphia. It was early May.

The Constitutional Convention Opens

Daniel Webster was a giant figure in American politics in the first quarter of the nineteenth century. Not the most famous American of his day—that title would probably extend to Thomas Jefferson and then later to Andrew Jackson—Webster was still famous in his own right. Though he started his career supporting the states' rights position, he quickly realized the value of a strong and energetic national government. For most of his time in politics, he supported initiatives that would stimulate the national economy, including the introduction of a national bank. He advocated for protective tariffs and infrastructure improvements. He successfully argued some of the most important cases of the early nineteenth century, including *McCulloch v. Maryland, Dartmouth College v. Woodward*, and *Gibbons v. Ogden*. Indeed, American law was largely shaped by Webster's mind.

But it was mostly his oratorical skills that set him apart from his peers. He could persuade and regale small and large audiences alike. His contemporaries in the U.S. Congress regularly marveled at his ability to weave intricate ideas and thoughts together, often culminating in a crescendo of power and persuasion. It was fitting, then, that he would be selected to join 130 other delegates, sent by their respective states, in Philadelphia in the summer of 1825.[5] The time had come for constitutional renewal.

It would be the first time that Jefferson's generational constitutional stance would be invoked. It was a test, of sorts. Could the delegates take what had been learned about America's experiment with written constitutionalism and improve upon the 1787 Constitution? Would the citizens then ratify the product of their labors? Delegates to the 1825 Constitutional Convention in Philadelphia were well aware that states themselves were experimenting with constitutional designs over the past three decades. In fact, eighteen states had added new constitutions since the U.S. Constitution was written in 1787. Eleven—Kentucky, Vermont, Tennessee, Ohio, Louisiana, Indiana, Mississippi, Illinois, Alabama, Maine, and Missouri—were granted statehood during this period, and as a condition of joining the Union, they had to draft their own constitutional documents and present them to Congress for approval. An additional five states—Pennsylvania, South Carolina, Delaware, Connecticut, and New York—used conventions in the early nineteenth century to fundamentally rewrite their Revolutionary War–era constitutions. Two states—Georgia and Kentucky—redrafted their constitutions twice during this almost four-decade period. Moreover, the knowledge and experience in the Assembly Room in Independence Hall was impressive. Many of the delegates to the convention had been primarily responsible for framing the various state constitutions. Familiar with constitution-making in the first place, they also had the political and social credibility to back up what they produced.

Fittingly, Jefferson took up the elder statesman role at the 1825 Constitutional Convention. It was the least the delegates could do to honor the man who insisted on periodic constitutional conventions in the first place. Of course, Jefferson had retired from public life in 1809, returning to his beloved Monticello near Charlottesville, Virginia. Now that his goal of establishing a world-class university was almost met, he could set his sights on another, perhaps final, civic act. He would enjoy his well-earned victory.

Jefferson's invitation to the 1825 Constitutional Convention was not without its detractors. He was beloved in the Commonwealth of Virginia, but outside his home state, many found Jefferson to be, shall we say, controversial and slightly out of touch. Most delegates understood that they were beginning to live not in Jefferson's agrarian America, but in Alexander Hamilton's America—where urban centers were the fuel of economic growth and industrial capitalism was the country's future. Delegates were also well aware that Jefferson was a major player in the advent of political partisanship in America. He hated the Federalist Party, and individuals wondered whether he could put his partisan inclinations aside and help to draft a new constitutional document. Still, he was present, and his influence was unmistakable.

Also present and influential were Daniel Webster, Henry Clay, John C. Calhoun, John W. Taylor, Andrew Stevenson, Rufus King, Andrew Jackson, and on and on—all the major political figures of the day. The delegates believed that the credibility of their enterprise was symbolically—or, even, spiritually—tied to the original framing convention in 1787. They knew how to play to a skeptical American public, one that still worried about the concentration of power and the long-term merits of written constitutionalism. They might gain favor, the delegates thought, if they replicated as many of the particulars of the original constitutional convention as possible. Most of current assembly viewed the representatives of the 1787 Convention as heroic, icons of a revolutionary and virtuous generation. As planned, they gathered in Independence Hall—a bit more cramped this time around as there were more than twice as many delegates—and called the convention to order on May 27th, exactly thirty-eight years to the day after the opening of the initial constitutional convention.

The first order of business, much as in 1787, was to deliberate on the specific rules that would govern the meeting. That would take some time; there was a lot to discuss. Eventually, the delegates would agree to many of the conventional procedural rules that govern these events: decisions would be determined by simple majority vote; verbal "yeas" and "nays" would be the electoral choice; a quorum of delegates *and* states was needed for any proposal to pass; committees were to be constituted by ballot; requests for the day's adjournment had to be seconded; straw polls would be taken; and so on. Parliamentary procedures would rule, the delegates determined; indeed, the entire project was to be, as much as possible, subject to the procedures that had governed the constitutional convention thirty-eight years earlier. With one significant exception: the delegates in 1825 agreed to abandon the 1787 rule that voting would be allocated to individual states, replacing it with a rule that granted a vote to each delegate. This represented a major, and quite surprising, departure from the 1787 Constitutional Convention rules, especially given that the future of slavery would no doubt be on the docket. But a majority of delegates found the prospect of not being tied to their state delegation more appealing than adhering to tradition.

There was one task, however, that caused a bit of political hand-wringing. Unlike the case in the original federal convention, the selection of a presiding officer to direct the gathering was not a foregone conclusion. There was no George Washington among this group, the man who had led the 1787 Convention by total consensus. His military record, combined with his decision to abandon public life at the height of his popularity rather than seize power, had made him the obvious choice. No American was considered more virtuous or more honest.

That kind of consensus was absent in 1825: in part because no one else could be "a Washington" and in part because partisan bickering had so permeated politics since the turn of the nineteenth century that there was no obvious choice for the leadership role. Andrew Jackson might have been a good choice, but it was well-known that he was still stinging, and bitter, from the contingent election defeat he had suffered in the House of Representatives. Plus, he was decidedly a regional voice, not the national unifier that was needed in this moment. He would not do. Daniel Webster might have been a good choice, but he made it known that he would decline, preferring instead to influence the proceedings from the floor. He was an orator, and he knew that the precedent set by Washington was for the President of the convention to remain mostly silent. Henry Clay? He might have been good, but he was so tarnished by Jackson's supporters for his role in ensuring John Quincy Adams' presidential victory that his candidacy was undercut from the start. How about James Madison, even then considered the "father of the American Constitution"? Could he lead the effort? The former President had largely stayed away from public affairs after his term in the White House ended in 1817. He advised Andrew Jackson from time to time on various matters, and he occasionally let slip his concerns about such policies as the Missouri Compromise and Nullification. But most understood that he no longer had the charisma (if he ever did) or the stature to preside in this moment. Fragile and sickly, he somewhat reluctantly decided to stay home.

Eventually, the convention would turn to Jefferson to be its presiding officer. It was a fitting tribute, of course. Folks knew that Jefferson had advocated long and hard for this convention. He was rarely shy about repeating his belief that "the earth belongs to the living" and that such a sentiment applied just as much to constitutions as it did to laws, traditions, and norms. The most prominent minds of the time were familiar with his argument, and these were the statesmen pegged to attend the convention. An argument could also be made that he was the elder dignitary of the lot. In no way equivalent in popularity to Washington, at eighty-two years old he nevertheless qualified for the chief position because of the respect he had earned throughout his impressive public career—and because of his senior status. It was decided. May 27th, 1825, would be Jefferson's day.

Now that the question of leadership was settled, and the details of the procedural rules were in place, the group could move on to the business at hand. Having studied James Madison's notes from the first federal constitutional convention, the *Federalist Papers*, the works of anti-Federalists, the editorials from the major newspapers of the time, and other materials surrounding the 1787 Constitutional Convention, Daniel Webster opened the substantive portion of the meeting by describing the importance of the moment. The first generation of Americans was unified by a common cause, a common purpose: independence and self-government. The second generation of Americans, Webster reminded his fellow conventioneers, was not blessed with a similar common purpose. Identifying the ingredients for a "more perfect Union," he said, was fundamentally different from cooking the stew.

The work of the convention would be arduous. Delegates would experience a range of emotions, including anger, frustration, and yes, even despair. But have no fear, Webster continued. They would also feel a sense of compassion and joy, duty and accomplishment, satisfaction and pride. He had no doubt that the product of their deliberations would be a better constitutional text, a constitutional instrument that would more effectively put them on the path toward a "more perfect Union." They simply had to trust the process and have faith that everyone in the room shared the same ultimate goal: a stronger and more unified country.

Webster saved his most powerful oratorical punch for last. He had heard whispers during the pre-convention socializing that the hardest task for the delegates would be to determine what language from the 1787 Constitution should go and what language from that document should stay. What is more, a few delegates had voiced a certain anxiety over how they might craft *new* constitutional provisions out of whole cloth. If they were to consider language relating to such contentious issues as judicial independence, suffrage, Electoral College reform, universal public education, slavery, and so on, these delegates wondered, what in the 1787 Constitution could be used as guidance? The word *education* does not appear at all in America's Constitution or its Bill of Rights. Nor does the term *slavery*. Webster understood that he had to address this seeming deficit. He began by announcing that he had heard those concerns, but that he did not share them. The Massachusetts statesman then reminded the delegation that it had useful templates—exemplars, models, prototypes, if you will—right under its nose. The *state* constitutions provided useful ideas, clauses, and language that they could "borrow"—or "transplant"—as they undertook their necessary work. The eighteen state constitutional conventions that successfully produced constitutional texts in the period between the drafting of the U.S. Constitution in 1787 and the convening of this convention in 1825 were, in fact, a good place to start, Webster declared. We should lean heavily on the work of those in this room, he said, who have committed so much to the enterprise of ordering their individual state polities.

"No one begins writing a constitution from scratch."[6] Such a sentiment has been shared by constitution-makers throughout modern history. If imitation is the sincerest form of flattery, constitutional drafters have been dabbling in flattery practically since the first written text was adopted. The constitutions of colonial North America, for example, were remarkably similar in structure, style, and language. Many followed the basic outlines of the early constitutional adopters—South Carolina, Virginia, New Jersey, and Delaware—in embracing bicameral legislatures, written bills of rights, independent judiciaries, and separate executives. By the time of Cornwallis' 1781 surrender at Yorktown, ending the Revolutionary War, all thirteen states had fully embraced the principle of written constitutionalism. Eleven of those states—all but Connecticut and Rhode Island, which continued to rule under their original colonial charters—had constitutions that were products of constitutional imitation.

The two primary sources that provide guidance on any polity's new constitution are the *existing* constitution (if there is one) and the constitutions that order other jurisdictions in the polity's backyard.[7] I call the former phenomenon "constitutional baselining," and the latter is known as "constitutional borrowing." Both are essential components of any drafting process. Constitutional baselining emerges from a simple fact: most new constitutions are in some ways a reaction to or reflection on the constitution about to be replaced. The U.S. Constitution was influenced mightily by the vices of its predecessor, the Articles of Confederation. Indeed, by almost every measure the U.S. Constitution is a *reaction to*, and not necessarily a *reflection of*, the Articles of Confederation. And yet most in the late eighteenth century still believed in the first principles that gave rise to the call for independence, the push for self-rule, and the need for liberty. Consequently, the Framers of the U.S. Constitution attempted to preserve several of the defining principles, sacred tenets, and basic protections of America's founding document even as they rejected the text itself.

That said, it is more in the arena of constitutional borrowing, not constitutional baselining, that the Framers of the 1787 Constitution did their best work. Constitutional borrowing "takes place when drafters of new constitutions encounter a particular problem and look to *other constitutions* for solutions."[8] And Webster knew that. He concluded his lengthy opening monologue with a promise always to lean on the brilliance and dedication of his forebears—at both the national and state levels—when imagining new constitutional possibilities.

The substantive work of drafting a new constitution was thus at hand. The first few weeks of the convention were spent discussing the broad contours of a new constitutional document. The prospect of altering the primary dimensions of America's governmental structure seemed reckless to most in the room. Simply because they had the opportunity to dispose of major elements of the American political system did not mean the delegates were in favor of wholesale change. Just the opposite, in fact. Enough was working under the 1787 Constitution to recommend a basic continuation of the original political architecture. It was thus decided early in the proceedings that the 1825 Constitution would transplant many of the design features of the original 1787 text. That was especially true for Articles I and II of the Constitution, the articles devoted to the legislative and executive branches.

Congress would, for instance, retain the bulk of its powers as described in Article I, Sections 7 and 8, the delegates concluded. The authority to tax, regulate interstate commerce, raise revenue, coin money, "promote the sciences and the useful arts," declare war, and so on, would be preserved. Further, Congress would remain a bicameral institution, with the lower chamber—the House of Representatives—consisting of 213 members and the upper chamber—the Senate—consisting of 48 members. The convention delegates felt confident that representation in the House should still be determined by population and that statehood should remain the determining factor in the Senate. The two-year term for Representatives and the six-year term for Senators would also be retained, as would the particulars surrounding the elections of these public figures. Finally, the qualifications clauses in Article I, Sections 2 and 3 would remain undisturbed.

Identical thinking characterized the debate about executive power. For the most part, delegates to the convention were satisfied with how the presidency and the executive branch were developing. The Qualifications Clause, Compensation Clause, and the Emoluments Clause all seemed functional at this point. The powers entrusted to the President, including those related to appointments, treaty making, his role as commander in chief, and his capacity to pardon, also seemed reasonable. Indeed, the fear of an autocrat assuming the office that so consumed the 1787 Philadelphia Convention was largely mitigated by the precedent established by George Washington and by the actions of ensuing chief executives. That's not to say violations couldn't happen, some delegates warned, but there was enough faith in the evolution of the office that the convention-goers left that issue, along with other questions of executive authority, alone.

But it was the workings of the Electoral College, or rather, the process of electing the President in general, that required adjustment. The "corrupt bargain" that resulted in John Quincy Adams becoming President in 1824 had shaken the population's faith in fair presidential elections. Even with the addition of the Twelfth Amendment, political commentators were beginning to recognize that state political leaders had considerable influence—perhaps *too* much influence—in selecting individuals for the Electoral College. In 1825, the nation had twenty-four states, and in six of them, state legislators directly elected members of the Electoral College; in the other eighteen, where the electorate had more of a say, the influence of state legislators was hardly less.[9] Voter turnout had been disappointingly low in those states with some mechanism for popular election, especially given the contested nature of the election and the correlated decline of two-party rule. Only 26.5 percent of eligible voters nationwide went to the polls to select a President that year.[10] Surprisingly, some of the most politically active states saw even less turnout in 1824: Pennsylvania 19.6 percent; Virginia 11.5 percent.[11] Cynicism was the most frequently cited emotion when individuals were asked about the 1824 election mess.

Furthermore, sectional divisions that had simmered just below the surface for most of America's electoral history—especially as they related to presidential politics—reappeared in the aftermath of the 1824 election. The Democratic-Republican Party pushed even harder for policies and positions that were considerably more popular in the South: states' rights, the expansion of slavery, agrarian sensibilities, greater popular sovereignty, universal White male suffrage, manifest destiny, and so on. Followers of Andrew Jackson railed against the disproportionate influence of political elites, and they called for a greater distribution of political power among everyday citizens. Interestingly, they also called for greater power to be vested in the President and the executive branch, especially at the expense of Congress. They reconciled the seeming inconsistency by insisting the Congress, and not the President, was the bastion of privilege.

The delegates to the 1825 Constitutional Convention thus knew that any proposed modification of the Electoral College would have to take account of the swelling support for these Jacksonian priorities. This was exactly the fear that had gripped Daniel Webster earlier that spring. The problem was that there were genuine philosophical differences among factions of delegates. On the one side were the Jacksonian Democrats, who favored greater democratization of the entire political system, including the selection of a President. On the other side stood the Federalists, descendants of a founding generation who were not convinced that the "common man" could truly be trusted. These individuals, hailing mostly from New England, insisted that republican ideals should still prevail. A standoff was inevitable.

Martin Van Buren, a Senator from New York, was the first to stand and propose amendments to Article II, Section 1, the portion of the 1787 Constitution that deals with the Electoral

College. Van Buren came from common beginnings as the son of a tavern keeper and a farmer. Like Daniel Webster, he had found his way into politics via the legal profession. He had been elected to the U.S. Senate in 1821, knew the political game, and maintained national ambitions. Van Buren stood and prepared to speak. His typically optimistic and smiling face had grown more serious, even formidable.

A disciple of Thomas Jefferson, Van Buren was not a fan of the nation's newly elected President. He had recently soured on the whole process of selecting a President from a body of specially chosen electors, and he wanted to democratize the procedure a bit. Van Buren was ideologically more aligned with the Jacksonian positions on issues like manifest destiny and states' rights, and thus he believed that the individual citizen was capable of selecting the country's chief executive. But he was also an independent thinker and a savvy political mind. If he did not play his cards right in the beginning, his goal of supplanting the Electoral College with a more direct system of selection would be finished.

So, he proposed a modest and simple revision to the electoral process. All in attendance that day knew that Article II, Section 1 of the 1787 U.S. Constitution empowered *state legislatures* to determine the method of selecting electors. Van Buren proposed that the delegation simply remove the clause authorizing the state legislatures to identify candidates for the Electoral College and replace it with a provision giving that same power to state citizens. Most states were trending in this direction anyway, he noted.

The proposed new language revealed Van Buren's bias in favor of more expansive popular rule. He read the proposed language out loud: "Resolved, in the matter of the election of the United States President, the following language be inserted in Article II, Section 1, Clause 2: Each state shall elect a number of electors, equal to the whole number of Senators and Representatives to which the state may be entitled in the Congress: but no Senator or Representative, or person holding an office of trust or profit under the United States, shall be an elector." He repeatedly cited the recent presidential election and the "corrupt bargain" as examples of how the system favored the privileged few. Elites held enormous power, he lamented, at the state level and, apparently, at the national level too. He preferred a less aristocratic manner of selecting inhabitants of the White House. The room went momentarily silent. Van Buren knew his actions would send a potent message to the political establishment and especially to the anti-Jacksonian faction of the convention. Make no mistake, he was not calling for the direct election of presidential candidates. He recognized that any proposed eradication of the Electoral College itself would be met with tremendous resistance.

John Gaillard, the senior Senator from South Carolina, quickly seconded Van Buren's proposal. A Democratic-Republican, he, too, was a disciple of Jefferson's political view. Gaillard was near the end of his life, and he had spent more than two decades in the upper chamber of Congress. He had earned widespread respect both in Washington and in Philadelphia for his statesman-like demeanor. Elected President pro tempore of the Senate no fewer than ten times, he was well-known for carving out the compromise position on most major issues of the day. He was never the first to get behind a controversial issue. In fact, standing to support Van Buren so quickly was a little out of character. Nonetheless, Gaillard felt strongly that a revision to the Electoral College was in order. Martin Van Buren had secretly huddled with Gaillard as he contemplated a revised presidential election process. They decided on the proposed language together.

Gaillard's support for the provision was met by a vocal objection from Horatio Seymour, a Senator from Vermont. Seymour had been elected to the Senate in 1821 and had spent four mostly unremarkable years in the chamber. This was his chance to move the delegation. He opposed the proposed resolution because any rejection of the republican principles underpinning the election of the President would disrupt the delicate balance among the three elected institutions. The House of Representatives, he argued, was the "democratically elected" branch. Not the President. And the original Framers of the 1787 U.S. Constitution had thought long and hard about the wisdom of various selection

processes. In a subtle sleight of hand, he even insisted that Senators, who were still appointed by their respective state legislators,
could not be the only federal officials elected by fully indirect
means.[12] The influence of the upper chamber of Congress, he
insisted, would erode over time if it was seen as the sole body
populated by limited and elitist methods. Others agreed and a
fiery discussion ensued. In the end, though, Seymour's points
were not persuasive enough. The convention voted 71 to 60 in
favor of the Van Buren resolution. The vote fell roughly along
party lines. It was a major victory for the Jacksonian Democrats.

The issue of suffrage was next up on the list of debate topics.
Extending the vote beyond White property owners had created
a frenzy at the state level in the decades leading up to 1825, and
there was every reason to believe that the issue would be contested at the convention. It was, in many ways, the signal issue
that defined the divide between the old Federalists and the new
Democratic-Republicans.

The 1787 Constitution devolved the power to grant or deny
suffrage to the states. Since the creation of the Union, states
had considered the franchise question from many different perspectives and had reached very different conclusions. In most
cases, the issue came down to the role of property. In the late
eighteenth century, all thirteen of the original states required
White males to either own property or pay taxes in order to vote.
By 1790, Delaware, Maryland, North Carolina, South Carolina,
and Virginia had even upped the ante by requiring White men to
own at least fifty acres of land to qualify to vote. In Pennsylvania
and Georgia, White men who paid their tax dues were permitted
to participate in elections.

However, things began to change in the early nineteenth century, as states began to expand the franchise to more White
men. By 1825, only six of the twenty-four states still had property qualifications, and only twelve maintained their tax-paying

requirement. It is perhaps most telling that none of the states admitted to the Union after 1790 chose to require a property qualification, though some held on to the tax-paying barrier.

In some states where the tax requirement lingered, the threshold was low. In New Hampshire, as well as in many of the new Western frontier states, the imposition of a relatively inexpensive poll tax enabled the enfranchisement of most White males. In other states, however, the effect and intent of tax requirements was the same as a significant monetary qualification. Massachusetts and Connecticut, for example, retained relatively strict tax-paying requirements that privileged only the wealthy electorate.

A growing number of other states had, in contrast, opted to forgo any monetary or property qualifications at all, deciding instead to expand the suffrage to *all* White males. This national trend was one of liberalizing the requirements and enlarging the electorate. Beginning with Kentucky in 1792, Alabama, Illinois, Indiana, Maine, Maryland, Missouri, and Vermont all had permitted universal White male suffrage by 1825. What was interesting was that the expansion of the franchise under state jurisdiction mirrored in many ways federal movement on the issue. Although the federal government could not force the states to adopt liberal suffrage laws, it *did* have the ability to enforce suffrage laws in the territories it governed. In 1808, Congress liberalized property qualifications in the Northwest Ordinance territories. Three years later, Congress enfranchised all free White males who paid taxes and lived in what would soon become Indiana, Illinois, Michigan, and Wisconsin.[13] New York delegate Nathan Sanford put it succinctly: "the course of things in the country is for the extension, and not the restriction of popular rights."[14] He was right.

In 1825, one of the convention committees assembled was a special committee on suffrage, composed of delegates from states whose voting qualifications ranged from universal White male to a freehold system. The committee members met in private rooms to discuss minute details, and in the hotels and taverns around Philadelphia to engage in philosophical and ideological discussions about politics and the nature of democracy. Progress was slow. Finally, though, the suffrage committee presented its report to the convention on July 6th, after pausing to observe Independence Day. Nathan Sanford addressed the delegates. As he spoke, conflicting noises of agreement and dissent rose in volume and in pitch. Sanford quickened his pace slightly but remained otherwise unperturbed as he barreled on toward his conclusion. His short speech culminated in a controversial proposal: universal White manhood suffrage for each and every state—the forced liberalization and standardization of voting qualifications through the elimination of all property and tax requirements. Sanford's eyes swept the crowd as he uttered his last syllable, and the listeners erupted in a frenzy of opinions.

The committee's proposal to enfranchise all White males in the United States smacked of the kind of populist, democratic fervor that was enveloping the country. The trend of liberalized voting requirements was perhaps the most evident facet of the divisive political movement that was sweeping across the United States in the 1820s. Personified by Andrew Jackson, a push was emerging to open up the American political system and to democratize the United States government. Moreover, the idealistic vision behind Jacksonian democracy—a newfound respect for the common man and a departure from the Jeffersonian emphasis on education as a prerequisite for politics—was only one piece of the motive behind shifting political ideals, particularly when it came to expanding the polity.

There were other reasons to support the expansion of White male suffrage. During the War of 1812, recruiting soldiers and keeping them in uniform proved problematic. Certain states sought to address this problem by enfranchising militiamen, because voting men would be more inclined to fight for their country.[15] Between 1817 and 1820, Connecticut, New York, and Mississippi chose to exempt militiamen from existing electoral requirements. Similarly, in the South, the desire to preserve slavery incentivized states to reward military men with the right to vote. Give all White men the vote regardless of their status as property owners, some southerners argued, and you had a stronger and more invested militia during a time of growing rebellion among the enslaved. Further, a financial crisis, the Panic of 1819, had resulted in the nation's first major economic depression. The South and the West were hit hardest by the Panic of 1819, but economics played a role in the politics of other regions as well. In the Midwest, for example, economic motivations encouraged the expansion of the electorate in order to entice people who would otherwise not have settled in frontier territory. That, in turn, would increase property values and improve other aspects of the economy. The delegates understood that this was a complex issue with a lot of overlapping tentacles.

So, they asked: What was the best way to protect the Union and guide it through this revision process without those on one side of the suffrage issue alienating those on the other side? If the majority of the delegates wanted universal White male suffrage, the only way to keep peace and unity in Philadelphia that summer might be to assuage them. And yet Webster had his doubts. He was next to speak. As he prepared, he recalled a short yet impassioned speech John Quincy Adams had made a few years earlier. Through a reasoned understanding of history, Adams sought to persuade his audience to preserve the balance between population and property by maintaining the pecuniary qualifications. History, he said, had furnished examples of republics destroyed by a disregard for property ownership. In at least three places—Rome, France, and America—persons of no property greatly outnumbered those with property.[16] In both Rome and France, the masses' incursion into politics was facilitated by political elites—by the Senators of Rome and by the Dukes of France. These men were eventually overrun and displaced by the very force they sought to empower. The radicals who sought to enfranchise the masses, Adams concluded, would condemn America to the same fate.

Although Webster agreed with Adams' sentiment, his tone would have to be softened. Webster was well aware of the populist momentum; he would have to appeal to history and to principle if there was any hope of defeating the Sanford proposal. Rising to speak, Webster began by echoing much of what he had said at the Massachusetts State Constitutional Convention of 1820 and had then reiterated in his famous oration at Plymouth shortly thereafter. Many in attendance had heard one or both of these speeches, but Webster wanted to slowly build his case. At the Massachusetts convention, Webster had spoken not of universal White male suffrage but of legislative apportionment.[17] Webster's position on that issue served as a clear indicator of how much stock he placed in property and its correlation with power in government. Webster reminded the delegates that he favored a property qualification for Senators as a distinct check on the House of Representatives. Webster said, again, that he believed there must be "some difference of character, sentiment, feeling, or origin" in the Senate in order for it to maintain some power over the House.[18] Property served as that difference. This, Webster explained, was how balance worked. It was not about placing checks on the people, but rather maintaining balance in the government.

As was typical of his style, Webster cited history—of the ancient philosophical variety, as well as a few recent American examples—to support his argument. Webster gestured toward Aristotle who warned of property and wealth in excess, but who also favored "sufficient and middling" property for all those engaged in politics. The seventeenth-century political theorist James Harrington had said something similar. He had argued persuasively, Webster emphasized, that there existed an inextricable link between power and property. Harrington believed that when King Henry VII took wealth away from the nobility, he irrevocably upset the balance of power in England. The gentry had acquired land, and with that land they expected political power. This was the natural order of things. Once the King tampered with the balance of land and power, the only option for England was to become a republic.

Webster pointed out that more recently still, the American Revolution was inextricably linked to the importance of property. "Our own immortal Revolution was undertaken, not to shake or plunder property, but to protect it."[19] As Webster hoped, that line had a noticeable effect on many in the audience. Some shifted in their seats, others closed their eyes in consideration of the idea. After building the credibility of his argument with this historical backing, Webster paused. For just a moment he went silent, losing himself in reflection, in his own history. His mind wandered briefly to his humble beginnings, assisting his brother and father on the farm. He thought of the mortgage his father had taken out on that land, land that he had bought and built and brought to life himself, in order to give his son an education and an avenue into law and politics. He thought, too, of the reverence he automatically felt for the cultured figures he had met during his early law days on Massachusetts' south shore, and of how their claim to property gave them some stake in the development of the nation. He thought about his accumulated debts, his property ventures, and the root of his occasional carelessness. Power grew from property as a farm grew from seed. Property and power in two different social classes, indeed in two entirely different social worlds, would threaten the balance a nation needed to thrive.

To his audience, the pregnant pause appeared merely as a dramatic touch. Webster regained his mental composure. "Will you forsake what has been built by our founders?" He began, his deep and intentional cadence brought him to a crescendo: "Will you condemn to ruin the very government that you have been elected to serve, to protect, and to strengthen? Will you upset the delicate balance of property and power upon which we all stand? Will you leave our land, our nation, vulnerable to the violent and clamoring frenzy of revolution, to every whim of popular opinion? Will you not guard the principles of Christianity, philosophy, and democracy that the founders penned into the spirit of this nation? Will you not stand united and defend the nation in which you have so great a stake?" This repetition of questions was a technique Webster had perfected, and one that had proved particularly successful in his Plymouth Oration.[20] Webster remained standing as he fixed his audience with one last gaze meant to chill and ignite.

Next to express his opinion was Martin Van Buren, who, more than anything else, surprised his fellow delegates by rising again to speak. At the time, Van Buren did not relish the spotlight. And yet he believed strongly that voting was a right rather than privilege. He had advocated as much at the New York State Constitutional Convention of 1821. In order to preserve a republic, its enfranchised citizens must retain some virtue, he argued. The right to vote must be earned, either by the payment of taxes, military participation, or work on public roads. But the exercise of rights didn't depend exclusively on the good fortune of land ownership. He spoke ardently in support of the enfranchisement of the emerging middle class—the working men who comprised the strength and mettle of America—the "bone, pith, and muscle" as he had called them at the New York convention four years earlier.[21]

Van Buren tackled the vision of the future, a vision that divided Federalists from Democratic-Republicans. The former predicted the coming of an "urban proletariat" with the rise of manufacturing.[22] The latter, folks like Van Buren himself, argued that such a fear was without merit.[23] Farmers would always remain numerous. America would remain agrarian. Federalists held fast to the idea of suffrage as a privilege to be bestowed on those who were capable enough to protect the interests of the people and the nation. Followers of Jefferson and Jackson felt differently. One of the more unconvincing arguments, Van Buren said pointedly, rested upon that fear of the urban proletariat, their potential for rebellion, and even more specifically, the ability of manufacturing bosses to manipulate dependent employees and thus manipulate the system. Even some of the shrewdest politicians, he argued, could not predict the changes that would alter the physical and societal landscape of America.

In the 1820s, a working-class, urban-dominated America was some sort of nightmare futuristic tale and not much more. For an increasing number of Americans, it was unconscionable to compromise egalitarian sentiment by cheating the propertyless man of his vote, so long as he pulled his weight. Unconscionable, too, for Martin Van Buren. He would not jump at some distant, ghostlike vision of the future. He was a reformer, and he had his own vision of America's future. Scoffing at another delegate's comment about the inevitability of manipulated votes and political chaos if transient manufacturing men gained suffrage, Van Buren decided to change the course of the conversation.

He was not known for oratorical skill, but Van Buren spoke sharply, enunciated clearly, and tapped into a purely American energy when he transported the other delegates back to the origins of the conflict that had given rise to the Union. As he grew more excited and impassioned, Van Buren's faint Dutch accent—a vestige of his rural past and his immigrant parents—crept ever so slightly into his speech. He spoke of parliamentary exclusion and of the subsequent violent and bloody revolution. He spoke of the men who worked hard and who contributed to the nation's success. What of these men? Contribute to society, Van Buren contended, and you deserve a vote in your government. Bear the financial brunt of the country by way of taxation, and you deserve a say in how the country's government operates. Voting, then, was a right, but a right with some limitations. Van Buren wished to end with an enthusiastic declaration, one intended to stir all the men present. "No taxation without representation!" he boomed, and the men were moved.[24] His words served as a reminder and a chastisement, a subtext warning to his fellow politicians to steer clear of hypocrisy.

A close friend of Van Buren's stood next. He was Nathaniel Macon of Warrenton, the son of a planter from North Carolina. By 1825, the sixty-seven-year-old Macon had already served ten years in the Senate and twenty-four years before that in the House of Representatives. Macon did not seek the political spotlight, but always accepted his positions out of a sense of duty. He was an ardent anti-Federalist, a leader among Jeffersonian Republicans, and had served as Speaker of the House during Jefferson's administration. Thomas Hart Benton, a Senator from Missouri, famously called Macon "the real Cincinnatus of America," referring to his virtuousness and principles.[25] Thomas Jefferson called

Macon "Ultimus Romanorum," or "the last of the Romans."[26]An uncompromising moral compass and reverence for individual liberty guided Macon's advocacy for a most open suffrage requirement. He had voiced some version of his opinion in a letter to Jefferson in 1822:

> Let the most numerous branch of the legislature be elected by all free Whites of the age of 21 years, except paupers, lunatics, & those who have committed crime, & every elector be eligible, let the other branch be elected by the same sort of people above a given age; every elector as in the other case to be eligible, The age for this branch ought not to be less than 30 years, perhaps forty would be better; The right to vote for both branches would depend on age & moral character; The object to let every man have a part in the government, & one branch at an age beyond youthful heat.[27]

In addition to reiterating his opinion that all free Whites of the age of twenty-one years (except the lunatics, paupers, and criminals) should have the right to vote, Macon came prepared with data. Maryland required substantial property qualifications for suffrage in its original state constitution (1776), Macon noted. Later, in 1802 and 1810, however, Maryland expanded its electorate to include all White citizens with permanent residence in the state.[28] Similar changes toward a more expansive voting population had recently taken place in South Carolina, Connecticut, and Massachusetts. Since 1790, Pennsylvania had allowed all citizens who paid taxes and all their sons between twenty-one and twenty-two years of age to vote.[29] No harm had come to these states, big or small, Macon insisted. Constitutional revision at the state level had augmented freedom in ways that reflected the times and the needs of the people. Macon expressed his impatience with a government that catered to the rich rather than to the moral.

As he continued to speak, he invoked Jefferson's language: "a government is republican in proportion as every member

composing it has his equal voice in the direction of its concern."[30]
It was the will of Thomas Jefferson that brought us here today
to congregate and to amend, was it not? No man should think
himself so powerful as to deny the vote to another. That is unjust. And worse, it is tyranny. With that, Macon subsided. He was
a Republican of the old variety, a veteran of the Revolutionary
War, and a seasoned politician with none of the pretense. The
delegates respected him.

John C. Calhoun of South Carolina joined Macon as another
southern politician with an open view of suffrage. While serving
in his state legislature, Calhoun had chaired a committee establishing a clause that guaranteed White manhood suffrage in the
Constitution of South Carolina.[31] To assuage those concerned
about changes written into the 1825 U.S. Constitution trumping
the rights of the states, Calhoun conceded that he understood
the aversion to such changes. He went on to explain that a government can more accurately and properly accomplish its ends
when it embodies the will of the people through universal White
male suffrage. "I call the right of suffrage the indispensable and
primary principle," Calhoun drawled, "for it would be a great
and dangerous mistake to suppose, as many do, that it is, of itself,
sufficient to form constitutional governments."[32]

Webster winced at Calhoun's remarks. The idea that a nonse-
lective electorate could somehow balance or aid the Founders'
Constitution in governing the country baffled him. He looked
to Henry Clay to gauge his thoughts on Calhoun's speech, but
Clay's face remained impassable. James Kent of New York arose to
voice his conservative view. He agreed with Webster ideologically,
and returned again to the emerging, uneducated, and rootless
mass that seemed to grow by the day in manufacturing centers.
The poor, he believed, would always covet the material goods of
the rich. A constitution that mandated universal White male suffrage would leave the country with two options, Kent explained:
a redistribution of land among the poor, or a revolution. In either case, Kent cried emphatically, "You condemn the Union!"[33]
He ended powerfully: "The tendency of universal suffrage is to

jeopardize the rights of property and the principles of liberty." It is to fashion a government from "[factory workers, retail clerks, and] the motley and undefinable population of crowded ports."[34]

No sooner had Kent taken his seat than Josiah Quincy of Massachusetts echoed his fervor: "What of women? Of minors?" Suffrage, Quincy believed, was not meant to be entirely equal, and in that inequality there resided protective liberty. "Is the spirit of our constitution not *limited* liberty? Of the careful control that constitutes a balanced governance?"[35] Webster nodded gravely in approval. He thought of the history that had taken place in this room, history not yet recorded nor appreciated for its full gravity. Seventeen eighty-seven was all too recent. Webster considered rising again, speaking out in protest for a second time, but he decided against it. He had not had time to prepare further remarks. He had accomplished all he could with this issue. The votes were then cast and counted.

The decision on suffrage turned Webster's skin a clammy gray despite the heat. By a slim margin, it would be universal White male suffrage for the Union. Jefferson had won again. Jefferson's views on suffrage, comparatively liberal for his time, aligned with the result of the Convention of 1825. As he had written in 1776: "I [am] for extending the right of suffrage (or in other words the rights of a citizen) to all who [have] a permanent intention of living in the country."[36]

While delegates would either celebrate or revile the liberalization of suffrage requirements, few would give serious consideration to those who had lost or been excluded from the conversation and from the right to vote. So much attention had been paid to an opening up of democracy and the potential implications of a constitutional change. A closing—though not many would have considered it as such at the time—also took place at the 1825 Convention. The language of the proposed and ultimately accepted resolution was exclusionary: "universal *White male* suffrage." By enfranchising all White males, the delegates vastly expanded the electorate in 1825 and converted America into a more democratic society—on its face. The success of the suffrage amendment also had the effect of disenfranchising a small portion of previously enfranchised people. In the states where race was absent from the elector qualifications, as in Georgia, Maine, Massachusetts, New Hampshire, New York, Rhode Island, North Carolina, Tennessee, and Vermont, previously enfranchised African Americans were disenfranchised in 1825.[37] In the states of New Jersey and Rhode Island, where gender was absent from elector qualifications, previously enfranchised women were disenfranchised by the convention. These previously enfranchised small pockets of Americans unequivocally lost a right. The decision of 1825 remained progressive only for a moment in American history.

Broad issues of representation, popular sovereignty, voting, and electoral influence are always the subjects that generate the most heated exchanges at constitutional drafting conventions. The 1787 Philadelphia Convention was mired for weeks in deliberations about the fair allocation of elected representatives and the proper way to select those officials. The 1825 Constitutional Convention was no different, and by mid-July, nerves were frayed and feelings hurt. Several delegates from New England even resigned in protest. But most got through this difficult period, beginning to produce an altered version of the old constitutional order.

The delegation could now move on to other pressing concerns. Though a full generation had passed since the original constitutional Framers met in Philadelphia, the political leaders of 1825 were acutely familiar with some of the "mistakes" of the 1787 Constitution. One such blunder, they thought, involved the question of whether to include a bill of rights. Most delegates to the 1787 Convention subscribed to the Hamiltonian view that a list of individual freedoms was not necessary because a constitution "is *itself*, in every rational sense, and to every useful purpose, a Bill of Rights."[38] Hamilton insisted that a constitution is legitimate only if it includes both *delegated* and *limited* powers; each branch of government, in other words, retains only those few powers clearly delineated in the actual words of the text. Consequently, powers *not* authorized to the government through the constitutional document are not retained by the government. Congress, Hamilton said, has no authority to limit an individual's freedom of speech because nothing in the text gives the legislature the power to do so. The same is true, he continued, for all the safeguards that might find their way into a proposed bill of rights. Hence, he concluded that a bill of rights was completely unnecessary; it was redundant, superfluous, even silly.

Unfortunately for him, many state Ratifying Conventions thought otherwise. The most ferocious opposition to endorsing the 1787 Constitution came from anti-Federalists who insisted that a list of freedoms had to accompany any new constitution. Anti-Federalists simply did not trust that individuals in power could resist the temptation to act in their own self-interest. Power corrupts, they argued, and so often the first protections sacrificed are the "unalienable rights" persons are "endowed" with, the ones that act as a bulwark against unbridled political authority. Give us the insurance of a written bill of rights, anti-Federalists insisted, or we won't ratify the text. It's as simple as that. Ever the politician, James Madison saw the writing on the wall and he agreed to this critical anti-Federalist demand. On June 8th, 1789, Madison proposed to the House of Representatives a list of seventeen amendments to the Constitution. Twelve of those amendments were eventually passed by the Senate, and ten of those were ratified in due course by the states. By 1791, the anti-Federalists had remedied the apparent omission from the U.S. Constitution. A Bill of Rights had been added to the country's fundamental law.

Ever since that moment, state constitutional conventions had refused to omit bills of rights from their fundamental law. They were not going to make the same mistake the Philadelphia delegates made. In fact, they were going to go one symbolic step further. Many state constitution-makers in the late eighteenth and early nineteenth centuries decided to *frontload* the list of liberties in the charter they were creating, in many ways sending the message that the bill of rights should be viewed as paramount to the institutional design portions of the state constitution. Maine's 1820 Constitution—the one that granted it statehood—*begins* with a list of individual freedoms. So does Alabama's 1819 Constitution. And Connecticut's 1818 text. And Mississippi's 1817 Constitution. And the 1816 Indiana one. And on and on. Such was the favored practice of state constitutional draftsmen; they placed their list of rights immediately following the Preamble and immediately preceding the description of the state's legislative body.[39]

Familiar with this unique state constitutional practice, several delegates came to the 1825 Constitutional Convention with a plan to frontload the Bill of Rights in that document. The assembly had agreed to transplant, almost verbatim, the entire Preamble from the 1787 document—as Webster had anticipated, the feeling in the room was that those lofty words still reflected the spirit of American optimism and the promise that many engendered.[40] Now they focused on those freedoms embedded in the original Bill of Rights. The process was a simple two-parter. First, the convention-goers had to decide if the ten amendments to the 1787 Constitution still accurately captured their own sense of the scope of Americans' freedoms, and second, they had to determine where in the 1825 Constitution they should list those rights. They tackled the second question first.

John W. Taylor hailed from rural, upstate New York. A member of the U.S. House of Representatives since 1813, he had twice been elected the Speaker of the House. Everyone in the room was familiar with his character, his public persona, and his political leanings. Though he would later self-identify as a Whig, he was currently a Democratic-Republican. Famously, he had represented New York in the deliberations about the Missouri Compromise. He opposed the extension of slavery to the territories, and he was a vocal champion of individual liberty. Ever since his days as a country lawyer in upstate New York, he had been steadfast in his belief that protecting individual liberty was the primary task of a written federal constitution.

Hence, it was he who stood in front of his fellow delegates to propose that any bill of rights ought to be located at the beginning of the constitutional document and not at the end. Individual safeguards have a sacred legacy, he said. They are the manifestations of an American ethos that dates back many decades and that saw its greatest defense in the opening passages of the Declaration of Independence. To bury the most tangible articulation of our individual freedoms in the body of the constitutional document, or God forbid, at the end, would denigrate their importance to this generation of countrymen. He thus proposed to do exactly what state constitution-makers had done: place the constitutional list of freedoms immediately after the Preamble and before any discussion of the government's institutional design. He then sat down. He was pleasantly surprised to witness what came next: a second from Gabriel Holmes, Governor of North Carolina, and then a nearly unanimous vote in favor of the resolution. The Bill of Rights—now dubbed the Declaration of Rights and located as Article I of the draft document—would have a far more prominent place in the new American Constitution.

But what should be included in said Declaration of Rights? Should the attendees propose a simple transplant of the first ten amendments to the 1787 Constitution? Or should additional safeguards be added? Perhaps some of the original protections in the Bill of Rights should be eliminated, some wondered. To these questions, the convention now turned. It was early August, and the humidity in Philadelphia was downright oppressive.

Several delegates prepared for a fight. The committee on rights had been remarkably discreet about its deliberations, but some rumors had circulated that changes to the original Bill of Rights might be in order. Virginian Philip Pendleton Barbour, a former Speaker of the U.S. House of Representatives, had been appointed the Chair of the Rights Committee back in May, an appropriate assignment in light of Barbour's legal training and his well-known support for a strict construction of the Constitution. Barbour was a Madisonian. Prior to joining the assembly at the Philadelphia convention, he declared himself a devotee of both the Jeffersonian and Madisonian perspectives on political power. Consequently, his view on the importance of protecting individual liberty was unwavering. It was, in fact, the primary reason he agreed to the invitation to attend the constitutional convention. When he was chosen by his fellow delegates to chair the Rights Committee, Philip Barbour considered it a personal triumph.

The members of the committee, Barbour knew, were committed to a broad set of privileges and immunities, including those that safeguarded speech, religious practice, assembly, the press, and the myriad protections for the criminally accused. There was a clear sense fairly early on that the first eight amendments to the 1787 Constitution ought to remain mostly intact. Perhaps some language might be tweaked just a bit in the new Bill of Rights, but for the most part the committee understood that it should simply transplant the old list into the new text.

With one exception, though. Most members of the Rights Committee subscribed to the Jeffersonian ideal that an educated citizenry was an essential ingredient in a thriving and energetic polity. Jefferson's views on universal public education were legendary, of course, though neither Jefferson nor his contemporaries believed in truly *universal* public education. Certain populations were not eligible for schooling, he said. Nonetheless, Jefferson often sprinkled his letters with advocacy statements on the value of widespread education.[41]

Several things were clear. Jefferson was ahead of his time, for sure, but others had caught on. In fact, it seemed the trend to expand the scope of common schooling was part of the larger democratization effort that also spawned a broadening of suffrage. The common man, in the early nineteenth century, was having a field day. The second thing that was clear was that Jefferson believed in the *decentralization* of educational oversight. Local communities ought to maintain authority and control over their educational systems, he thought; Governors and legislators were simply not capable of understanding the local particulars essential to the proper education of the American citizen.[42] In his *Notes on the State of Virginia* (1781), Jefferson proposed a "Bill for the More General Diffusion of Knowledge," in which he famously described, in considerable detail, the specifics of a public school system organized by counties and townships.[43]

The Virginia Assembly eventually rejected Jefferson's proposed law, but not before it made an impact in the commonwealth and beyond. People regularly referenced the specifics of Jefferson's plan. Some even contend that it was those details that became the core architecture for the common school movement that emerged in the 1830s. Of course, the delegates to the 1825 Constitutional Convention were among those most familiar with Jefferson's plan (he was not shy about mentioning it to fellow delegates over a drink or two at the local Philadelphia taverns), and many believed that some allowance for public education should be recorded in the new constitutional document. They were not beholden to Jefferson on this matter or any other, but many, including fellow Virginian Philip Barbour, felt a strong sense of loyalty to the former President. Barbour wanted to please his mentor. He knew he had to reconcile Jefferson's defense of *localized* control over education with a declaration in the Constitution of some *federal* involvement. First, he would lean on the growing state movement to constitutionalize educational support, in order to try to soften Jefferson. Then, he would remind the elder states-man that placing some protection for public or common school education within the text's new Declaration of Rights would do more to further Jefferson's dream of universal public education than practically anything else. He hoped it would work.

There was a movement afoot. In the years leading up to the 1825 Constitutional Convention, several states had embedded protections for universal education in their state bills of rights. The Bill of Rights in the 1803 Ohio Constitution provided a ready example for the delegates. It read: "No law shall be passed to prevent the poor in the several counties and townships, within this State, from an equal participation in the schools, academies, colleges and universities within this State, which are endowed, in whole or in part from the revenue arising from donations made by the United States, for the support of schools and colleges; and the doors of said schools, academies and universities, shall be open for the reception of scholars and students and teachers, of every grade, without any distinction or preference whatever, contrary to the intent for which said donations were made." Connecticut's 1818 Constitution also provided an interesting model. Connecticut chose to protect universal public education by embedding within its constitutional text a provision that established and protected a "School fund"—a monetary account for the "support and encouragement of the public or common schools throughout the state, and for the equal benefit of all the people thereof." The Rights Committee was also aware that other state constitutions— Indiana (1816), Alabama (1819)—included specific provisions protecting and supporting common public education.

Philip Barbour was ready when Jefferson called for a report from the Rights Committee. After discussing the merits of extending the entire list of rights and freedoms from the 1791 Bill of Rights to the 1825 Constitution, and reminding the delegation that it had already determined the proper placement of the list within the Constitution itself, Barbour spoke easily and confidently about the importance of including a provision addressing the federal protection of public education. He cited Jefferson's many public writings on the subject. He also cited Rousseau's *Émile*. He aimed to persuade his fellow assemblymen of the somewhat radical notion of implanting a clause in the federal Constitution that both sent an unequivocal message about the virtue of public education and ensured the further spread of education across the nation. The federal government was going to get into the education business.

He and his colleagues on the Rights Committee had a problem, though. Two problems, in fact. First, federalism was a powerful component of the American political design and to suggest that the national government ought to be involved in such local affairs as the proper way of educating muddied the relationship between the states and the federal government. Second, there was the problem of style. If public education was now going to fall within the jurisdiction of the federal government, how should the provision be written into the Constitution? Barbour and his colleagues were convinced that the language in Ohio's 1803 Bill of Rights was the most consistent with the style of writing throughout the U.S. Constitution's Bill of Rights. Ohio's clause read like a negative right. It spoke of a prevention *against* the exercise of government power—a style identical to the language in the 1791 Bill of Rights—and not an affirmative right *to* a public education. That was an important distinction. Barbour and the Rights Committee tried to remain as faithful as possible to the style of America's first Bill of Rights.

Barbour read the resolution slowly and carefully, emphasizing certain words for full effect. "Neither Congress nor the States," he began, "shall prevent any freeman from an equal participation in the schools, academies, colleges, and universities of the United States and the various states." He stopped. That was it. It was short and simple. He was not sanguine that including jurisdiction over the states would fly with his colleagues, but he and the Rights Committee had discussed the issue over and over again and concluded that only preventing the federal government from the prohibition would be much ado about nothing. There had been talk—significant talk, in fact—of establishing a "National University" to promote, in Madison's words, "national feelings" and "liberal sentiments," but nothing had yet come of it.[44] The idea, though, had had a lot of backers throughout America's short history, including Benjamin Franklin, James Madison, Thomas Jefferson, Benjamin Rush, John Adams, and John Quincy Adams. America's National University would most likely be located in Washington, DC, and would, in theory, stand alongside the three major branches of the federal government as an institution founded to help perpetuate the principles of democracy, freedom, and constitutionalism. Until the National University was established, however, the federal government had no "schools, academies, colleges, and universities" to direct. The proposed provision in the new Declaration of Rights was thus useless without the mention of the states.

Of course, this was not the only reference to the states in the Declaration of Rights, but, should the proposal pass, it would be the most disquieting. It seized at least one of the powers "not delegated to the United States by the Constitution." The Tenth Amendment had long stabilized the system of federalism in the country, and this proposal, while not turning the Tenth Amendment on its head exactly, certainly encroached on an area long assumed to be reserved to the states. But no mind, Barbour thought. He plowed ahead with the resolution. And he gained some confidence that it might pass when, of all figures, Thomas Jefferson himself stood to voice a second. Violating the unwritten rule that presiding officers should remain largely silent on the substance of proposals, Jefferson felt compelled to proclaim his support. He wanted to see any nod to broadening education find its place in the constitutional document.

Sadly for Jefferson, even his endorsement could not convince the loudest skeptics to favor the proposal. Barbour's resolution was met with fierce opposition right from the start, and it ultimately went down to defeat. Even those in the assembly who favored an expansion of the vote, or a refinement of the Electoral College in favor of less elite influence, could not get behind a constitutional provision that shifted so much power from the local authorities to some broad and amorphous national entity. Sure, the common man would probably benefit from federal oversight of public schooling, especially in those states that still didn't allow for universal public education. And sure, the proverbial common man had triumphed in virtually every battle in the constitutional convention thus far. But there was a very real difference between promoting the democratization of state and federal political systems and the dismantling of the basic scaffolding of federalism. Or at least, that's what many in Philadelphia thought. Even the followers of Jackson (who, interestingly, was not formally educated) could not see their way to supporting the interests of the free common man if that meant states had to relinquish control over their own educational systems. First, education would shift to federal jurisdiction, and then it would be only a matter of time before other historically sacrosanct police powers would be sacrificed. Any true conception of federalism, many thought, would soon disappear. The vast majority of delegates to the constitutional convention simply could not stomach that possibility.

By this time, the summer was almost over and the delegates were, to put it mildly, fatigued. Many of them wanted to return home. Many, though, were also feeling relatively good about what they had accomplished. As the terrible heat of August gave way to the first hint of fall in September, those assembled realized they still had one significant matter to discuss. What to do, if anything, with an increasingly powerful federal judiciary? It was a question that had frequently permeated discussions throughout the convention, in part because the delegates were often fixated on maintaining an appropriate balance among the different branches of the federal government. A shift in power here or there could disrupt that approximate equilibrium.

Still, there was also another reason the power of the federal judiciary remained in the back of the delegates' minds, a reason that was hard to pinpoint, hard actually to articulate. In many ways, the federal judiciary had *surprised* those delegates in Philadelphia's Independence Hall. Its development over the decades, especially since 1801, when John Marshall began serving as the Supreme Court's fourth Chief Justice, was somewhat unexpected. It was clear to most that the federal judiciary's power had expanded considerably in the years following the founding. It had seized power, intentionally and unintentionally, by carefully crafting rulings and opinions that often subtly placed it in a relatively heightened position. For many, this power grab was astonishing. Indeed, the Supreme Court had most assuredly startled the American public with its bold and fearless ambition.

You see, constitutional Founders in the late eighteenth century were uneasy about the relative power of the federal judiciary.

Some expressed concern that an independent judiciary, with few checks on it from the other branches, would be far too powerful. Others were worried that the judiciary was not powerful enough. Remarkably, Publius addressed both sets of worriers in *Federalist* 78. After explaining the importance of judges' receiving lifetime appointments so long as they maintained "good behavior," he goes on to calm those convinced that an independent judiciary wields too much influence:

> Whoever attentively considers the different departments of power must perceive, that, in a government in which they are separated from each other, the judiciary, from the nature of its functions, will always be the least dangerous to the political rights of the Constitution; because it will be least in a capacity to annoy or injure them. . . . It may truly be said to have neither FORCE nor WILL, but merely judgment; and must ultimately depend upon the aid of the executive arm even for the efficacy of its judgments.

The problem for many was that the "judgment" Publius tagged to the judiciary had proven lethal, in some ways even more lethal than the "force" or "will" of other branches.

Chief Justice John Marshall wielded that "judgment" to great effect. He was a fervent Federalist, appointed to the bench by President John Adams to carry on the platform of the party even after Adams' unceremonious defeat in the 1800 election. What is more, he had become a considerable thorn, first in the side of Jefferson and then in the side of most Democratic-Republicans. Distant cousins by birth, Jefferson and Marshall hated each other. Marshall was a vocal proponent of the nationalist inclinations of George Washington and John Adams. Indeed, Adams' masterful plan to pack the courts with Federalists so as to maintain his party's presence in the federal government had worked almost to perfection. The party was dead in the elected branches, but far from it in the judiciary. Many at the 1825 Convention wanted to remedy that problem.

Though few would recognize it at the time, Marshall took his place on the Supreme Court with a plan to bolster the stature and authority of the judiciary in relation to the legislative and executive branches and to establish the superiority of the national government over the states. He accomplished both, sometimes simultaneously. By the time the delegates met in Philadelphia in 1825, the Marshall Court had exercised its authority to decide the constitutionality of legislation,[45] sent clear messages that the Supremacy Clause allowed the federal judiciary to retain jurisdiction in most state civil cases and most state criminal cases,[46] established the almost infinite expanse of the U.S. Constitution's interpretive power and Congress' scope,[47] and set a precedent that the judiciary would be the protector of Congress' general authority.[48] The consequence of all these rulings was that the federal judiciary, and, in particular the Supreme Court of the United States, had arrived and was not to be messed with.

The decision in the *Marbury v. Madison* case was a particularly bitter pill for followers of Jefferson. The case was fairly simple. It involved a dispute over a commission—an appointment—that Marbury believed was rightly his. That commission (to become a Justice of the Peace) had been "signed" and "sealed" but not yet "delivered" when President Adams had to depart the White House. When Jefferson took over as President of the United States, he promptly ordered his Secretary of State, James Madison, to discard the commission. Marbury sued Madison, and the case was sent directly to the Supreme Court. Jefferson originally tried to embarrass Marshall and the Court by refusing to allow government lawyers to argue the case, citing "executive privilege." Marshall, in turn, roundly embarrassed Jefferson by engaging in a bit of judicial statecraft: he ruled in favor of Jefferson. It was a brilliant move on Marshall's part, because this way Jefferson was forced to accept the ruling in his favor—and to accept all that came with it. And Marshall seized the opportunity to decry Jefferson's actions as reprehensible, shameful, and completely dishonorable. Friends of the President never forgave Marshall for that slap in Jefferson's face.

Nor did they forgive the Chief Justice for his role in other cases that swung in the Federalist Party's favor. Perhaps most telling was that Jefferson and his colleagues occasionally hinted at impeachment, particularly around the time of Aaron Burr's 1807 trial for treason. Marshall presided over parts of that trial. Several commentators at the time believed that Jefferson was more interested in procuring Marshall's impeachment than he was in securing a guilty verdict against Burr. Their mutual hatred swelled.

The 1825 Convention delegates were quite familiar with other tales of judicial impeachment as well. Most famously, in 1804, Samuel Chase, Associate Justice of the U.S. Supreme Court, was impeached by the House because he was unapologetically promoting political views from the bench. He was reviled by Jeffersonian Republicans. It got so bad that Republicans in the House took the extraordinary step of handing down articles of impeachment just to get him to shut up. It didn't work. He was impeached by the House of Representatives, but he was never convicted by the Senate. He lived out his days as a Justice of the Supreme Court, dying in 1811. Still, the whole sordid affair contributed to the idea, at least among Democratic-Republicans, that an independent judiciary might not be all that it was cracked up to be.

Fast forward to the 1825 Constitutional Convention. To be sure, some members of the assembly were quite comfortable with Marshall's determined attitude and with the Federalist imprint he left on American jurisprudence. Daniel Webster certainly was. Still, many at the convention were upset by the turn of judicial events over the past twenty-five years, and others were just plain irritated by the ongoing Federalist presence on the federal bench.

One who was troubled by the expansion of federal judicial power was Thomas J. Oakley, a former New York State Attorney General and a former member of the U.S. House of Representatives from the Empire State. Oakley was a somewhat surprising choice to represent New York at the constitutional convention.

An unremarkable man by most standards, he was probably best known for being on the losing side of the Gibbons against Ogden case a year earlier. He and Thomas Addis Emmet had represented Aaron Ogden in that interstate commerce case. On the other side of the dispute stood Gibbons' attorneys: Daniel Webster and U.S. Attorney General, William Wirt. Oakley never doubted Webster's and Wirt's legal acumen—he considered them especially skilled adversaries—but he was still frustrated that the Court, and in particular that John Marshall character, had manipulated certain facts and legal reasoning to guarantee a particular outcome. To Oakley, the decision was the epitome of judicial bravado. The Court had ruled in favor of Congress and against the states, but it had also managed in the process to substantially augment its own power. Oakley wasn't going to have it. He thought he had powerful ammunition on his side. He was mindful that states had experimented with independent judiciaries and many were now regretting those decisions. Several states, in fact, had amended their constitutions to place greater checks on the judicial branch. Those checks typically took three forms: term limits, legislative appointments, and/ or popular elections. Oakley favored all three over the current system of federal judicial appointments. Now, all he had to do was convince his fellow delegates of their merits.

He cited Georgia's 1798 Constitution first. Section 1 of Article III was absolutely clear, he said. It read: "The judges of the superior court shall be elected for the term of three years, removable by the Governor, on the address of two-thirds of both houses for that purpose, or by impeachment and conviction thereon." Elected judges and fixed terms—these, Oakley insisted, were the makings of a checked federal judiciary. He continued: Ohio's 1803 Constitution allowed judges to be appointed by a "joint ballot of both Houses of the General Assembly" and to "hold their offices for the term of seven years." Indiana's 1816 Constitution similarly limited the appointment of judicial officers to seven years, he noted next. High court judges in Connecticut, as per the state's 1818 Constitution, were appointed by the legislative branch, not the Governor. As were the judges in Illinois. They were scheduled to hold their positions until 1824, as stipulated by the state's constitution, when their commissions were to expire. Oakley's point was that states had turned their backs on the idea of independent judges with no accountability to the people and no recourse for their periodic review or removal. It was time to do the same at the federal level. Unspoken was Oakley's antagonism toward Marshall and his Federalist instincts, as well as the long shadow the Marshall Court had thrown on the nation. He didn't have to say a word about that. The entire assembly understood his stance on the matter.

His resolution had two components. He didn't want to swing the pendulum too far to the side of judicial accountability, but he wanted some check on the courts. He thus proposed that federal court judges from then on would be appointed by the U.S. House of Representatives, and confirmed by the Senate, for an initial term of seven years. He emphasized the word "initial" because he was prepared to assent to the view of advocates for an independent judiciary that there should remain some mechanism for lifetime appointment, but only after the appointee successfully navigated the seven-year probationary period. In other words, Oakley proposed that all federal court judges serve a lifetime appointment *only after* they were reappointed at the seven-year mark. Federal court judges would earn their independence by demonstrating to the Congress that they could be trusted. He closed his remarks by reminding delegates of the unfortunate story of John Pickering, U.S. Federal District Court Judge for New Hampshire. Pickering was impeached and thrown off the bench for drunkenness and mental insanity. A seven-year probationary period, Oakley argued, would have prevented that embarrassment.

Oakley saw these changes to the existing appointment method as a reasonable fusion of the current process—lifetime appointment was, after all, preserved—and the interesting models of accountability materializing at the state level. Legislative selection would bring these judges a bit closer to the electorate. Similarly, a seven-year probationary period allowed for some review—some degree of oversight—from the people. That was positive.

Oakley liked these changes, but he was unsure if others would as well. At a minimum, though, he knew he had the partisan support for the resolution. There were more Democratic-Republicans in Independence Hall than there were Federalists. He felt fairly confident that he could get this resolution through. He predicted accurately. Several members moved to change the seven-year probationary period to five years, but those proposed emendations were ultimately rejected by the assembly. In the end, Oakley's proposal passed. The 1825 Constitution would include a dramatically different process for populating the federal bench. It was perhaps the most significant change to the country's outgoing constitutional design.

All that remained was for the delegates to tie up a few loose ends and then sign the new constitutional document. Ratification, of course, was a different story altogether, but most delegates simply basked in the glow of a job well done. They were satisfied that this new proposed Constitution reflected the new America they inhabited. They prepared to adjourn.

The Convention Adjourns
The date was September 22nd and Independence Hall hummed with patriotic sentiment and political excitement. The energy in the room somehow proved powerful enough to overcome the languid heat of a Philadelphia summer. Temperatures had remained warm or very warm on most days of debate and deliberation, and the men came clad in professionally formal attire no matter the humidity. Little air moved through the high-ceilinged chamber, as windows and doors remained shut against prying eyes and curious ears. Now, as Jefferson called for order in the room, the atmosphere changed palpably. The boisterous conversation gave way to a hush, punctuated by a chair leg scratching the floor, a nervous cough, or the faint drumming of fingers against a wooden table. The delegates were like schoolboys who would soon hear either that

they had failed an exam and would have to return home with bowed heads, or that they had earned highest marks and could march out to recess with chests puffed proudly.

It was time to sign the document. Of the original 131 delegates, a respectable 118 remained. Federalists and Democratic-Republicans alike filled the room. A few were disappointed in the overall document and almost all were in some way uneasy about specific portions of the text. But that is what any constitution-maker must face up to. If written well, constitutions are compromises. They reflect the interests of many constituencies and of varying visions "for a more perfect Union." The 1825 Constitution certainly was that. A compromise. Those from New England who, coming in, might have been cautiously optimistic that this text would capture some of the Federalist flavor were probably the most disappointed. But even they felt that the proposed constitutional text was acceptable. They lived in a different world from that of their forebears thirty-eight years ago. They lived in a more democratic world now. As such, they took their rightful place in line alongside their Democratic-Republican colleagues and added their signatures to those that came before.

A few days later, as Webster prepared for his trip back to Marshfield, he ruminated on the convention and what its outcome meant for the Union. He folded his blue suit. The sun had set on the Federalist vision for America and the new horizon loomed ominous and uncertain for Webster. The changing winds of constitutional revision and an expanding electorate were upon the nation, stirring its dust and rattling its windows.

Twenty-five years ago, Webster had predicted a time in which "American blood shall be made to flow in rivers, by American swords!" and he still saw that threat as a real one.[49] The convention had not touched the issue of slavery, and though Webster had opposed it vocally in his speeches, he saw the reason for silence. The country was too fragile and too varied. Webster still sensed strife in the distance, but at least the topic of suffrage had revealed a mostly united Union, even if the delegates came to the issue with various angles and motives. Chaos had been delayed a little longer. Even Webster could stand behind that. His mind then wandered to Jefferson, who had returned to Monticello— eating his French-style dinner, contemplating higher education, and remaining ever the advocate of the greatest and most American cause: independence. Webster then thought of returning safely to New England where he, like Jefferson, might sit and contemplate the world from the comfort of a parlor chair. Two men who represented differing visions of politics in a country they were immensely proud of and yet somewhat estranged from.

Webster sighed audibly as his thoughts returned again to his children, to Charles, so recently deceased, and to little Grace, dead long before him. He thought of Edward, Julia, and Fletcher, the last of whom would be the only one to survive his father. Webster knew he would be dead by the time the Union faced its gravest challenges yet, and as he ruminated silently he thought of the possibility that Jefferson might actually have been right in some small way.

Webster believed that men of talent and intellect set things in motion. They made people feel as they felt when they commanded the pulpit and governed nations with their written word. It was Jefferson who had penned the title deed of American liberty. It was Jefferson, too, who had always known what Webster was now beginning to understand: a great man must eventually step out of the way of the thing he set in motion. Neither the Constitution nor the nation had ever been static, and Webster—indeed the Convention of 1825—occupied only a small place in history. Yes, on this one particular matter in this one specific instance, Jefferson had been right. The past retained its influence on the present, but the world would always belong to the living.

1863 ———

ABRAHAM LINCOLN WAS ANXIOUS. Again. The feeling he experienced when he was particularly worried differed from any other he came across in his daily life. The top of his head throbbed. Sadly, he experienced this sensation frequently these days.

What triggered the President's anxiety was the prospect of endorsing the upcoming federal constitutional convention. It was February 1863, and the scheduled convention was a mere three months away. He was fielding inquiries about the status of the constitutional convention, as if the decision to push forward or call it off were his alone. It was not. Technically, the delegates were now the only participants who could put a halt to the gathering, or more likely, suggest a reasonable postponement. Northern state legislatures had issued invitations, and delegates were now making plans to gather in Philadelphia for the meeting. Some were even readying to start the journey. A courtesy invitation had gone out to each of the legislatures in the Confederate States of America, but it had been ignored. That wasn't surprising, even if it was disappointing to Lincoln. Everyone recognized that the President's actual role in the convention proceedings was minimal. He would not be attending the actual convention. Still, leaders from across the North looked to him for guidance and direction on the essential question of whether to hold the meeting at all.

Lincoln had an opinion, of course. The President simply could not imagine drafting a brand-new constitutional text right now. Not now. The Union was fractured and there appeared no end in sight to the devastating Civil War. The latest skirmish—the Battle of Stones River in Murfreesboro, Tennessee—had contributed approximately 20,000 more casualties to the already gruesome tally, and neither side could confidently claim victory. When Lincoln was feeling most generous, he could convince himself that the Union forces had fought the entire war to a draw. But when he was most reflective—when he was truly honest with himself—he knew that things were not going well. 1862 had not been a good year for the northern armies. He had replaced generals and witnessed southern tactical superiority. The Confederate states were digging in, both in battle and in their crusade to maintain a way of life that so clearly violated the natural law principle that "all men are created equal." The country was more divided now than ever.

How could convention delegates reasonably craft a fair and just governing charter at this time, when almost every imaginable vision for a united America was unclear? Lincoln never doubted that the North and South would eventually reunite, whether through peaceful negotiations or, if need be, through relentless violence. He would see to it that the United States was whole again. But he knew that the precise moment of reunification was, to put it mildly, far off.

For some time now, Lincoln had wondered if the 1825 Constitution—the current Constitution—was failing. It concerned him that his instincts leaned toward the affirmative. His training as a lawyer had taught him the importance of an organizing document, a single written text that self-consciously orders a specific polity. He had come to revere the 1825 Constitution, in part because it so closely resembled the 1787 Constitution. The President believed the 1787 Constitution was a magnificent invention, a supreme example of human ingenuity and originality.

But now he was far less certain of the eighteenth-century Constitution's virtues, and that meant he was decidedly less confident about the current document's capacity to "promote the general welfare," "secure the blessings of liberty," and irony notwithstanding, "form a more perfect Union." He wasn't President of a complete Union anymore, he thought. The country was divided, and the ordained Constitution could do nothing to change that. Lincoln understood that the states were most assuredly not on the path to a "more perfect Union." The question he puzzled over was whether a new Constitution—a fresh Constitution— would prove a better navigator. He wasn't entirely sure. His head throbbed even more.

Abraham Lincoln was a spiritual man, a superstitious man. He had an irrational fear of disappointing his greatest idols, even if they were long deceased and couldn't do anything about his choices. It was silly, he knew. But he so admired Madison, Washington, Hamilton, Adams, and others who had sacrificed much to birth a nation that was the greatest in human history. He thought of these figures often as he chose paths for himself. He had done so throughout his life.

Lincoln felt a certain paradox when he thought of Thomas Jefferson, though. He did not care for Mr. Jefferson's penchant for backstabbing and deceit. In fact, he was mildly disgusted by the stories he'd read of Jefferson's legendary reputation as someone who was willing to do almost anything to prevail in a contest. Nor was he keen on Jefferson's nostalgic allegiance to an agrarian economic system that, to Lincoln, seemed perilously short-sighted.[1] He did not share Jefferson's affection for the simple life. Memories of his childhood had cured him of that misguided fondness.

And then there was the issue of slavery. Lincoln despised the institution of slavery, even as he recognized early in his presidency that he could do little to erase it. He accepted that the Civil War started in part because of an intractable disagreement between northern and southern states about the authority of the federal government to restrict the spread of slavery into the territories. The central pillar of his presidential platform, after all, had been a pledge to establish all new states as free states. Slavery, he recognized, would eventually tear this country apart because it flew in the face of one of the nation's most basic founding principles.

That was why he had a hard time reconciling Jefferson's oft-repeated stance on liberty, equality, and justice with the Virginian's silent defense of slavery. Sure, other founding figures also owned slaves, including the "father of the Constitution," James Madison. But none of those folks were responsible for penning the most magnificent expression ever written in favor of human dignity and equality. Jefferson alone held that title. His claim in the Declaration of Independence that "We hold these truths to be self-evident, that all men are created equal," rang somewhat hollow to Lincoln. Fair or not, Lincoln viewed Jefferson as a hypocrite. It forever clouded his view of the famous Virginian.

Still, Lincoln did share Jefferson's esteem for the majesty and power of words. The language of the Declaration of Independence had stirred a citizenry and started a revolution. Paine's *Common Sense*, his *Rights of Man*, his *Age of Reason*, and countless other pamphlets inspired thousands to examine their instinct to be conservative and maintain the status quo. The Preamble to the 1787 U.S. Constitution was sublime in its elegant forcefulness. Lincoln was convinced that the eighteenth-century founding generation was more gifted than any other in revealing truth through the force of the written word. He had read the writings of the Founders over and over again, and if anything, they filled the tall statesman with a sense of inadequacy.

As a result, he was terribly uneasy about moving forward with a constitutional convention that was *all about* the power of words. Constitutions, he knew, are unique beasts. The words of a constitution have no force; they command no armies. They rely on the integrity of those who utter them, and integrity often finds an enemy in self-interest. Constitutions, therefore, can be ignored just as easily as they can be followed. And that is what scared Lincoln. If the southern states were not present at a constitutional convention, what would ensure any degree of allegiance to a set of words and clauses they had no part in crafting? A new Constitution forged by northerners would never include southern traditions, habits, institutions, and customs. Presumably nothing would ensure allegiance then, short of the Constitution's being imposed, by power and might, on southerners, as if they were mere subjects of a northern tyranny.

Nonetheless, Lincoln was also a political realist. If Confederates were going to break away from the Union, northerners could seize this chance to create a constitutional text in *their* own image—one that got us closer to a "more perfect Union." Or at least a more perfect northern vision of a Union. Lincoln had come to the conclusion that Jefferson's call for generational constitutional change was meant precisely for these moments. It would not have been his choice to draft a new Constitution right now—Lincoln was a resolute Madisonian in that respect—but he had convinced himself that periodic constitutional conventions were intended as a safeguard against the type of political decay that ruined nations.

The American public, in fact, had known about this upcoming convention for at least a decade now. Officials had planned this moment so carefully. It was the rarest of historical rarities: an intentional and premeditated sunsetting of a current constitutional text in favor of a new one.

And yet, at the same time, the President found himself in the middle of the most ruinous crisis the country had ever experienced. America had a solid infrastructure in the middle of the nineteenth century, but it still could not escape the cultural, economic, and societal problems that lead to war and that so often force the decline of a constitutional text. The irony was rich. A planned constitutional convention was likely to be seriously affected by a monumental internal crisis. Not the other way around. Lincoln was knowledgeable enough to realize that the demise of constitutions in places like France was brought on by internal strife, and that new constitutions sprang from the ashes of the old. On the eve of another constitutional change in America, Lincoln wondered whether history would remember this moment as it remembered France in 1789.

Lincoln was one of the few who recognized that the Civil War was what Charles and Mary Beard would later call America's "second revolution."[2] War could be cleansing, he thought. As horrific as it is to think that thousands—*hundreds* of thousands, in fact— would lay down their lives in sacrifice to ensure a specific vision of self-rule, Lincoln couldn't help but imagine the possibilities that could arise with a Union victory. Collectively, he, his colleagues, and the entire citizenry could "rebirth a new nation," just as the Revolutionary War–era generation had done.[3]

Lincoln understood that history was, in many ways, repeating itself. And he was powerless to stop it. The American Revolution of the late eighteenth century was a battle among brothers about fundamentally differing visions for a collective future. So was the Civil War. The Revolutionary War started because of a declaration of independence. So had the Civil War. The revolution ended with an expression of compromise—the 1787 Constitution. Lincoln was convinced that the Civil War would end that way too. This constitutional convention, he thought, presented a unique opportunity to alter the direction of America's democratic republic. It could realize an extraordinarily rare occasion to engage in a genuine constitutional founding. If only the North could get the upper hand in the fighting. Maybe then, southerners would relent and attend the convention proceedings.

Months later, in early May, things only got worse. All eyes were focused on Chancellorsville, Virginia, where Major General Joseph Hooker's Army of the Potomac—nearly 100,000 strong— crossed the Rappahannock River and arrived on General Robert E. Lee's doorstep. Hooker's goal was to push Lee farther into Virginia's wilderness. The southern army was outnumbered almost two to one, but it had something that the Union forces sorely lacked: a leader of the courage and quality of Thomas Jonathan "Stonewall" Jackson. A ferocious and fearless commander, Jackson had proven himself a critical piece of the successful southern campaigns. On that day, Jackson took 30,000 infantry troops and surprised Hooker along his eastern flank. It was a bold idea and a brilliant strategic move. And it worked. Despite being significantly outnumbered, Confederate soldiers forced Hooker to abandon his position; they emerged victorious in perhaps the most astonishing battle of 1863. The only setback for General Lee and his southern troops at Chancellorsville was that Stonewall Jackson suffered a mortal wound during the skirmish. His death would fundamentally alter the entire course of the war.

At a mere sixty miles away, Chancellorsville was dangerously close to the Union capital in Washington, DC. From Washington, it was just another short hop to the city of brotherly love. What separated Philadelphia from Chancellorsville, Lincoln thought, was a couple of hundred miles and a northern army in which he had little confidence. There was no way a constitutional convention could be held in Philadelphia this year, and so talk turned to identifying an alternative location.[4] Northern leaders such as Stephen A. Douglas, John P. Hale, Salmon P. Chase, Charles Sumner, William P. Fessenden, Edwin Stanton, and others, considered various sites. Most surprising perhaps, these individuals batted around the idea of relocating the constitutional convention to, of all places, Columbus, Ohio. Looking west to Columbus was an unexpected choice—an audacious choice, even—as it did not carry the same gravitas or historical cache as cities on the eastern seaboard. But the sense among this group was that a decision to relocate the convention to Columbus would reinforce the importance of the less established states west of the Appalachians.

New York and Boston were safer choices, to be sure. New York was quickly dismissed because it was well-known that the city on the Hudson was more sympathetic to the southern cause than most other northern cities. Fernando Wood's sympathetic posture toward the Southern Confederacy as Mayor of New York, and his call to make the downstate island a "free city," apart from the rest of the United States, was both baffling and unacceptable. To relocate the convention to New York would send the wrong message to northerners and southerners alike. Perhaps Boston might work. The cultural and economic capital of New England was an interesting choice, a nod in some ways to the misfortunes and eventual triumphs of the revolutionary era. It seemed fitting to many that Boston would be the site of another historical transition in the midst of civil war. Battling the crown was somewhat different from battling countrymen who seceded in protest. Nevertheless, it felt in some ways familiar. It was settled. Boston it was.

Joseph Wightman considered himself a skilled and amiable host. A two-term Mayor of Boston, Wightman was comfortable accommodating visitors to City Hall and to the many social functions he attended while in office. Recently, he had been selected by the Massachusetts state legislature to represent the Bay State at the 1863 Constitutional Convention in Philadelphia, an honor he gladly accepted. He had looked forward to debating fellow lawmakers about the future of the United States. But now that the convention was being moved to his home city, he saw his role just a bit differently. He would be expected to advise convention delegates on the finest meeting parlors, boarding houses, and grand hotels in his beloved city. Immensely proud of his home city, he relished the assignment.

Wightman understood that relocating the convention to Boston was a matter of necessity, but it also posed a few challenges. An influx of Irish immigrants had pushed the population to almost 200,000. The city was crowded and, in Wightman's estimation, never more energized. Finding a location for the delegates to do their work was not difficult: the Massachusetts statehouse on Beacon Hill could more or less accommodate the gathering. The number of invited delegates was less than anticipated just a few years ago, given that southern representation would be absent.

Still, 232 delegates were expected to attend, a number equal to the membership of the United States Congress. Of course, seventy-seven additional seats in Congress had been vacated as a result of the South's protest against Lincoln's 1860 election to the presidency and the subsequent secessionist movement. Those seats would not be taken at the Boston constitutional convention.

The delegates began to arrive in mid-May, just as the flowers in Boston Common were starting to bloom. Wightman got to work welcoming the delegates arriving from far and wide. He successfully located lodging for those who asked, and he alerted local restaurateurs to the importance of these men. They were to be treated with the utmost respect and hospitality. We must impart the right impression to our esteemed guests, Wightman warned. This was a big deal for the city of Boston and for its reputation. By Sunday, May 17th, the transition was complete. Most were comfortable and felt welcomed. The delegates could commence their important work.

The Constitutional Convention Opens

In many ways, the delegates entered a political echo chamber when they took their seats in the Massachusetts Statehouse on Monday, May 18th, to begin deliberations on a new constitution. At first glance, it seemed most of these northerners held roughly similar views on the major issues of the day. A majority of northern citizens, for example, supported the emerging Republican Party and its coalition partners, meaning they were largely in favor of increased power in the national government and a corresponding decrease in state authority, a higher degree of economic protectionism, the benefits of railroad expansion, enactment of the Homestead Act, further sponsorship of education, and perhaps most importantly, the abolition of slavery.

Pulling back the curtain a bit, though, it was equally clear that there were divisions among party elites. Some Republicans might be defined more as moderates or pragmatists, including Abraham Lincoln, while others were decidedly more radical or progressive in their views. The pragmatists were fixated on maintaining the Union, and if that meant they had to mollify southern Democrats, especially around slavery, so be it. They often struck a more conciliatory tone in the early days of the war. These moderate Republicans were opposed to slavery, of course. Lincolnian Republicans were especially (and vocally) opposed to the *spread* of slavery into new states and territories; keep slavery confined is what they would say. And yet the moderate Republican wing often conceded that slavery could continue in those areas where it had gained a historical foothold. They convinced themselves that the institution of slavery was not the manifestation of hell; that would occur only with the dissolution of the Union.

Meanwhile, the more progressive, or radical, wing of the Republican Party believed that emancipation and abolition was the end game. Radical Republicans offered a number of arguments against the enslavement of fellow human beings, but perhaps their strongest argument came from their religious beliefs. Slavery, they insisted, was an insult to God's teachings, an evil that debased the dignity of man and corrupted the entire nation. In fact, most Radical Republicans thought that the Civil War was God's punishment for slavery. Of course, secession was also an outrage; but it was enslavement that most triggered God's wrath. The Radical Republicans were a powerful lot, and their ideas were gaining traction every day. A full ten of the seventeen declarations in the 1860 Republican Party Platform dealt in some way with slavery.

It was probably the proposed Corwin Amendment that most exposed the country's political differences. The amendment's roots were planted on November 6th, 1860—election day. On that day, Lincoln was elected President, the single most critical event in a series of events that started the cascade of southern states seceding from the Union. By inauguration day on March 4th, 1861, seven states had divorced the country and founded the Confederate States of America. Fearing a complete constitutional crisis, the outgoing President—James Buchanan—used his final weeks in office to lobby Congress to propose a constitutional amendment that would decisively declare that states could retain the institution of slavery.

Buchanan, a Democrat from Pennsylvania, was morally opposed to slavery. Yet he believed that the Constitution protected it, or at least did not outlaw it. He felt sure that the country was barreling headlong into a civil war and thought a possible solution was to introduce into the Constitution an "explanatory amendment" on the general topic of slavery. He thus approached Representative Thomas Corwin of Ohio to draft a constitutional amendment that would essentially prohibit the federal government from interfering in the "domestic institutions" of a state. Should the amendment pass, no federal authority could touch slavery in the South. It was Buchanan's attempt to pacify southerners and avert the outbreak of hostilities. It didn't work. Not only was Fort Sumter bombarded a few months later, on April 12th, 1861, but the Corwin amendment never gained traction among state legislatures. It was passed by Congress and, in a highly unorthodox and completely unnecessary move, signed by President Buchanan (constitutional amendments do not require presidential approval). But it could only muster the support of five states, far fewer than the twenty-six needed at that time to pass the threshold for ratification.

The Crittenden Compromise[5] and the Washington Peace Conference[6] were also efforts to pass amendments intended to avert war. Any number of proposals—legislative, executive, and constitutional—were introduced in an attempt to stave off the inevitable. Most in some way tried to locate the very fine line that would, essentially, perpetuate the status quo. But all in some way failed. The existing Constitution could not save the Union. It had to be changed.

By 1863, the Republican Party was clearly Lincoln's party, and from the outside, it felt more or less unified. The perceived unification of the Republican Party had come about in part because Lincoln himself moved in the direction of the radical wing. In September of 1862, for example, he had signed the Emancipation Proclamation calling for the complete emancipation of slaves.

It went into effect on January 1st, 1963. Further, he wanted to textualize the liberation of the former slaves in the constitutional document, and he began a campaign to amend the 1825 Constitution to do so. His politics looked a good deal different in the early months of 1863 from what they had been when he was campaigning in 1860.

In contrast, members of the opposition party, the Democrats, split along geographical lines. Northern Democrats were slightly more progressive than their southern counterparts, especially on the issue of slavery. They supported Stephen A. Douglas from Illinois during the 1860 presidential election, while southern Democrats backed the sitting Vice President, John C. Breckinridge from Kentucky. These Democrats, like Breckinridge himself, were enthusiasts for Andrew Jackson's political ideals, and their base would eventually be concentrated mainly in the American South. They were agrarian in spirit and isolationist in temperament.

With no real opposition present to push back, it seemed highly likely that the 1863 Constitution would reflect most of the priorities of the Republicans. And yet an uneasiness set in among some of the more intellectual convention-goers. The members of the 1863 federal Constitutional Convention in Boston were familiar with the distinction between the superiority of a constitution and the inferior nature of standard legislation. They understood, for example, that the proposed Corwin amendment, Crittenden Compromise, Peace Conference, and so on, represented higher-level attempts—constitutional attempts—to resolve fundamental differences among slave and free states. They understood that more routine attempts—legislative attempts—were less likely to yield long-term success. And yet there was something rare about what they were embarking upon, something unique about *this* moment and *this* constitutional convention. Monumentally important regulations, laws, and ordinances had been introduced in the twenty years prior to the convention, and each now had a chance to find firmer grounding in the new constitutional text. To many in Boston, a Constitution that emancipated the slaves, guaranteed some manner of equal rights for all, and prohibited the return of any form of involuntary servitude was long overdue.

-+>-<+-

Delegates arrived, committees were formed, and the convention was called to order. In all, 232 representatives from twenty-four states were sent to Boston. These twenty-four states included nineteen free states, where slavery was outlawed, and four border states, states that allowed slavery but had never seceded from the Union or joined the Confederacy. Representatives from West Virginia were also invited to the proceedings even though that commonwealth would not be recognized as a fully independent state until a month after the opening of the convention. New York, with the largest population in the Union, sent the most delegates: thirty-five. Several states, including Delaware and Kansas, sent only three representatives. Every state was represented by at least one delegate on the three major committees: the Rules Committee, the Committee of Detail, and the Committee of Style. Those committees, and the more specialized ones, were tasked with doing their work in parallel with the general conversations that took place on the convention floor.

Charles Sumner, senior Senator from Massachusetts, was elected President of the convention on the official opening day, a clear nod to the most famous delegate from the host state. At first glance, it was a somewhat surprising choice. Sumner was a powerful orator and a firebrand against the institution of slavery. A member of the radical wing of the Republican Party, he often clashed with Lincoln and the President's fellow moderates on strategies to end slavery. Throughout his long career, he was never silent—never timid—about the causes he most believed in. Some members of the convention delegation immediately saw the irony in making him president, while others secretly maneuvered to make it so. A controlled Sumner was a more productive Sumner.

The attendees knew, from the prior conventions of 1787 and 1825, that procedural matters ought to be considered first. The 1863 Convention was no different, even though the procedural decisions seemed trivial in comparison to the weighty issues that awaited. In the days leading up to the event, delegates concluded that it was the most important meeting of statesmen since the federal Convention of 1787. Northern newspapers confirmed that appraisal, even going so far as to call the convention a "reckoning with the past and an opportunity for a dramatically fresh beginning."

One procedural issue raised almost no objections. The assemblage decided right away that it would maintain the practice of debating in secret. The proceedings of the 1787 Constitutional Convention had famously progressed without so much as a single inadvertent leak to the press. Sure, there were times when delegates continued discussing their business within earshot of tavern patrons, but remarkably, almost no information about the new Constitution found its way to the major newspapers. Delegates to the 1825 Constitutional Convention tried to repeat that practice, but they had considerably less success. Either that assembly's lips were looser or the newspapermen of the time were more clever in their methods of scooping details, because some information did slip through that convention's pledge of secrecy. The convention members in 1863 were thus adamant that they needed to follow the example of 1787.

Almost immediately, the delegates turned to discussing more substantive issues. Conversations about the continued effectiveness of a bicameral legislature, a unitary executive, and an accountable federal judiciary occupied the early committee meetings and floor debates. Should we maintain the basic structure of the federal government, delegates asked? What about the system of federalism?

Not surprisingly, the first truly explosive issue involved the future of slavery. It was David Wilmot, a Republican Senator from Pennsylvania, who started the conversation—a conversation, incidentally, that would occupy the convention's attention practically from its opening to its concluding day. Wilmot was an interesting politician and an even more interesting historical figure. He was well-known among the delegates for his staunch support of northern labor and his moderate stance in opposition to the expansion of slavery. Most knew he also maintained that, if left alone, the institution of slavery would die under its own weight. "Wilmot explained the South's expansionism by pointing to the exhaustion of southern soil by slave labor. The ever-pressing need for new and fertile lands made the extension of slavery an economic necessity for the South. 'Keep it within given limits,' he told a New York audience in 1847 'and in time it will wear itself out. . . . Slavery has within itself the seeds of its own destruction.'"[7] In this regard, his early allegiance to the Free Soil Party was an appropriate reflection of his fundamental values.

The failed Wilmot Proviso was his main calling card. In 1846, a full seventeen years prior to the 1863 Constitutional Convention, Wilmot had attached a controversial rider to an appropriations bill that paved the way for the annexation of Texas and the end of the Mexican-American War. Wilmot's rider was unequivocal: it prohibited the extension of slavery into any lands acquired from Mexico.[8]

This proviso passed the House of Representatives—twice—but it failed in the crucial Senate vote. It went down to defeat in late 1847. And yet its legacy most assuredly endured well beyond its defeat in Congress. In fact, it may be one of American history's most famous legislative failures in that it can be tied directly to the outbreak of the Civil War. Wilmot's name would forever be associated with a congressional attempt to stop the spread of slavery into new territories and new regions. For that reason, he was hated by most southerners.

As he stood to present a resolution that he believed would eventually end slavery, Wilmot knew the position he had staked out for himself was the moderate one. He was now a full-fledged member of the Republican Party (indeed, he helped to found the Republican Party in Pennsylvania), and yet he still believed that the best course of action was to let the institution of slavery wither away gradually and slowly. He would not champion any constitutional article or provision that would eradicate slavery in one swift and decisive action. Let the southerners have their slaves for the foreseeable future, he argued. But do not allow slavery to find a foothold in any new state or any existing territory. He continued: "eventually, slavery will be eradicated, but we cannot hope to welcome our southern brothers and sisters back to the Union if we cut them at the knees. They have no say in the outcome of this convention, and thus we must be mindful of their interests when we design a Constitution for this generation."

It was a sensible argument, for sure. Plenty in the assembly agreed with him. Wilmot was not prepared to offer a resolution this early in the proceedings, as certain procedural and routine tasks were still left to do. But he wanted to alert his fellow delegates to the fact that he was prepared to fight for the pragmatic position on slavery. He would take on any who called for its swift and complete eradication.

Wilmot was still describing the rationale for his position when opposition voices erupted. Thaddeus Stevens of Pennsylvania and John C. Fremont, representing the border state of Missouri, practically knocked each other over to register their disapproval of any moderate position. Both were Radical Republicans who, loudly and consistently, called for the immediate emancipation of slaves and the eradication of all forms of inequality and racial discrimination. Of the two, Fremont had the more colorful past. He was an explorer of national fame, a Senator from the new state of California, and an unsuccessful presidential candidate for the nascent Republican Party. During the Civil War, he tasted defeat at the Battle of Wilson's Creek in Missouri, taking much of the blame for the loss. He witnessed the Confederate siege of Springfield, Missouri, a critical town west of the Mississippi, and then he and his troops managed to recapture the town a few months later. Impressed with his courage and his reputation, President Lincoln placed Fremont in charge of the Department of the West and then watched as he defied orders and issued his famous "emancipation edict," freeing all the slaves in Missouri. The year was 1861, and Lincoln was nowhere near ready to issue his own Emancipation Proclamation. John C. Fremont could not wait for his boss. He was fired shortly thereafter.

Thaddeus Stevens took a different path to Radical Republicanism. Born in Vermont to a struggling farming family at the end of
the eighteenth century, Stevens suffered as a child. He had a club
foot, forcing him to limp his entire life. His father abandoned
the family when Thaddeus was just a teen, leaving his mother to
make the best of a bad financial situation. Young Stevens would
ultimately relocate to Pennsylvania, setting up his law practice in
the small town of Gettysburg. From there, he would advocate for
universal public education, claiming several important statewide
victories in that policy area. Rumors circulated that he enjoyed a
common-law marriage with his live-in, African American house-
keeper, Lydia Hamilton Smith, and that she greatly influenced his
moral and cultural stances. Eventually, he would enter politics,
first as a member of the Whig Party and then later as a Republican. He would win election to the U.S. House of Representatives
in 1848, and it was in Washington where he began to formulate
his fierce opposition to slavery and inequality. It would become
the great cause of his life.

Both Fremont and Stevens saw the world in the same way:
there would be no compromising on the issue of slavery. In this
setting, Stevens was the more vocal of the two. He relished the
debate; in fact, he was particularly proud of his skills in oratorical battle. Trained as a lawyer and also fearless, Stevens often
pointed out the hypocrisy of the situation, and of his opponent,
when attempting to win an argument. He could hardly wait to
put his debating skills to work during the convention.

Fremont was similarly fearless, but less confident of his rhetorical skills. Fresh in his mind was the pleasure of watching President Lincoln finally issue the Emancipation Proclamation eight
months prior. This was precisely what abolitionists had been fighting for. Sure, they had secured important victories in Congress
over the past twelve months, including, first, a joint resolution
calling for a federally compensated emancipation plan; second,
a war resolution prohibiting northern armies from returning
escaped slaves; third, the abolition of slavery in the District of Columbia; fourth, the outlawing of slavery in the federal territories;

fifth, the Second Confiscation Act, effectively allowing the freeing of slaves in southern territory occupied by the Union Army; and sixth, a revision of the Militia Act, allowing African American men to join the Union Army. But what Fremont most desired was for the exact objective of Lincoln's Emancipation Proclamation to find its way into the 1863 federal Constitution. He knew that the Emancipation Proclamation carried the weight of the President's signature, but he was also aware that it could easily be ignored by rebellious southerners. He needed something more. He needed to *constitutionalize* emancipation; it was the only solution. He and Stevens had a plan.

The 1825 Constitution had cleverly altered the way federal constitutions were organized. By placing the list of rights and freedoms immediately following the Preamble, the framers of the 1825 Constitution sent a powerful message about the relative importance of constitutional rights protections. These rights were not simply additions—addendums or amendments, if you will—to the basic architecture of a polity; they now enjoyed equal standing with the critical design features of America's constitutional document. Fremont and Stevens pounced. They eagerly backed a proposal by James M. Ashley and John A. Bingham, congressmen from Ohio, to embed a distinct section in the new Constitution's Article I—its Declaration of Rights—that would not only emancipate the entire enslaved population but also secure that population's equal rights. The new constitutional section would guarantee the equal status of all Black citizens as well as erase most of the legislation and court cases—the Fugitive Slave Act and the *Dred Scott* decision among them—that had so successfully oppressed an entire race.

Ashley and Bingham formally proposed their resolution on Friday, May 29th, 1863. The wording of the proposed new section was clear. The first clause read: "Neither slavery nor involuntary servitude shall exist within the United States, or any place subject to its jurisdiction." The second clause stated: "All persons born or naturalized in the United States and subject to the jurisdiction thereof, are citizens of the United States and of the State wherein they reside. No State or Federal entity shall make or enforce any law which shall abridge the privileges and immunities of citizens of the United States; nor shall any state or federal entity deprive any person of life, liberty, or property, without due process of law; nor deny to any person within its jurisdiction the equal protection of the laws." Finally, the third clause of the proposed constitutional provision said: "The Congress shall have the power to enforce, by appropriate legislation, the provisions of this section."

The language was plain and simple, but that did not guarantee its eventual passage. The issue of slavery and its place in America over the next generation occupied the convention's deliberations for weeks with no side—moderate Republican, Radical Republican, or northern Democrat—coming any closer to claiming victory. Still, Stevens and Fremont were convinced of the section's eventual ratification. Moral righteousness would eventually prevail, they thought. Surveying the room, though, they expected some temporary opposition. They got it from George Hunt Pendleton.

Pendleton was a fervent Democrat, or more precisely, a fervent Copperhead, a peace-loving subgroup within the Democratic Party that opposed the Civil War effort. And yet he was often a thorn in the side of Lincoln and the Republicans. Pendleton was also a descendent of the Jacksonian wing of the Democratic party, which favored federalism and states' rights. Unsurprisingly, then, he was deeply troubled by Lincoln's regular attempts to manage so many aspects of state police powers from the nation's capital. And that included the emancipation from slavery. States should decide for themselves whether to permit slavery, Pendleton thought.

It was these federalist instincts that eventually formed the basis of Pendleton's opposition to the Ashley-Bingham proposal. He rose to speak as soon as Thaddeus Stevens finished seconding that proposal. His voice boomed, for he was a large man with a deep baritone. "I do not sympathize with the southern cause for slavery," he began, "but I most certainly do agree with my absent southern brothers that any legitimate Constitution—new or old—must protect the rights of states that are so essential to a functioning republic. No one in this room, or in the history of this great nation, can doubt the genius of American federalism. It was the prescription for peace for two generations before this horrific war broke out, and it will be the prescription for stability after the hostilities are over. We cannot simply discard the principle that states are independent sovereignties when the urge directs us. No, indeed, selective enforcement of federalism sows the seeds of political decay. It is thus our responsibility—our duty—to defend the very principle of dual authority that has to this point defined the American political temperament."

He went on. Citing Publius in the *Federalist Papers*, Pendleton ticked off the many virtues of a strong federalist structure. He relayed the importance of preserving a governmental structure that is neither wholly national nor wholly federal. He called such a structure a "composition of both" and he insisted that, if maintained, it gave the country the best chance of preventing the rise of tyranny.[9] He continued for some time in this vein. In all, he bellowed on for almost twenty-seven minutes, drawing again and again on the advantages of federalism and the disadvantages of concentrated power. It pained him, he admitted, but he could not support any proposal calling for the immediate emancipation of slaves and the delivery of equal rights without a corresponding constitutional guarantee that allowed states some degree of self-determination. This, he said, was especially true when talking about a primarily economic interest. States, he reminded the delegation, were more capable than the federal government of regulating state-level commercial activities because regional and sectional variations were so pronounced. Why have states in the first place, he asked, if their authority over local markets can so easily be subsumed under the jurisdiction of the federal Constitution?

But what about Congress' power under the Commerce Clause? Could that be a vehicle to get at slavery? Pendleton said no. The Supreme Court, he reminded the crowd, had issued several major decisions allowing the federal government broad powers to regulate interstate commerce, but none involved the slave trade. In his mind, slaves were not articles of *interstate* commerce. He understood that abolitionists, including several in this room, had tried to sink the slave trade by placing it under congressional regulatory jurisdiction. He was not one of those advocates. He simply did not believe that slavery could be attacked that way. Ignoring decades of debate on this very subject, Pendleton confidently announced his stance that the institution of slavery could not fall under Congress' power to regulate interstate commerce.

Certain provisions in *former* Constitutions, he continued, were of no help either. He reminded the delegation that the Migration Clause in the 1787 Constitution, which technically granted Congress the power to outlaw the "migration or importation of persons" after 1808, had been removed in the 1825 Constitution. Southern interests had prevailed in the 1825 Convention, and now the Constitution was largely silent on the issue of slaves crossing state lines. Silence, Pendleton argued, presumes impotence. If the Constitution does not explicitly grant authority to the federal government, or unambiguously prohibit the states from exercising that authority, power is "reserved to the States respectively, or to the people." The Ashley-Bingham proposal, he concluded, just went too far.

In addition, he claimed to be attending the convention on behalf of the "working man," and said that he took his responsibility to protect the wage laborer quite seriously. Emancipation, he argued, would have a profound impact on employment. "The abrupt end to slavery and the establishment of a racially equal society," he continued, "would be profoundly threatening. The image of millions of illiterate, unskilled Blacks living amongst Whites, competing with Whites for jobs, and driving down wages would not be a welcome one."[10] His conscience told him to take up the abolitionist cause, but his brain told him to be more practical, to consider the impact emancipation would have on virtually all corners of American society. In addition to all the reasons he cited earlier, Pendleton would thus oppose the new language, he said, in the name of employment security.

Concern over the influx of Blacks into the workforce was very real. Even Radical Republicans worried about the impact millions of laborers would have on jobs throughout the country; it would be impossible to absorb so many looking for work. Moreover, most recognized that jobs were just part of the challenge. Delegates began whispering about the challenge emancipation would have on the welfare of the newly freed people of color and, secondarily, on the core components of a stable society. How would the freed slaves find food for their stomachs, clothing for their backs, shelter for their protection, and land for their cultivation, they asked? How would Blacks receive an education? Or medicine? Or legal help, when it was needed? Or any other basic necessity? Pendleton's hostility toward the Ashley-Bingham resolution focused primarily on the effect of newly emancipated Blacks in the labor force, but the liberation of over three million slaves at a single moment in time would also strain the economic, social, and cultural foundation of a nation still trying to find its footing. Delegates would be asked to consider how a constitutional document could effectively manage a "refugee" crisis; how words on a page could ensure stability in an expansive nation with only a rudimentary infrastructure. It was a tall task, to be sure. Many in the room did not think a fresh constitution could remedy all of these expected complications.

He was done. He had said all he wanted, and he felt good about his performance. Pendleton sat down, and immediately, the room came to life. Delegates rose simultaneously as if standing could guarantee a louder retort. The noise was impressive, and for a time the meeting was thrown into verbal chaos. Finally, though, President Sumner's pounding gavel got the upper hand, and the delegates began to settle down. Many were angry and confused by Pendleton's monologue, but they bowed to decorum just the same. And yet Pendleton's speech in opposition to the Ashley-Bingham proposal had achieved one thing: it raised issues that had yet to be verbalized. Several questions still hung in the air: how should the delegates attempt to solve the inevitable refugee crisis? Is it the responsibility of constitution-makers to establish some office or department to oversee the transition from slavery to freedom? If so, what does that office look like? Is it part of the executive branch?

The legislative branch? Or is it yet another power best allocated to the individual states? Finding answers to these questions would occupy the delegates' thoughts for the next several weeks.

Thomas Dawes Eliot, a shy congressman from Massachusetts, saw his chance. Long an advocate of establishing a "freedmen's bureau"—a federal department that could provide needed support to the emancipated population—Eliot recognized that his opportunity was now. He was concerned about his role, and the role of his fellow constitutional framers, in protecting these new citizens. He took seriously the charge in the Preamble that the Constitution was intended, among other things, to "promote the general welfare."

In preparation for this moment, he had spent some time huddling with colleagues, hoping to convince them that such a government organization could be "founded by this august body" and that it could "reside under the broad authority of the Congress to establish." He reminded his fellow framers that Congress should have the power to establish the department, much as it retained control over the creation of "inferior courts," but that the actual body should reside in the executive branch. Either way, he preferred that identification of the Department of Freedmen's Affairs (as he called it) somehow be embedded or entrenched in the new Constitution and that its existence be concretized and legitimized by the constitutional text.

And yet he recognized the complete lack of precedent for such an action. There are no administrative bodies mentioned in the 1825 Constitution (nor in the 1787 Constitution, for that matter), unless one considers Congress' power to "establish Post Offices," or the reference to "offices" in the "executive Departments" that appears in Article III. Declaring the creation of some Department of Freedmen's Affairs in the constitutional text would be unprecedented. But Eliot would not be deterred. He knew the department would carry far more weight if it was backed by constitutional force.

Also unprecedented was the administration of such an operation. He would have to create the organization out of whole

cloth. Eliot thus sought to convince fellow delegates of the proposed department's critical mission in two ways: first, by carefully
describing how it might eliminate some of the unknowns that
come with mass emancipation; and second, by appealing to the
delegates' republican spirit. Indeed, he "insisted that a minimum
degree of economic security and education were central conditions of freedom and full citizenship."[11]

He started by talking about land redistribution. Assuming a
northern victory in the Civil War, Eliot argued, southern lands
could be possessed and carved up. "Spoils of war," he uttered,
mostly under his breath. Freed slaves could then be relocated to
these confiscated lands, and if all went well, a certain order would
be restored. The freed Blacks could live mostly independent lives,
working their small parcels of land, and suitably provide for themselves and their families. They could be self-reliant.

Newly liberated people would need shelter, of course, and that
would be both expensive and complicated. But not impossible. Eliot imagined that "camps" could be set up. These refugee camps
would not establish a permanent solution, he insisted, but rather
be an initial step toward full and complete independence.[12] He
even suggested that they could be constructed in close prox-
imity to remaining northern troop stations in the South. Eliot
expressed some concern about potential health hazards threatening the former enslaved population living in such camps,
but the Department of Freedmen's Affairs could deal with that
in good time. The key, for now, was to ensure the most basic
necessities—food, clothing, and shelter. The rest could happen
a bit later. Next, Eliot continued, the department could focus
on basic infrastructure: schools, country hospitals, law offices,
and public services. The department would set up small villages
for the freed slaves, and these villages would provide all kinds
of aid and assistance.

Of course, a secondary goal of the entire refugee project,
he secretly hoped, was to maintain a level of control over the
formerly enslaved population; for most northerners, he recognized, were hardly different from their southern neighbors in

subscribing to a belief in the superiority of the White race. He knew that the majority of men in the meeting room were not truly in favor of full equal rights for Blacks. Almost all the delegates were prejudiced in that they judged people of color to be largely uneducated, intellectually unsophisticated, and morally inferior. Should the Constitution be ratified, Eliot thought, the Ashley-Bingham section would rightfully erase, on paper at least, all forms of legal discrimination. That was the just and right thing to do. But all the constitutional language and legal principles in the world cannot change the minds of men, he reasoned. They never do. But make no mistake, the new "emancipation" and "equal protection" clauses of the Constitution would be sufficient—abundantly so—to achieve some degree of peace after generations of racial strife and years of civil war. And wasn't that the primary objective here?

Something else troubled Thomas Eliot. The Bay Stater also suspected that most in the room were still frightened by the prospect of some violent uprising. Enslaved or not, Eliot figured, Blacks would quickly recognize the economic disparity that plagued most parts of the South and that would not be erased when they were liberated. Even a defeated White southerner was far more likely than a freedman to enjoy access to basic needs. The situation would perpetuate tensions that went well beyond race. In fact, Eliot estimated that two-thirds of all tenant farmers in the South—sharecroppers, if you will—would be White. That worried him. Poverty, he knew, was a powerful bonding agent. Poor Whites and freed Blacks could form a powerful alliance and threaten the existing economic state of affairs. Armed insurrection along the lines of John Brown's 1859 raid on the armory at Harpers Ferry, West Virginia, was thus very possible.

It was clear at that point that most members of the 1863 Constitutional Convention recognized what we now know: that slavery would be the single greatest moral abomination in the country's history, an irremovable stain on a nation that held more promise than any ever organized before. It would have ripple effects for generations to come, and it would forever define America's uneasy relationship with race and privilege. Even those, like Pendleton, who were opposed to any constitutional provision eliminating the institution of slavery, recognized its foul stench could never be erased. They were willing to live with that troubling reality if it meant that statehood would remain a legitimate and meaningful concept. Others, of course, were not. Sensing that he was running out of options for compromise, Sumner then suggested a recess through the weekend. It was the 5th of June—a Friday—and the convention could use a time-out.

The weekend passed without incident, at least in Boston. Deep in the South, however, the Civil War raged on. In the early morning of Sunday, June 7th, the Union Army outlasted the Rebels in an important battle at Milliken's Bend. Part of the Vicksburg campaign, the skirmish was one of Grant's critical victories on the banks of the Mississippi River. He and his generals ultimately defeated the Confederate Army on this day using the superior firepower of gunboats and occasional resorts to hand-to-hand combat. It was a fitting victory in light of the deliberations in Boston, for the Battle of Milliken's Bend is probably best known for the participation of freed slaves on the Union side.

News of the victory at Milliken's Bend would not reach the constitutional convention for several weeks. Still, the sacrifices made by Black infantrymen, and by the entire Union Army, would prove inspirational to the convention delegates. Freed Blacks were now soldiers fighting for their freedom and for the reunification of all the American states. They were equal in the eyes of patriots like Thaddeus Stevens and John C. Fremont, and they deserved the kind of protection only the U.S. Constitution could guarantee.

And so the delegation had come, after almost three weeks of debate, to the moment for a vote on the Ashley-Bingham language. President Sumner carefully reviewed the details of the proposal to include in the new Constitution a set of clauses that, upon ratification, immediately freed the enslaved and granted them equal rights. It was, sensibly, determined that Eliot's proposal to create a constitutionally protected Department of Freedmen's Affairs could be introduced after the vote on the Ashley-Bingham resolution.

That resolution was officially entered into the record on Tuesday, June 9th. When the time came, President Sumner took great pains to call on each delegate, methodically going through the roll call and carefully recording the votes. In all, it took more than two hours to poll the 232 members present. A few early "nays" were recorded, mostly from northern Democrats who aligned with George Hunt Pendleton. But quickly the "yeas" overtook the "nays," buoying the abolitionists' spirits. Stevens and Fremont shared a quick smile from their seats across the room. The final tally was not close. Pendleton and his supporters had failed to convince Radical Republicans of the merits of their argument. Instead, they had alienated a few delegates who were on the fence. By a vote of 149 to 83, the emancipation of slaves and the corresponding protection of their equal rights was placed into the proposed 1863 Constitution in Article I, right after the section that protected freedom of speech and of the press, and the right of the people to peaceably assemble. The Radical Republicans had won a major victory, and they let the assembly know their elation with a spontaneous cheer. Most understood that the new constitutional section would change the entire trajectory of the nation.

Later that afternoon, with most of the assembly still savoring the emancipation victory, delegates began pondering Eliot's formal proposal to create a Department of Freedmen's Affairs. It would prove a much quicker discussion. Consideration opened with the Massachusetts representative reading his official resolution into the record: "The Congress shall have Power to . . . Establish a Department of Freedmen's Affairs, to which shall be committed the supervision and management of all abandoned lands, and the control of all subjects relating to refugees and freedmen." Eliot argued that more detail was not required. It was not necessary to flesh out the specifics of the department's duties in the constitutional document; those details were better left to the men who eventually ran the organization. For now, what was necessary was that Congress be granted the authority to establish such an operation.

The language included a few nuggets that were neither surprising nor altogether controversial. For example, it seemed obvious to Eliot that the clause should appear in what was now Article II, Section 8 of the Constitution, the article detailing the scope of *legislative* power. He reasoned that Congress, the people's governing body, should retain license over initiatives aimed at protecting the general welfare. Further, he insisted that the clause's language include important terms such as "supervision," "management," and "control." These terms were deliberately chosen to ease the fears of delegates who were suspicious about the potential turmoil that would likely result from a massive influx of refugees. It wouldn't work. Even before he finished his impassioned defense of the proposal that day, opponents were already registering resistance.

The underlying question for most delegates centered on whether a constitutional provision establishing a Department of Freedmen's Affairs was even necessary at all. Wouldn't Clause 3 of the recently passed Ashley-Bingham provision, the clause that empowered Congress "to enforce, by appropriate legislation, the provisions of this section," include jurisdiction over the creation of a freedmen's bureau? How necessary was it for this one, lone department to be identified in the constitutional text when other departments, organizations, bureaus, and the like, could be initiated through routine legislation? To make matters worse for Eliot, some even wondered aloud whether the Necessary and Proper Clause of Article II, Section 8, especially as the U.S. Supreme Court had interpreted it in *McCulloch v. Maryland* (1819), gave Congress the ability to launch a freedmen's department. These were good, and devastating, questions, which effectively raised doubts about the clause's credibility. And so, in the end, Eliot's proposal to initiate a Department of Freedmen's Affairs and anchor it in Article II of the 1863 Constitution failed to win a majority vote.

➤⚫◀

Fatigued by such strenuous debate, the delegation was relieved to consider other constitutional matters, though most understood that the discussion about slavery was far from over. In fact, several state delegations worried that the scars of slavery would shape virtually all deliberations henceforth. It was too easy and convenient to think that constitutional language, as powerful as it can be, would erase centuries of racial bigotry and abuse. That was not going to happen during this convention.

To no one's surprise, the proceeding's discussions again pitted the radical wing of the Republican Party against more moderate voices. This was especially true when conversation turned, as it regularly did, to questions of constitutional ratification and the inevitable end of the Civil War. The word *reconstruction* was rarely uttered at the convention, but few in the assembly could escape the truth that should the North win the Civil War, the South would have to be rebuilt and probably strong-armed into accepting a new social and political order. That new reality included the elevated status of people of color.

Ratifying a new Constitution could be simple, many thought. In essence, the federal government would hold southerners hostage. In exchange for the promise (and the funds) to rebuild the devastated South, Lincoln and his colleagues would insist that southerners accept the new Constitution, with its emancipation and anti-discrimination provisions, and pledge an oath of allegiance to the Union. Some in the delegation felt uneasy about any scheme that forced constitutional ratification on unwilling subjects, but they saw no real alternative. The only option for the framers of the 1863 Constitution was to finish their work, set the terms of ratification, and hope that, over time, the new Constitution was authoritative enough, or at least moral enough, to survive.

Radical Republicans urged the rest of the delegation to leverage that powerful bargaining position into more sweeping constitutional change. What is more, these Radical Republicans insisted that the table had been set by the states to do just that. The framers at the convention were well aware that almost all state constitutions drafted since the 1825 U.S. Constitution continued the trend in favor of populism (especially as it concerned voting), support for public education, and greater accountability in the selection of judges. Indeed, constitutional trends were a real phenomenon, many remarked. Once framers in one jurisdiction constitutionalized a political impulse, others tended to follow. West Virginia, for instance, copied many other state constitutions when it applied for entry into the Union. The state's fundamental law included protections for public education and, reinforcing the 1825 federal Constitution, universal White male suffrage. It also included a few more idiosyncratic clauses, ones that were based on that state's desire to split from Virginia: first, equal apportionment based on population, and second, loyalty oaths. What is fascinating is that these types of constitutional safeguards would become far more present in the next round of state constitution-making. In fact, the legacy of the Jacksonian Democrats was quite evident in state constitutions at the time. The protection of the common man and the extension of rights to the everyday citizen had, over the prior four decades, become a fundamental part of the country's ongoing political and cultural narrative.

Hence, the time was ripe for the convention delegates to consider a proposal—*any* proposal—to extend the franchise to all Black males. Most delegates in Boston recognized that the added emancipation and equal rights section covered a lot of territory. What it did *not* include was any guarantee of the vote. After weeks of debate, the delegates were mostly supportive of ensuring the *civil* rights of freedmen, but they were not as comfortable with extending *political* rights to the newly freed slaves.

It seemed appropriate that a discussion on freedmen suffrage should follow the lengthy debate on how the new Constitution could ensure emancipation and equal rights, almost as if one led directly into the other. To do otherwise would be to emasculate the Ashley-Bingham clauses. Radical Republicans reminded the delegation that upon ratification, *Dred Scott* would be no more.

But the ill effects of the *Dred Scott* decision (that said slaves were not citizens) would haunt the country as long as Blacks were prohibited from voting.

In some ways, the conversation about extending the vote would be more heated and difficult than the one just concluded. Abolitionists in the room were very interested in expanding some of the moral and political arguments that characterized the debate about liberation and equality, while others, including some moderate Republicans, were wary of going too far in this new Constitution. Doing so would not only guarantee an uphill battle during ratification, but it also might deter southern sympathizers—men like Andrew Johnson, a former Representative, Senator, and Governor from Tennessee—from the Union cause. Moderate Republicans in the constitutional convention thus urged restraint.

James F. Wilson, from Iowa, was the first to raise the issue in any consequential way. He did so subtly, using the recently passed emancipation section to frame his remarks. The Ashley-Bingham section, he began, provides for the equality of citizens of the United States in the enjoyment of "civil rights and immunities." "What do these terms mean? Do they mean that in all things civil, social, and political, all citizens, without distinction of race and color, shall be equal? By no means can they be so construed. Do they mean that all citizens shall vote in the several States? No; for suffrage is a political right which has been left under the control of the several States, subject to the action of Congress only when it becomes necessary to enforce the guarantee of a republican form of government. Nor do they mean that all citizens shall sit on the juries, or that their children shall attend the same schools. The definition given to the term 'civil rights' is very concise, and is supported by the best authority. It is this: 'civil rights are those which have no relation to the establishment, support, or management of government.'"[13]

Benjamin Butler, of Massachusetts, was furious. A colorful figure, Butler had a political career that was a puzzling mash of odd allegiances, curious stances, and controversial positions. Prior to the outbreak of the Civil War, Butler vocally endorsed several efforts to maintain slavery in the South. He even backed Jefferson Davis at the 1860 Democratic National Convention in Charleston, South Carolina, believing that Davis, a relatively moderate southerner at the time, represented the best hope for preserving the Union. And yet by the time he joined the Union Army less than a year later, his more radical views were starting to emerge. He found himself questioning his pro-slavery stance, and one of his more innovative ideas on this front was to label slaves as "contraband," thus allowing the Union forces to seize them during the war and subsequently free them. It was an idea that never got off the ground, but it represented Butler's growing hatred for the institution of slavery.

He carried that hatred back to Boston as a chosen delegate from the Commonwealth. By that time, Butler had denounced his affiliation with the Democratic Party and was now considered a devoted member of the radical wing of the Republicans. He immediately protested Wilson's interpretation of the emancipation section, claiming instead that political liberties were every bit as important as civil liberties, and that one set of rights could not effectively function without the other. How could one ensure the equal rights of all citizens if certain people were prohibited from participating in the democratic process, he wondered? How can we even claim that the freed slaves are "citizens" in the truest sense of that term if they are not allowed to exercise the vote? He insisted the broad and sweeping language of the Ashley-Bingham provision ensured more than liberation. It encompassed a standard of equal justice that allowed all who have a stake in the political system to also have a voice in that system.

He confessed the emancipation provision did not include specific language allowing newly freed Blacks to vote. But that could be remedied easily enough. All that was needed was another constitutional section, again embedded in Article I, that prohibited the disenfranchisement of any male citizen regardless of race. After all, he pressed, didn't the delegation wish to remain faithful to the very best features of the 1825

Constitution, even as the document itself was slated for replacement? Jeffersonian constitutionalism, Butler reminded the delegation, didn't call for the wholesale invention of an entirely
new constitutional form. It called for each generation to write
its own fundamental law, and that could include most or all
of the previous generation's favorite constitutional elements.
Butler had a resolution at the ready.

Butler carefully read his proposed resolution. "The right of
citizens of the United States to vote shall not be denied by the
United States on account of race, color, or previous condition
of servitude." It was a simple constitutional provision, but it
went straight to the point. Butler wanted to keep it clean, unequivocal.

Still, a heated debate ensued. Several delegates immediately
voiced opposition to Butler's proposal, echoing the general sentiments of James F. Wilson. The freedmen cannot possibly contribute to the electoral process, these delegates said. They don't
have the moral compass, or the intellectual capacity, to make informed judgments about the qualifications of various candidates.
Freed slaves simply cannot be trusted to share in the democratic
process. Daniel Woolsey Voorhees, Democratic Congressman
from Indiana, even went so far as to cite John Brown's raid on
the Harpers Ferry armory as reason to fear the accumulation of
rights in the hands of former slaves.

Of course, reactions to the Harpers Ferry raid far outweighed
the magnitude of the event. The revolt took on a life of its own
in several respects: Brown was widely viewed as a fanatic or a
madman, the skirmish took place in a federal arsenal that stored
thousands of weapons, and southerners worried that the clash
was just the first note of an orchestrated campaign of slave re-
bellions that would eventually destroy the region's carefully tailored social and political hierarchy. Southerners were scared,
and they roundly condemned Brown for his actions. But so did
most northerners.[14] If Brown was looking for sympathizers in
progressive states like Massachusetts and Rhode Island, he would
not find them. Most northern Whites saw Brown as unstable and

his attempt at Harpers Ferry as foolhardy. They, too, were scared, and they, too, recalled how the battle made them think that an armed Black man is often a violent Black man. And now Butler was proposing to arm Black men, not with guns but with votes. If Blacks feel emboldened by their new status as equal citizens, what's to stop them from taking up arms when elections, or any other political outcomes, do not go their way? Put too much power at their disposal and violence will inevitably erupt. We must proceed cautiously, Voorhees insisted.

Back and forth the debate continued. In all, the delegation considered Butler's proposal, or some variation of it, for more than a full week. Several amendments were proposed, and all but one were voted down. The one amendment that stuck actually extended the rights of freed slaves even further. It came from John Alexander Logan. Logan was a somewhat surprising choice to represent Illinois at the constitutional convention. At thirty-seven, he was younger than most, and he was relatively inexperienced. He had been a Democrat for most of his adult life, entering the political realm first as an elected county clerk in 1849 and then later as a member of the Illinois House of Representatives. He held the dubious distinction of helping his state legislature pass an 1853 ordinance prohibiting Blacks from even settling in Illinois. That law, he now knew, was hard to square with his evolution as a politician and a human being concerned about equality and freedom. By the time he reached Boston in the spring of 1863, he had denounced that legislation as immoral and had ditched his loyalty to the Douglas wing of the Democratic Party. He announced that he was a Republican, and a radical one at that.

It was John Logan's proposed amendment to the voting clause that gained the most traction. Having experienced the potential of *state* legislatures to obstruct certain political rights, Logan suggested an important addition to Butler's proposed language. It would prove critical in the decades to follow. Specifically, Logan wanted to see that the clause included some mechanism for jurisdiction over states as well as the federal government. In other words, he wanted to include language in the proposed constitutional clause that would prevent *states* from thwarting the Black vote. He reminded his colleagues that the recently passed Ashley-Bingham constitutional section is quite explicit in regulating state activity designed to discriminate. As such, he insisted Butler's proposed new section be modified to read as follows: "The right of citizens of the United States to vote shall not be denied by the United States *or by any State* on account of race, color, or previous condition of servitude" (emphasis added). More complete coverage is needed, he warned.

The inclusion of states under the passage's regulatory umbrella again raised the ire of the strong federalists in the room. Folks like George Hunt Pendleton, John Brough of Ohio, and Horatio Seymour of New York repeated their opposition to any constitutional language that so significantly eroded the system of shared political authority that the principle of federalism, as they knew it, would no longer exist. State power, they chimed, is sacrosanct and must be protected. They were not taking a southern or Confederate position here. There is a difference, Brough argued, between hoping to preserve critical elements of federalism and treasonously seceding from the Union. To accept some oversight capacity on state elections from Washington, DC, would be to turn our backs on almost one hundred years of state sovereignty.

To no avail. The arguments vocalized by the Douglas Democrats like Wilson and Seymour were not convincing enough to derail the effort by Radical Republicans to push a voting rights provision through the framing process. Though the tally was closer than the one that secured the passage of the Ashley-Bingham resolution, on Wednesday, June 24th, a constitutional provision ensuring the extension of the vote to all freed Black males successfully passed the constitutional convention, Logan amendment and all. The pieces of the Radical Republican agenda were coming together nicely, Stevens thought.

Exactly one week after the passage of the voting rights provision, the fate of this Constitution and the entire United States changed dramatically. Though no one recognized it at the time, the Battle of Gettysburg marked the beginning of the end of the Confederacy. In hindsight, Lee's arrival in Gettysburg was the high-water mark of the Confederacy because it represented a bold maneuver to take the campaign to the North. And yet a mere three days after the commencement of hostilities, Lee retreated, a defeated and demoralized general. His forces had suffered over 28,000 casualties. The final insult had been the outcome of "Pickett's Charge," a suicidal, frontal assault on the Union Army that had the Confederate infantrymen marching more than a mile over an unobstructed wheat field. It was a massacre. No rebel army would ever get farther North or closer to ultimate victory. Neither Lee's army nor the will of the Confederacy would ever recover.

The eventual ratification of the 1863 Constitution was directly tied to the North's triumph at Gettysburg. Had the battle unfolded a little differently—had Lee not ordered Pickett's Charge, for example—the Confederacy might have expanded its control over northern territory and, eventually, forced Lincoln and his Union generals to concede. But it didn't turn out that way. As the delegates read reports of McClellan's Union Army victory at Gettysburg, their courage and fortitude were bolstered. They had two more major issues to confront: equal apportionment and loyalty oaths. The first represented a logical extension of the successful voting rights provision, which would now be included in the new constitutional text. The second represented a prayer, a hope (and nothing more), that the war would conclude with a Union victory and that southerners would accept, willingly or not, the authority of a constitutional document they had no hand in drafting.

Article II, Section 2, Clause 3 of the 1825 Constitution had to be modified. That much was clear. This particular clause was ostensibly about apportionment, but it included a few, shall we say, prejudiced punches that reflected the unconcealed discrimination of America's past. Specifically, the clause laid out the formula for calculating each state's number of members in the lower house of Congress. It stipulated that state delegations in the House of Representatives, in contrast to the Senate where each state enjoys an equal number of Senators, would be determined by a complicated formula made up of the total number of "free Persons" plus a percentage of the Black population: specifically, each Black person counted as three-fifths (60 percent) of a "free Person." The clause also spoke to two other important issues: first, the timeline for determining future apportionments; and second, the precise ratio of population to representation. It reads: "The actual Enumeration shall be made within three Years after the first Meeting of the Congress of the United States, and within every subsequent Term of ten Years, in such Manner as they shall by Law direct. The Number of Representatives shall not exceed one for every thirty Thousand, but each State shall have at Least one Representative."

The convention's Committee of Detail had flagged this particular constitutional section for alteration, and for good reason. It no longer reflected the progressive nature of the emerging constitutional document. The Three-Fifths Clause, for example, no longer applied, given that the framers had written the emancipation protection into the 1863 text. Relatedly, delegates urged that the reference to "free Persons" be removed altogether. All would be free once the new Constitution was ratified.

Equally problematic was the orientation to the practice of apportionment. A whole host of problems arose from this constitutional language. The clause read simply enough: representative apportionment would be based on the "respective numbers" of the various states. Those numbers—or state populations, in more direct language—would ostensibly come from the decennial census, a practice initiated in 1790 by the federal government. America's national census occurs every ten years and is used in lots of ways. Among them is the routine of using census data to determine roughly equal apportionment in the U.S. House of Representatives. As the population has grown, so has the size of the lower legislative chamber. In fact, the increase in the number of Representatives has been startling, from 65 in 1789 to 182 in 1813. By 1835, the number of Congressmen had ballooned to 242, but by 1861, on the eve of the Civil War, membership in the House of Representatives had dropped to 178 because of the absence of southerners in Congress. By 1869, the number of Congressmen had rebounded to 243; four years later, it was 50 more than that (293).

Framers of the 1787 and 1825 Constitutions tried to ensure roughly equal apportionment. That is why they entrenched a very precise ratio: one legislator for every "thirty-thousand" inhabitants. But exact apportionment is always elusive. Malapportionment, constitutional engineers know all too well, can often creep into the system, especially when reapportionment efforts are undertaken a decade or more apart. State systems are especially susceptible to faulty calculations and shady negotiations. Politics invades state legislatures just as regularly as federal ones. For that reason, the drafters of the 1863 Constitution endeavored to at least appear honest and irreproachable. But they were worried. They were averse to specifying in too much constitutional detail how the apportionment might be managed, and yet they needed to identify some ratio for the next generation of Americans. Would they specify a clear threshold again, as they did in 1787 and 1825? Surely, the number would be more than the now outdated 30,000 that remained in the constitutional text.

And then there was *the* fundamental question, the one on everybody's mind: who should count? Should apportionment be based on total population, or should it be based on the voting-age population? Should Congress determine that only voting-*eligible* persons can count, or should apportionment be based on average statewide voter turnout? How about aliens? Would they be counted? And minors? Should they be included? Minors may not be able to vote, several delegates argued, but they need representation in Congress just the same.

In many ways, state constitution-makers were more proactive on the apportionment issue, or at least more experienced. Several states had embedded fairly sophisticated provisions in their constitutional texts that sought to clarify the situation. In the years leading up to the Civil War, state legislatures regularly favored one of two counting systems to determine apportionment for their statehouses: total population *or* total number of registered voters.[15] Census population—total population, that is—was overwhelmingly preferred by most states, but the remaining states had opted to base statehouse representation on the number of voting-eligible citizens within the state. Now it was the federal constitutional framers' turn to discuss the issue.

Throughout the entire debate surrounding apportionment, the question of the emancipated slaves kept coming up. Unlike the situation faced by earlier drafting conventions, a whole influx of citizens would *immediately* join the voting rolls after this new Constitution was ratified, especially in the southern states. Likewise, former slave states would immediately see an increase in voting power as a result of the shift from counting enslaved individuals as three-fifths of a person to counting freed individuals as whole persons. This addition to the population would significantly alter the balance of power in a unified and fully populated House of Representatives, delegates feared. The former Confederate states would benefit from the recalculation.

As constitutional convention delegates in Boston prepared to finalize an apportionment plan, they looked to the census data for insight. The 1860 census revealed some interesting, if not altogether surprising, facts related to aggregate population and the institution of slavery. The soon-to-be freed slaves constituted a large percentage of the population in most southern states: 45 percent in Alabama, 26 percent in Arkansas, 55 percent in Mississippi, 57 percent in South Carolina, 44 percent in Florida and Georgia, 31 percent in Virginia, and 30 percent in Texas. Delegates supposed those percentages would only increase over time. Birth rates among the enslaved populations showed signs of increasing at a greater rate than birth rates among Whites in the South. Moreover, mass migration of freed people from the South to the North was not likely to happen, at least not in the short term.

Of course, the constitutional drafters in Boston appreciated that the population in northern states still far outpaced that in the southern states: New York was the most populous state in 1860, with close to 4 million inhabitants, while Pennsylvania had close to 3 million and Ohio had approximately 2.5; only four Confederate states (Georgia, Kentucky, Tennessee, and Virginia) had more than a million residents apiece. Still, with a decision to set total state population as the mechanism for congressional apportionment would come the worry that the relative power of the northern states would diminish. That concern was in many ways absurdly overblown. At the time, most of the delegates to the 1863 Constitutional Convention were only vaguely aware that a possible reconstruction effort would include the suppression of any real southern political power. The war was still raging, and they had not given much thought to how the South might eventually be restored. The more forward thinking among them, however, knew that the South would eventually look to the North for help, and that it would probably do so from its knees.

The delegates went round and round. At certain times, it seemed as if the conservatives would prevail and force the drafting party to come up with an elaborate mechanism for determining apportionment. Perhaps the best strategy, the conservatives said, would be to *ease into* a full counting of people of color—deliberately, and over a long period of time. So, a state might get *partial* credit for its suddenly larger population, and then in a certain year—say, 1880—it would enjoy *full* credit. Earlier constitutions, they reminded the group, had incorporated analogous transitional schemes directly into the text—think of the clause in the 1787 Constitution that prohibited Congress from outlawing the slave trade before the year 1808. We could do the same with apportionment, a few argued. Some in Boston thought such a strategy could work.

More progressive voices disagreed. Strongly. They highlighted two major faults with the argument that the new Constitution should stipulate a gradual buildup of population numbers in certain states. First, it was immoral and unjust. Sure, penalizing southern states by mandating separate counting schemes in free and former slave states might be appealing as payback for the devastation brought on by the Confederacy. To some, it seemed almost meek to punish the South this way. Still, it was unjust. The North, in addition to fighting to retain the Union, was also fighting that bloody war in protest of manifest intolerance and discrimination. To then perpetuate the tradition of counting people of color as less than fully human was, to put it mildly, hypocritical. Plus, it had consequences that many considered wholly unacceptable. Progressive-minded thinkers like Thaddeus Stevens and John Fremont worried that the dilution of political power in states with large Black populations would inevitably harm the emancipated. Stevens, in fact, imagined that some congressional districts in the South would elect former enslaved persons to Congress. He was prescient, of course. History reveals that there were more Blacks elected to public office, including the House of Representatives, in the Reconstruction period immediately following the Civil War than in practically any other period since. He feared that calculating apportionment based on figures that did not account for full human beings would only increase the difficulty of ensuring adequate representation for freedmen.

There was a second line of reasoning for the progressives. It was grounded in constitutional theory. Horace Greeley, founder and editor of the widely circulated *New York Tribune*, championed this line of thinking. The newspaperman had traveled to Boston to cover the proceedings—as best he could, given that the assembly had decided to maintain strict confidentiality. He wielded significant influence at the time, though, and he personally knew a lot of the delegates. He was also quite outspoken.

Again, the decision in *McCulloch v. Maryland* (1819) would claim the intellectual spotlight. Greeley was convinced that any rational definition of constitutionalism followed the more popular interpretation of Marshall's opinion. Marshall's statement, "We must never forget that it is a constitution we are expounding," Greeley reminded his friends, must be read in the context of what Marshall says next. A constitution's nature, Marshall wrote, "requires that only its great outlines should be marked, its important objects designated, and the minor ingredients which compose those objects, be deduced from the nature of the objects themselves." A constitution, in other words, is the fundamental law, the law that governs all other laws. It should not be troubled with the directions and details that are better left to routine legislation. Any constitution with the "prolixity of a legal code," Greeley insisted, quoting Marshall again, could "scarcely be embraced by the human mind."

He was quite adamant about this. To Greeley, there was no other way to comprehend a nation's constitution. Others in Boston agreed; several delegates brought Greeley's arguments back to the chamber. As debate ensued, the progressive position started to gain the upper hand, until, suddenly, it was over. Confident that he had support on his side, Thaddeus Stevens called the question on Tuesday, August 11th.

The outcome was never in doubt. As the votes were uttered, it became evident that the progressive view would again carry the day. Article II, Section 2, Clause 3 would be completely reworked to reflect the character of the rest of the new Constitution. There would be no mention of the country's oppressive past, no reference to fractional personhood or indigenous tax status. The clause would deal exclusively with apportionment—nothing else. The delegation further determined that there would be no stipulated ratio of population to representation, as had been the norm in constitutions past. That would allow for future flexibility and growth before the next generation's convention was called. Finally, the assembly rejected any attempt to introduce a phased approach to counting bodies. Freed individuals would be counted just as white individuals always had been. The proposed new clause would thus read as follows: "The House of Representatives shall consist of Representatives, who shall be apportioned among the several States, according to the number of inhabitants in them respectively; and to this end the Congress shall cause an enumeration of all the inhabitants of each State to be made in the year 1870, and every ten years thereafter, and shall make an apportionment of the representatives among the several States at the first regular session of Congress after each enumeration; which apportionment, when made, shall not be subject to alteration until after the next census shall have been taken: Provided, That each State shall be entitled to at least one representative."[16] The clause passed easily.

The convention was coming to an end. The delegates could see the finish line now that most of the major structural, rights-based, and substantive pieces were in place. The Committee of Detail had penned an early draft of the new Constitution during the first week of August, in part to give the delegates a bird's-eye view of what they had agreed upon and what was left to do, and in part to give the entire assembly a much-needed few days off. The plan was for the Committee of Style to take its turn to carefully edit the document once the convention was completely finished with its work. The entire assembly would then reconvene, one final time, to cast a deciding vote on the Constitution itself, and then, if all went well, delegates would impart their signatures to the document. It was late August, and the delegates were eager to return to their homes.

One final piece remained, however. The last consequential debate of the 1863 Constitutional Convention underscored the ongoing rift between moderate and Radical Republicans. It concerned the correct approach to receiving southerners back into the Union, should the North win the war. This was a big issue for many in Boston that summer, even if it was optimistically premature. The Battle of Gettysburg had given the northern army a much-needed morale boost, but the conclusion of America's bloodiest war was still too far off to predict. Even so, delegates to the constitutional convention were now absorbed with the process of reunification. They often spoke about plans that were rumored and ideas that were floated. What would it take, they wondered, for us to be confident that history will not repeat itself and sectional war can be prevented? How can we be sure that southern Whites will not try their secessionist antics again?

Abraham Lincoln worried during the summer of 1863 that reconstructing the South would require a firm but delicate hand. Too much coercion and the South was likely to turn its back yet again on the idea of a nation of *united* states. What is more, Lincoln feared that compelling southerners to abide by certain conditions in order to rejoin the Union placed the whole concept of emancipation in real jeopardy. What was to stop southerners from restoring some form of slavery? They might not be able to reestablish *legal* modes of slavery, but, Lincoln feared, they could easily devise informal ways to keep Blacks enslaved. He had heard rumblings from the radical wing of the Republican party that the only way to deal with southern traitors was forcefully, with little mercy. Lincoln disagreed. He tried to persuade individuals like Senator Benjamin F. Wade of Ohio and Representative Henry Winter Davis of Maryland that a temperate and restrained approach gave the North the best chance of reconciliation. Strong-arming the South into civic submission was simply a losing strategy, Lincoln thought.

Wade, Davis, and fellow Radical Republicans mostly rejected Lincoln's view because they disagreed with his central premise. The President believed that the act of secession was illegal and unconstitutional from the start, that southern states had no legitimate authority to break from the Union and form their own nation. The response to the establishment of the Confederate States of America could be less severe, Lincoln concluded, because the act itself was not as egregious as some thought. That didn't hold water with most Radical Republicans, especially after receiving reports of the intensity of the fighting and sacrifice on the battlefield. Hundreds of thousands of casualties implies a commitment to something greater than a mere illegal act. Lincoln was just wrong, they insisted.

Moderate Republicans were already outnumbered at the constitutional convention; it did not help that most in Boston disagreed with Lincoln's view of secession's dubious legal foundation. And so disagreement about the proper way to treat southerners once the war concluded reached a head when the specific topic of loyalty oaths was raised. Oaths were popular at the time. They were used widely as a way of demonstrating fidelity to a shared cause. Both the 1787 Constitution and the 1825 Constitution included provisions for the President to take a specific "Oath or Affirmation," the particulars of which are found in the executive branch's article in each Constitution. The 1787 text also included a mandate that most public officers take an oath to support the Constitution (Article VI, Clause 3). That requirement was preserved in the 1825 Constitution (Article VII, Clause 3). Now, it was decided that both the detailed presidential oath and the requirement that other public officers swear allegiance to the Constitution should stay in the 1863 text.

But an oath of office is subtly different from a loyalty oath. The former, in the United States at least, represents a statement of commitment to a grand principle, a pledge of allegiance to a noble experiment in collective self-rule and limited government. The latter, in this case, feels quite different. It represents a reflection of superiority, subordination, and power. It feels as though the vanquished foe is being coerced into affirming allegiance to an unfamiliar people and an alien way of life. Doubtless, southerners would be reluctant to take any loyalty oath at all, unless it was to the Confederacy. An oath to the United States would be completely out of the question. But northerners required some guarantee that their southern brothers and sisters would not go rogue again, that their treasonous activities would not repeat themselves.

Lincoln's closest allies were skeptical of any robust attempt to force citizens to take loyalty oaths, because to do so seemed discordant with the powerful and uniquely American version of liberty. They preferred a low bar here. Some southerners could be forced to take loyalty oaths—former officers of the rebel army, for example—but the common citizen should not be required to do so. Or at least not in the numbers and percentages that Radical Republicans wanted. In contrast, Radical Republicans favored a more significant and widespread demonstration of loyalty. To them, this was not a minor condition for readmittance; it represented a significant admission of the injustices perpetrated by those in the Confederacy. And it was a necessary first step toward readmission.

Lincoln himself had floated the Ten Percent Rule prior to the start of the convention, so players in Boston were generally familiar with his stance. The Ten Percent Rule required just that: 10 percent of the citizens in each former Confederate state had to pledge allegiance to the United States and its Constitution in order for that state to gain readmission.

Delegates were also familiar with Lincoln's preference for keeping the loyalty oath simple. A promise to support the Constitution of the United States and the full Union would suffice. The first proposal reflected that simplicity. It read: "I, ____ ____, do solemnly swear, in presence of Almighty God, that I will henceforth faithfully support, protect, and defend the Constitution of the United States and the Union of the States thereunder; and that I will, in like manner, abide by and faithfully support provisions of this Constitution with reference to former slaves, so long and so far as not repealed, modified, or held void by decision of the Supreme Court; and that I will, in like manner, abide by and faithfully support all proclamations of the President made during the existing rebellion so long and so far as not modified or declared void by decision of the Supreme Court. So help me God." Minimalism was best, the supporters of this oath argued. They suggested that this language appear in Article VII of the draft Constitution, right after the provision that requires Senators, Representatives, state legislators, and all executive and judicial officers to take their own "Oath or Affirmation."

The initial objection to this proposal came from Senator Wade of Ohio. Nicknamed "Bluff," Wade had enjoyed a long career in politics, and was widely known as one of the most radical of the Radical Republicans, advocating early on for, among other things, women's suffrage and Black equality. He was thrilled, of course, that the 1863 federal Convention had been such a triumph for the radical wing of the Republican Party. They could claim almost total victory if only he could get the assembly to follow his lead on the conditions of reunification. He wanted a lot from the Rebels. Why not mandate a more resolute loyalty oath, he asked? And the presence of Military Governors in the southern states? Why not include them in the mix as well? Wade did not believe southerners should govern themselves after inflicting such bloodshed on fellow citizens. They had relinquished, at least temporarily, the privilege of self-governing, he thought. They could earn it back, of course, but it should not be handed to the former Confederate states as soon as the war ended.

It thus irritated him that moderate Republicans and northern Democrats were pushing a tepid agenda. This was the moment, he thought, to fundamentally change the course of American history. In his mind, the act of secession was the most profoundly treasonous action in the history of the country. The draft 1863 Constitution would be a powerful response to southern aggression, he knew, as it repudiated all that the Confederacy stood for. Wade was convinced that constitutional transitions like this one inspired a kind of civic assimilation, a bonding of many peoples under a single Constitution into "one People." But southerners should not get a free pass to reenter the Union, to become part of this "one People."

He thus stood to propose an alternative to the loyalty oath currently on the floor. His was more forceful. It read, "I, ____ ____, do solemnly swear that I have never voluntarily borne arms against the United States since I have been a citizen thereof; that I have voluntarily given no aid, countenance, counsel, or encouragement to persons engaged in armed hostility thereto; that I have neither sought nor accepted nor attempted to exercise the functions of any office whatever, under any authority or pretended authority in hostility to the United States; that I have not yielded a voluntary support to any pretended government, authority, power or constitution within the United States, hostile or inimical thereto. And I do further swear that, to the best of my ability, I will support and defend the Constitution of the United States, against all enemies, foreign and domestic; that I will bear true faith and allegiance to the same; that I will abide by the dictates of this Constitution, especially as it relates to the emancipation of all slaves; and that I take this obligation freely, without any mental reservation or purpose of evasion, So help me God." Wade argued that *this* oath, in contrast to the other, would send a commanding message to the southern states. It was unequivocal. It included multilayered statements—anti-treason statements, statements in support of the Constitution, and a statement accepting the veracity of emancipation. It covered most bases, and in his mind, it was an ironclad requirement for southern reconciliation. On Monday, August 31st, he formally introduced it into the record of the convention. Henry Winter Davis of Maryland was quick to announce a second.

It seemed peculiar, in a sense, to be discussing the rules for reengagement when the war was not over and the South had given no indication of wanting back into the Union. And yet it also seemed perfectly normal to be thinking ahead. That seemed the American way, or at least the Union way. Lincoln and his Cabinet were constantly planning for what they saw as the inevitable reunification of the United States. Their eyes were mostly fixed on the future and the development of a just and prosperous America.

Two proposals were on the floor. Each enjoyed considerable support from particular members of the assembly. The Radical Republicans stood behind Wade's proposed language, while the more moderate band of the party advocated for Lincoln's preferred oath. The temperament of the overall assembly on the topic was hard to assess. What was not hard to gauge was everyone's mood. The delegates recognized the importance of this moment, but general fatigue and impatience had set in. The last week of August had been scorchingly hot in eastern New England, and the delegates' enthusiasm for constitution-making was fading. As a result, the debate over which loyalty oath to support was comparatively lackluster. The two sides made the same arguments that had been rehearsed in the taverns and boarding houses around town: what was the appropriate degree of pressure to put on southerners? Should we really insist that rebels go on record as never having given "aid, countenance, counsel, or encouragement to persons engaged in armed hostility" against the United States when we know that's exactly what so many did? Is it even appropriate to insist that all citizens, or even just all White males, take the oath?

In the end, the radicals had the votes. By a margin of 153 to 86, Wade's more intense language prevailed. It would be included in Article VII of the new Constitution. As a concession to those Republicans who were not sure how to vote right up to the last minute, the radical wing was willing to bend a little on the percentage of southern citizens required to take the oath before a state could be readmitted to the Union. Forty percent would be the number, not the 10 percent that Lincoln preferred or the 50 percent that Wade and Davis wanted. Forty percent represented a significant number of citizens, both radicals and moderates concluded, but it was just short of a majority. It felt right.

And so the task of sketching out a new Constitution in 1863 was now complete. The collective delegation had finished its work on the eve of September 1st, 1863, a few weeks ahead of schedule. The Committee of Style was then impaneled to work out the many particulars and present a finalized draft to the entire convention. The delegates not on that committee adjourned and retreated to their various places of lodging. They expected the committee's report in a few short days.

The Convention Adjourns

In some ways it was fitting that the final substantive debate on the convention floor was about oaths of commitment to the U.S. Constitution. A Constitution based on a belief that "We the People" can, collectively, form "a more perfect Union" should inspire a serious discussion about devotion and faith. Indeed, commitment to country has a powerful magnetic force, attracting many different people to a single shared purpose. The Constitutional Convention of 1863 represented a microcosm of that high virtue. The delegates had given their summer months—and a whole lot more over the course of their lives—to the principle that freedom and good government could be realized only if certified by an effective and celebrated Constitution. Their collective mindset harkened back to an era in the late eighteenth century when people were willing to give their lives for a shared public cause, when the ideal of civic virtue—of sacrifice triumphing over private interest—meant something. The interwar period between the Revolution and the Civil War had witnessed an erosion of that civic loyalty, but the Civil War had put it back on full display. Could there be a greater demonstration of sacrifice for one's country than taking up arms against a brother who shared a collective past? Could we ever doubt the commitment of those in the North and the South who were willing to die for their vision of a patriotic dream?

As the delegates packed up to leave Boston, they wondered how successfully this Constitution would ensure order in the reborn polity. They worried about ratification, of course. Constitutional founders *always* worry about ratification. But even more so, they worried about the next five years, the next decade, and the next generation. Could this Constitution withstand the types of crises that would inevitably arise? Could it help to guide government officials and private citizens in realizing "a more perfect Union"? The 1825 Constitution could not, in part because Daniel Webster, Thomas Jefferson, Henry Clay, John Taylor, and the scores of other constitutional framers in Philadelphia that year chose not to disturb the institution of slavery. They took the safer route—perhaps, with hindsight, even the cowardly route. And the country paid the price. The Civil War is still the most devastating war in American history. The 1825 Constitution could do nothing to prevent it.

The 1863 framers were more hopeful that the product of their labors would better deliver on the promises of the Constitution's Preamble. What they desired most was a certain degree of "domestic tranquility." Let's end this war, the delegates argued, and enjoy the inevitable calm that comes—perhaps because of exhaustion or because a certain sadness naturally befalls a nation concluding a war with itself—immediately thereafter. They recognized that the new constitutional document would not be all that popular in the South, and that the former Confederacy would likely protest many of the changes to the 1825 text. But those in Boston felt a strong moral obligation to fundamentally alter the American narrative. They understood that their unique place in the history of this nation was to drive a stake, once and for all, through the very heart of slavery.

And so they had done that. It wasn't always pleasant or easy, but in the end the document was signed by 206 delegates. It reflected a new vision for America. The vision was slightly more progressive than the one imagined by Abraham Lincoln, but it was close to what he wanted. As it turned out, he was pleased with the document and almost immediately signaled his steadfast support for ratification. Of course, most knew that Lincoln would always be the major figure of the 1863 Constitutional Convention, the proverbial elephant in the room. It was ironic that he was never in Boston at any time during that summer;[17] nor did he ever formally communicate with any of the convention's delegates. His considerable shadow unquestionably extended up the Massachusetts coast, though. In many ways, Lincoln provided the cover for delegates to secure the emancipation of the enslaved and extend basic constitutional rights to those newly freed individuals. The election of 1860 had seen to it that the future of slavery was in doubt. The Civil War just accelerated the process of emancipation. The Constitution of 1863 made it official.

It had been a remarkable constitutional convention. Most are, but this one had a special quality because of the moment itself and because the future of a unified and bonded United States was so indeterminate. What was perhaps most remarkable about the 1863 Constitutional Convention in Boston, however, was that Thomas Jefferson's name rarely made an appearance. We can only wonder if the 1863 Constitutional Convention symbolically marked the end of Jefferson's enduring influence. The next generation in the United States would be defined by the rise of commercial production and urban migration, two developments that would have puzzled, or perhaps even concerned, the lanky Virginian. The economic engine that the United States became in the last half of the nineteenth century would have been terribly unfamiliar to Jefferson. A slaveowner and a civil libertarian at the same time, Jefferson would likely have also been internally conflicted by the expansion of liberty in this Constitution at the expense of slavery. Sure, the practice of each generation crafting its own fundamental law would remain Jefferson's greatest legacy. But so many other components of his American dream were, quite simply, fading away.

1903 ———

CONSTITUTIONS ARE CURIOUS human inventions. They enter the world with such promise, such soaring potential. Fresh off the pen of the framers, they offer a crisp start, a new beginning to a polity that has lost its way. They have a very practical purpose—to order a political community around an agreed-upon set of rules and institutions—and yet to focus primarily on their utility is to grossly underestimate their broad and inspiring capabilities. There are qualities to constitutions that are not readily apparent from simply studying the words and phrases of the text. Constitutions can be emotive; they have the capacity to move a citizenry. They can rally patriots and disarm subversives. They can be a beacon of pride for an entire community of people. Constitutions are the opposite of mundane. Useful? Sure. But not mundane. They are unlike any other creatures in the modern body politic.

And yet sometimes constitutions are none of these things. Sometimes their promise fizzles almost immediately after they are signed and ratified. Such was the fate of America's 1863 Constitution. With all of its grand promises and far-reaching potential, it fell flat when the time came to use it to safeguard the transition to a post–Civil War America. It helped to spawn fringe groups like the Ku Klux Klan. It was not capable of ordering a diverse and multicultural society that was about to undergo the massive technological expansion associated with the second industrial revolution. The birth of the transcontinental railroad changed everything about the United States. So did the invention of electricity and mass communication, the rise of labor unions, the influx of tens of millions of immigrants, increased wages, private investment, urbanization, and so much more. And then there was the political arena. The intensity of the competitions among parties led to the rise of political machines, corruption, and scandal. Politics was a mess in the last third of the nineteenth century. The financial panic and severe depression of 1893 only added to the political chaos, leading to a political realignment in 1896. Overall, it was a period of massive change in the United States, and the Constitution of 1863 couldn't keep up. The Gilded Age, as the late nineteenth century came to be known, tested the very idea of a constitutional polity ordered by a single fundamental text. The document produced in 1863 failed that test.

Things started off well enough. America's 1863 Constitution was ratified in the months following its September 4th public debut. Most northern Governors and state legislators quickly endorsed the new plan for government and called on their state Ratifying Conventions to do the same. The Ratifying Conventions were more deliberate, but eventually enough came around. By June 1st, 1864, the text had been ratified by twenty-two of the thirty-five states, four more than was required by Article VIII of the 1863 Constitution, which mandated only that a "majority of States" agreeing was "sufficient for its Establishment." Still at war with the North in 1864, the states of the Confederacy did not recognize the legitimacy of the 1863 Constitution and hence did not assemble any Ratifying Conventions. Several states—Maryland, Kansas, and West Virginia—considered and then rejected the new text altogether. In one state—Maryland—two members of the Ratifying Convention came to blows over their differences of opinion on the merits of the new Constitution. The stakes are always high when constitutions are formed. But no matter, nothing could halt the new text's apparent momentum.

Inauspicious signs, though, began to surface right away. The 1863 Constitution did nothing to accelerate the conclusion of the Civil War. Hostilities would officially cease on August 9th, 1865. But fierce fighting had accompanied the Constitution's first two years of existence. Some claim that the progressive nature of the 1863 Constitution may even have *extended* the war; it gave southerners little incentive to rejoin the Union. Most southerners likely thought their way of life was slipping further and further from view because of this new constitutional document. Many insisted it would probably be better for the rebels just to fight on to preserve the antebellum way of life than for the South to accept a place in the newly reborn polity. The fighting that might have ended before New Year's Day, 1865, under a more moderate Constitution, continued for more than four additional months. The price was thousands more casualties.

It could also be that John Wilkes Booth had the 1863 Constitution in mind when, just six days after Lee's surrender, he placed a gun to President Lincoln's head, fired, and then jumped to the stage at Ford's Theatre. Rarely has a fresh Constitution endured so much in its first twenty-four months.

Tragically, things did not improve for the 1863 Constitution during Reconstruction. Federal forces maintained their presence in the former Confederate states so that they could enforce the provisions of the new Constitution. Southerners refused to oblige. They enacted Black Codes in an attempt to restrict the liberty of the freed individuals. These new laws essentially replaced the old Slave Codes, and were intended not only to discriminate but also to suppress any political power Blacks held. The repressive laws represented a blatant rebuke of the rights and freedoms extended to all Blacks in Article I of the new Constitution. Southerners also managed to keep most people of color in serious poverty. The codes forced Blacks into low-paying jobs that often resulted in rising personal and family debt. Ironically, the newly established Bureau of Refugees, Freedmen, and Abandoned Lands—the Freedmen's Bureau—was of little help. That institution was supposed to act as a shield against racial discrimination while providing basic necessities and support for the formerly enslaved. Its primary objective, it turns out, was inconsistent with its stated mission. That objective was to control the Black population.

Riots erupted in places like Memphis and New Orleans because of the Black Codes. Former Confederate soldiers in Tennessee founded the infamous Ku Klux Klan. President Andrew Johnson vetoed the Civil Rights Act of 1866 and the first three Reconstruction Acts. Johnson was then impeached, but later acquitted in the Senate by a razor-thin margin. Carpetbaggers and scalawags sought to profit from the South's despair. Sharecropper agreements benefited wealthy southerners at the expense of freed Blacks and poor Whites. The economic Panic of 1873 led to a worldwide depression. And the federal government began a systematic and brutal campaign to relocate Native peoples onto "reservations," where arable land was scarce and threats from Washington were plentiful. The failure of the 1863 Constitution lay in its inability to stave off these many crises that plagued the United States after the Civil War.

State constitutions began to reflect these tensions as well. For obvious reasons, there was a flurry of state constitutional activity throughout the Reconstruction era. Between the end of the Civil War and the conclusion of Reconstruction in 1877, twenty-seven new state constitutions were drafted and ultimately ratified across the country, and three additional state constitutional conventions were held where the proposed text was not ratified. Thirty separate attempts at constitutional revision in this twelve-year period is remarkable. In some states, framers even went to the drawing board more than once to draft new plans for government. Yet the bustle was not unexpected. As former Confederate states rejoined the Union, they often turned to the constitution-making process to shape their government's forthcoming expectations and to send a message of protest to Washington, DC. State constitutional framers in the South saw the process of crafting a new fundamental law as a powerful means to rebuff some of the Reconstruction-era policies.

Southern state constitutions in this period shared a number of common characteristics: they were a product of the contemporary political environment, both regionally and nationally; they were a reaction against Reconstruction; and they sought to restrict the power of government, and especially the legislature, in advancing any of the progressive policies of the time. Reconstruction spawned such a backlash among middle- and upper-class White southerners that the plight of freed people was always in some kind of jeopardy.

It was the period of southern "Redemption" that most frightened formerly enslaved people. During Reconstruction, African Americans, it can be said, enjoyed a degree of freedom never before experienced. They voted successfully; they built the first public schools for African Americans in the South; they moved about rather freely; they felt what it was like to be relatively equal in the eyes of the law. That soon changed, as White southerners called for a reversal of such rights.[1] Between 1873 and the end of the nineteenth century, southern lawmakers and private citizens participated in a systematic campaign to oppress and torment former slaves. They found ways around the constitutional guarantees of freedom, due process, and equality. They passed statutes that reversed a number of Reconstruction-era safeguards. They amended their state constitutions to marginalize all persons of color. They refused service to Blacks. These actions were deliberately calculated to intimidate and terrorize. And they worked.

Plessy v. Ferguson was the most infamous in a series of Supreme Court decisions that ultimately broke the 1863 Constitution's back.[2] The case involved a challenge to a Louisiana law that required separate racial accommodations on all state railroads. Homer Plessy, who was mixed race, purchased a first-class ticket and boarded the "Whites-only" car of a train headed to Covington, Louisiana. He recognized that his actions would invite the attention of law enforcement, but he still wanted to test the constitutionality of Louisiana's law. As expected, he was asked to leave the "Whites-only" car. He refused, citing his right under the new Constitution to equal treatment. Plessy was then detained and arrested, setting up the constitutional showdown in the Supreme Court. There, seven Justices—one short of unanimity[3]—ruled against Plessy. They reasoned that the state was perfectly within its constitutional authority to separate the races and that the clause guaranteeing "equal protection" required only roughly equal accommodations. In other words, a state could legally segregate the races as long as the facilities were more or less equivalent. Writing for the majority, Justice Henry Billings Brown concluded that, "the object of the Constitution's equal protection clause was undoubtedly to enforce the absolute equality of the two races before the law, but in the nature of things, it could not have been intended to abolish distinctions based upon color, or to enforce social, as distinguished from political equality, or a comingling of the two races upon terms unsatisfactory to either."[4] In dissent, Justice John Marshall Harlan seemed to say that when the Equal Protection Clause faced its first crucial test, it failed miserably.

Here, regrettably, was another strong argument against Jeffersonian constitutionalism: the 1863 Constitution (which, to many White southerners, was the equivalent of colonial rule in constitutional form) simply did not foster the degree of authority, loyalty, or standing needed to overcome the country's many troubles.[5] It simply never had sufficient time to amass the necessary credibility. Southerners worked assiduously to combat the very ideals the Radical Republicans in Boston most wanted to advance. They took direct aim at the very heart of the new Constitution—and it was not up to the fight.

The world changed more dramatically in the period between 1863 and 1903 than at any other time in American history. It is not too much of an exaggeration to say that the framers of the 1863

Constitution likely would not even have recognized their own country in 1903. America's population in 1860 stood at 31 million. By 1900, that figure was 76 million. Ten more states had been admitted to the Union. The average monthly wage for laborers in 1863 was less than $15. By 1900, that number had grown by over 250 percent. Alexander Graham Bell was awarded the first U.S. patent for the telephone in 1876. Just three years later, Thomas Edison harnessed electricity. Even the creation of Coca-Cola, movie theaters, and the zipper in the late nineteenth century helped to transform the expanding country into a fully commercial republic. America was a fundamentally different place in the years leading up to the 1903 Constitutional Convention.

What would have been tragically familiar to constitutional framers, however, was the continuing racial divide that tormented the country at the end of the nineteenth century. The explosion of Jim Crow laws in the South immediately following the removal of federal troops in the late 1870s was dizzying. State and local lawmakers in the former Confederacy used as many avenues as possible to introduce measures aimed at segregating the races. The goal was to demoralize and dominate. Segregated schools, restaurants, buses, water fountains, bathrooms—segregation in virtually every slice of public life—became the cultural norm in many parts of the country.[6] And so did lynchings. Thousands of Black people were lynched in the years leading up to the convention. Mississippi, Florida, Arkansas, and Louisiana were particularly likely to use the terrorizing threat of lynching to intimidate and repress, and few Whites were willing to raise any serious objections. Most simply stood on the sidelines and watched.

Nicholas Murray Butler was acutely aware of both the legal methods used to oppress people of color and the lawless activity that so often terrorized them. Born in 1862 at the beginning of the Civil War, Butler was a member of the exact generation that the 1863 constitutional framers were trying to reflect in the document. He was smart, and he was a master of self-promotion.[7] Butler would hold the top post at Columbia University for a record forty-four years.[8] He would later become the President of the American Academy of Arts and Letters and the recipient of the 1931 Nobel Peace Prize. He was an impressively intellectual fellow. The *New York Times* referred to him, on separate occasions, as "the incarnation of the international mind" and the "Prime Minister of the Republic of the Intellect."[9] And he had an out-sized ego to match.[10]

He was also heavily into politics. A regular at Republican National Conventions, he flirted several times with elected office over the course of his long career. The closest he would come to such a position would be as "adviser" to seven Presidents. He was popular among them; Theodore Roosevelt once even called him "Nicholas Miraculous" before they had a famous falling out over the expansion of unionization. Altogether, though, he was perhaps best known as an armchair expert on international affairs. He would in his later life maneuver his way into leading such organizations as the Carnegie Endowment for International Peace and the Pilgrims Society, but early on he would speak to anyone who would listen about global politics and America's place on the world stage.

Butler would take this interesting mix of immodesty, self-promotion, and intellectual bravado to Philadelphia in May 1903 to participate in the federal constitutional convention. He was selected by the New York State legislature to represent the Empire State at the convention primarily because of his international expertise. He was not really surprised by the invitation—his ego rarely allowed for surprise—as his network of colleagues, acquaintances, and confidants was deep and wide. He had a lot of friends in Albany, the state capital.

Butler's arrival in Philadelphia on Friday, May 15th, 1903, was not without drama. He arranged to take the first-class railroad car from Manhattan to Philadelphia and, coincidentally, was assigned a seat near Henry Cabot Lodge, Republican Senator from Massachusetts, who was also on his way to the convention. Lodge and Butler had a lot in common, but they differed on the extent to which America should display a heavy hand in foreign affairs. Lodge was more aggressive. He was a staunch supporter of the

Spanish-American War, and he advocated for the annexation of Hawaii and the Philippines. He was an imperialist through and through. Butler, in contrast, was not as keen on America's imperialist tendencies, preferring instead a more diplomatic approach to international relations. They got into a heated argument on the train ride to Philadelphia, an argument about internationalization that would spill out into the convention itself.

Butler and Lodge joined 265 fellow delegates in Philadelphia. The appropriate number of invitations was the topic of a flurry of discussion in the years leading up to the 1903 Constitutional Convention. How many delegates is too many? The 58th U.S. Congress consisted of 476 lawmakers: 386 in the House of Representatives and 90 in the Senate. Most felt that such a number was simply too high for any constitutional convention. It would be impossible for all members to experience any meaningful impact on the proceedings. The delegates had to be fewer. In studying the notes from the 1863 Constitutional Convention, organizers of the 1903 gathering realized that there was virtually no comment—and thus presumably no complaint—about the size of that conference. Two hundred and thirty-two delegates made up the congregation in Boston that year. Perhaps roughly 232 would do this time as well? To be sure, a membership numbering in the hundreds could not deliver the same intimacy and efficiency as the one in 1787 that consisted of only fifty-five delegates. But efficiency wasn't everything. Appropriate state representation and a diversity of voices were just as critical.

Back and forth went the discussions, in Congress and in the forty-five statehouses around the country. A commission was set up to study the issue and propose recommendations on the exact number of delegates and other logistical concerns. Finally, it was determined that 267 would be the number. It reflected a fairly simple formula based almost entirely on state populations. Each state was entitled to a delegation made up of *half* the number of representatives it sent to Congress. The host state of Pennsylvania, for example, was allotted seventeen seats at the constitutional convention, exactly half of the thirty-four seats (thirty-two

Representatives and two Senators) it held in Congress. Half of the 476 total lawmakers in Congress meant that the convention delegation would be at least 238 strong. But six states—Delaware, Idaho, Montana, Nevada, Utah, and Wyoming—held only three seats in Congress (two Senators and one, at-large Representative). Those states were awarded a second seat at the constitutional convention, adding six more to the total number. An additional eighteen states each had an odd number of lawmakers in Washington, DC. Those states, too, were awarded an "extra seat"—rounding up their total number of places at the Convention. Lastly, five territories were awarded one seat apiece. The Arizona Territory, the Hawaii Territory, the New Mexico Territory, the Oklahoma Territory, and the Puerto Rico Territory requested representation at the convention. Their request was granted.

The meeting was in Philadelphia. It felt right to be back in the capital of America's experiment in constitution-making. Finding a venue big enough to hold the entire drafting party, however, was a singular challenge. Independence Hall could not accommodate such a large gathering. The Pennsylvania State Capitol building might be sufficient, but it was 100 miles away in Harrisburg. The Philadelphia Commercial Museum, however, looked like a possibility. Built in 1897 to be a "permanent World's Fair museum," the neoclassical building on 34th Street near the University of Pennsylvania had successfully hosted the first International Commercial Congress, attracting representatives from over forty countries, and the 1899 National Export Exhibition, with over a million patrons visiting during the ten-week exhibition. For the constitutional convention, the museum could be transformed again. There was one room on the first floor that was large enough to hold most of the delegates, while the adjacent room had an entryway wide enough that delegates in that room could hear the proceedings too. The architecture of the rooms was sufficiently grand. It would do.

Housing America's federal constitutional convention in a venue other than a legislative building was not the only first for the 1903 gathering. For the first time in American constitutional convention history, people of color were invited. Not many, but a few. Booker T. Washington was one. Born into slavery in 1856, Washington would gain fame as the foremost African American leader at the turn of the twentieth century. Blacks admired him because he worked tirelessly to improve their condition; Whites appreciated him because he was not "radical." His 1895 "Atlanta compromise" speech was widely praised by both southern Blacks and southern Whites for its "sensibility" and "conservatism." In some ways, it became the calling card for his life.[11]

The Alabama state legislature endorsed Washington's seat at the constitutional convention. They did so as a demonstration of racial progress. Alabama was in the beginning stages of a relatively progressive period that included regulation of child labor and compulsory public education. Racial issues, however, were not part of the state's progressive agenda. The Ku Klux Klan was entering a peak period across the state, and lynchings were on the rise. Methods to prevent Blacks from voting were frequently employed. Poll taxes, literacy tests, and "grandfather clauses" that exempted people (that is, Whites) who were voters before the Civil War from such taxes and tests represented attempts by Whites in the South to thwart Blacks from exercising their constitutionally guaranteed right. When those tactics didn't work, Whites resorted to intimidation and terror.

Washington's invitation to attend the federal constitutional convention was originally championed by William Farrington Aldrich, a Republican transplant to Alabama from upstate New York. Aldrich defeated all the party odds at the time, winning several congressional elections in the heavily Democratic southern state. He was a member of the U.S. House of Representatives from 1896 to 1901.[12] Though he was not a member of the Alabama House of Representatives in 1902 when the appointments to the convention were issued, Aldrich remained very popular among the state's lawmakers. He was racially progressive by southern standards, which is to say that he was only mildly bigoted. Aldrich worked back channels to get Washington an invite, not because he was a complete fan, but because he believed it was a good public relations move. A skeptical North would appreciate such a gesture. Aldrich thought Washington was an ideal pick: the Tuskegee man was well-known—and he was a conformist.

Quanah Parker was the only other person of color invited to the convention in 1903. An American Indian born before the Civil War, Quanah had what can only be described as a checkered past among his Comanche brethren. His father was a powerful figure in the Comanche tribe, while his mother, who was later captured by the Texas Rangers at the Battle of Pease River, was White. Quanah's mixed-race heritage triggered suspicion from other tribesmen. Early in his life, he resisted the White settlement of sacred Indian land, even leading several major raids in Texas and the Oklahoma Territory. One skirmish, however, changed his life. He was wounded in the Second Battle of Adobe Walls, in 1874, and by the next year, he and his warrior colleagues had surrendered to federal forces. They were compelled by government officials onto a reservation in southwestern Oklahoma. It was there that Quanah discovered his true leadership abilities. He was appointed Chief of the reservation by federal government agents and, over the next quarter of a century, managed to win the respect of the others on the reservation. He built schools and expanded farming production. When he died in 1911, he was considered the wealthiest American Indian in the entire country.

Like Washington, he was also a favorite of the White man. In fact, the similarities between Quanah and Washington are striking. Both witnessed prejudice and intolerance first-hand. Both were ultimately forced to choose between two less than ideal options: succumbing to a system that restricted freedom and liberty or embracing violence and resistance that yielded only moderate gains. Both chose the former path. And both paid a price for their assimilation. And yet, here they were, sitting in Philadelphia's Commercial Museum along with the current generation's collection of constitutional framers. It was an important moment, one that history would celebrate.

Nicholas Murray Butler, Henry Cabot Lodge, Booker T. Washington, Chief Quanah—these men emerged as the James

Madisons of their time. The circumstances made their efforts in constitutional draftsmanship unique. They were part of a small collection of delegates who would prove instrumental in shaping America's newest constitutional text. They had few traditions in common and very different visions for a unified America. But they shared a particular set of qualities and skills that are critical during any constitution-making process. They were intellectually superior to most; they were creative and courageous; they understood the complexities of political design; and perhaps most crucially, they were capable of great compromise. Like Madison, they scorned the stubbornness and intransigence of their peers. They were willing to surrender the moral high ground in favor of pragmatism. They knew that the final product—the signed Constitution—was more important than any one part of it. Indeed, at the dawn of the twentieth century, this group of framers would help to restore the country's wavering faith in constitutional government.

The Constitutional Convention Opens

The delegates woke to rain on Monday, May 18th, 1903. It had rained, on and off, for about a week now, and the streets of Philadelphia were almost impassibly muddy. The gloomy start to the proceedings, however, did not dampen the festive mood in the convention hall. Hundreds of men were buzzing around in anticipation of the negotiations. Many had crossed paths before, either in Washington, DC, or other cities east of the Mississippi, so they greeted each other with the familiarity of old friends. The delegates were dressed appropriately for the occasion. Sack suits and single-breasted vests were the norm.

It was Quanah who really stole the show. He arrived at the convention dressed in a traditional Comanche chieftain's uniform. He wore a breechcloth and a buckskin shirt under a resplendent Buffalo robe that emphasized his broad shoulders. The beadwork on these beautiful pieces of clothing revealed Quanah's wealth and stature. His long hair fell across his back in the customary matching braids, and his headdress made him appear almost ten feet tall. The headdress was a feathered war bonnet, symbolic of the Chief's elevated position in the Comanche tribe. It was a magnificent sight—a stunning display of red, black, and white that extended almost three feet from the back of his head—and it was carefully calculated to convey his intention to play a significant role in the proceedings.

If there was a worry on opening day, it centered on the amount of detailed work the delegates had ahead of them. Several appointees expressed concerns that this constitutional convention might differ substantially from the previous three and that deliberations would likely take them well into the fall and perhaps even into the winter. Philadelphia winters could be brutal, and the delegates fretted that they had not planned accordingly. Most were unprepared to leave their law offices, political posts, classrooms, studios, and the like for more than four or five months. The delegates received no official compensation for their participation. Some worried about the debts they owed and the needs of their families. Their worries were well founded. The convention, which opened on May 18th, 1903, would not adjourn until almost seven months later, on December 14th. It would be the longest federal constitutional convention in American history, and it taxed all who attended.

Interestingly, a small contingent of the assembly approached this constitutional convention with a true Jeffersonian attitude. These delegates, including Butler and Lodge, arrived in Philadelphia intending to draft a new constitutional text from scratch. The previous two conventions had opened with the unspoken understanding that the proposed Constitution would retain the best features from the existing plan for government, and the assembly's job was simply to modify the current text to reflect the present generation's wishes. In contrast, Butler and Lodge were among several framers in 1903 who wanted to break from that tradition by constructing a new constitutional text, essentially from the ground up. Butler had expressed as much to three of his fellow New York delegates—Charles Evans Hughes (who would later become the eleventh Chief Justice of the U.S.

Supreme Court), S. Frederick Nixon (who was Speaker of the New York State Assembly at the time), and Michael E. Driscoll (who was a Congressman from Syracuse)—when he disclosed his readiness to scrutinize some of the basic structural features of the American political system: bicameralism, separation of powers, checks and balances, and even federalism. He knew the Jeffersonian approach was controversial. It would keep delegates in Philadelphia longer, and it might prove completely futile: the plan of government imagined by the delegates in 1903 could be identical to the one they were tasked with replacing. Still, Butler and others thought the exercise was worth the effort. If they ended up in the precise place they started, so be it. Any process of reconsideration, even if it leads eventually to ratifying the structural status quo, Butler thought, strengthens the eventual end product. A strong Constitution, he concluded, breeds a healthy nation.

The selection of a convention President was the first topic up. Few desired the appointment because of its mostly ceremonial status. Nonetheless, two delegates were nominated for the seat: Joseph Gurney Cannon and Lloyd Lowndes Jr. Cannon was a prominent figure. A lawyer and a Republican since the time of Lincoln, Cannon enjoyed somewhat of a storied political career as a member of the U.S. House of Representatives from Illinois. At the time of the constitutional convention, he was actively jockeying for the House speakership, a position he would gain in November 1903. What made him a viable candidate for the presidency of the constitutional convention was his track record of successful lawmaking combined with his animated personal style. He was a character, but he was a character with depth.

Lloyd Lowndes Jr. was a different kind of politician. Younger than Cannon, Lowndes was a one-term congressman from Maryland, having served as a Democrat in the 43rd Congress from 1873 to 1875. His term in Washington was unremarkable. After he switched his political party affiliation to the Republicans, however, he triumphed in the 1896 gubernatorial election in Maryland. He would serve only one term in that office as well. Northerners liked Lowndes because he was more progressive on racial issues than other Governors in the region. He presented an interesting contrast to Cannon. He was much less bombastic, much less full of himself. Perhaps his humility and self-effacing style led to his downfall in this race. Cannon had some debts to pay, for sure, but he secured the vote and achieved the post he coveted dearly. And as it turned out, he was a most capable leader.

On May 20th, Cannon took his seat at the front of the room and swung the gavel to open the proceedings. The roll was called. Not surprisingly, a few delegates from the far-flung states had yet to arrive, but the vast majority of invitations had been fulfilled. Immediately, Cannon turned the discussion to the question of secrecy. Should the work of the assembly follow the tradition of earlier drafting conventions, he asked, or was there reason to open the deliberations to outside observers? There were good arguments on both sides, he continued, and the times now were different from earlier convention periods. He then opened the floor for discussion. Those arguing for secrecy reminded the rest of the gathering that constitution-makers had to be free to speak their mind—utterly and completely—in order for a full range of ideas to surface. If the press were invited into the room, remarked Frank Naismith Parsons, robust conversation would simply stop.

Parsons was a proud son of the state of New Hampshire. The literal son of a famous Congregational minister, he had practiced law for over a quarter century before being appointed as an Associate Justice to New Hampshire's highest state court. Immediately, he validated the appointment, establishing himself early on as a stellar jurist. Recognizing his talent, Governor Chester B. Jordan elevated Parsons to Chief Justice of the New Hampshire Supreme Court in 1902, a year before the opening of the constitutional convention. Parsons was honored by his new position, and though not surprised, he was also enormously gratified to receive an official invitation from the state legislature to attend the federal convention.

Parsons felt strongly that politicians would grandstand if patrons and the press were allowed into the proceedings. He wanted a closed convention. Only then could the specter of showboating and electioneering be banished. James T. Lloyd objected. Lloyd was a Congressman from Missouri's first congressional district. A Democrat, he was the House Minority Whip at the time of the constitutional convention. What burned Lloyd was the combination of abusive power and the lack of government transparency he saw in Washington. He was particularly angered by Republican President Theodore Roosevelt's 1902 decree that all federal employees must secure permission from their superiors before being allowed to deliver any information to Congress. Lloyd thought, correctly, that such a rule was essentially a gag order cloaked in official administrative jargon. It was no wonder, then, that Lloyd supported a practice that expanded the transparency of the convention proceedings.

As it turned out, Lloyd prevailed. Perhaps seeing an opportunity to advance their political ambitions with a good showing at the convention, a significant majority of delegates—most of whom were elected politicians—voted with him. For the first time in American history, the daily activities of the constitutional convention would be recorded and reported in real time.

Four newspapers covered the proceedings extensively. The *Philadelphia Inquirer* sent a reporter to all but a few individual sessions, while the *New York Times* was present at least once a week. The *Philadelphia Tribune*, one of the oldest African American newspapers in existence, also followed the proceedings with considerable interest.[13] Together with other African American news outlets like the *Philadelphia Defender*, the *Philadelphia Standard-Echo*, the *Courant*, and the *Philadelphia Sentinel*, the *Tribune* provided the Black community with an important voice. The *Tribune*, in fact, would emerge as the convention's harshest critic, and delegates took notice. Circulation of dailies like the *Tribune* increased dramatically during the summer and fall of

1903, in part because of their continual coverage of the convention proceedings.

The most complete coverage of the 1903 Constitutional Convention came from the *Public Ledger*, a Philadelphia daily published by the owner of the *New York Times*, Alfred Ochs. The most popular Philadelphia newspaper at the time, the *Public Ledger* was known for its bold headlines. Perhaps the most alarming and sensationalist headline emerging from the convention came on Sunday, November 1st, when the *Public Ledger* proclaimed that the conventioneers were "Blindly Following Roosevelt into International Chaos." Both the crisis in Cuba that had led to war with Spain and the U.S. interventionism in Hawaii and the Philippines were fresh in the minds of American citizens, and media reports of an even more aggressive foreign policy proved unsettling. Of course, the general public probably suffered from a bit of amnesia, as most Americans likely assumed that the 1903 Convention would deviate from the radical impulses of prior federal conventions. That mindset proved erroneous, and the newspaper reporters in attendance were all too eager to point that out. In the end, though, the 1903 federal Convention would be influenced by the presence of newspaper reporters in the gallery. Frank Naismith Parsons would turn out to be prescient: grandstanding became the acceptable norm.

Like Abraham Lincoln during the previous constitutional convention, Theodore (Teddy) Roosevelt would emerge as the key figure affecting the 1903 Convention discussions. And like Lincoln, Roosevelt went nowhere near the meeting's headquarters.

By the spring of 1903, the country was clear about who Teddy Roosevelt was. The youngest President of the United States, Roosevelt brought fresh energy to the White House. He also brought a steadfast belief in the role of government as a mediator. Government would not stand by as tensions erupted between warring factions: labor and management, conservationists and developers, expansionists and isolationists. His "Square Deal" domestic policy attempted to block the rise of monopolies and trusts that could threaten consumer prices and protections. His plan also called for an end to organized labor strikes when worker demands were unreasonable. He was a true mediator on the domestic front. In the foreign policy arena, Roosevelt believed that government should mediate between those who called for expansionism and those who preferred American isolationism. He strongly preferred the former. In Roosevelt's mind, America was a leading world power.

Even so, Roosevelt's powerful influence, like Lincoln's before him, could not overcome all ideological differences. The contrast between the first few weeks of the 1903 Constitutional Convention and the beginnings of the 1863 meeting could not have been much greater. Unlike in 1863, when a group of reasonably like-minded men opened the convention with an intense focus on the single issue of slavery, the delegates in 1903 were anything but like-minded and anything but interested in a single issue. Delegates from the North saw the world very differently from delegates from the South. Delegates from the cities viewed the economic and political landscape far differently from those who hailed from rural districts, even when all were from the same state. Those who came to the convention to champion the interests of the working class wanted distinct outcomes, while those who socialized in more affluent circles pushed for particular constitutional values. A number of delegates—particularly those from urban settings—owed their invites to the political machines back home. They were primarily interested in maintaining power. They did not want to confront what others knew too: that corruption in state and local politics was a deep scourge that threatened the whole system. It was best to let a sleeping dog lie, they supposed. Such a factionalized gathering created chaos in the beginning.

The first major issues to attract sustained dialogue at the convention were the darlings of the Progressives. Constitutions, most Progressives thought, were good instruments with which to combat the social and political ills of the time. The most vocal champions of the Progressive agenda—men like Teddy Roosevelt, William Howard Taft, Jacob Riis, Eugene V. Debs, Thomas Edison, and Henry Ford, and women like Jane Addams, Grace Abbott, and Sophonisba Preston Breckinridge—advocated for sweeping reforms in both the public and private sectors.

The Progressive era, spanning approximately the last decade of the nineteenth century and first two decades of the twentieth, was a time of adventure and change, excitement and wonder. The old paradigms of society required reconsideration and renewal, just as the old patriarchy needed a dose of humility. Fairness and justice were back in vogue. The dignity of the worker, and of the previously marginalized, was underscored. Eliminating corruption in government was a popular project of the Progressives, as was modernizing manufacturing methods, improving labor market conditions, granting women the vote, and busting the monopolies and trusts of the period. Progressives understood the time was ripe for them to concretize their platform in a new constitutional document. What better place to begin a new era in American history than at the federal constitutional convention in Philadelphia?

It was Thetus W. Sims who first introduced the issue of women's suffrage during the convention. Sims seemed to those in the convention hall to be sympathetic to the suffragist position. Shouldn't the Constitution extend the right to vote yet again, he inquired, but this time to women? Wasn't that the logical extension of an ever-expanding American democracy? A republican style of government could gladly absorb more and more voices from the population, he insisted. The problem was that currently, the "citizenry" were just a subset of the general population: all adults were counted in the census as part of the overall population, but not all adults were defined by the Constitution as "citizens." Sims claimed he wanted to close that gap. He insisted that he wanted to bring women from inhabiting just one column and place them in the other as well.

Sims boasted of his friendship with Susan B. Anthony and her nephew Daniel Read Anthony. He spoke of his familiarity with their positions and his admiration for their wisdom and resolve. He even raised his voice slightly when he recounted the injustices and political slights suffered by women. He referenced a few famous examples. Susan B. Anthony and fifteen other women were arrested for illegally casting a ballot in the 1872 presidential election, he said. Sojourner Truth was, embarrassingly, turned away from the ballot box in her own local precinct. In 1878, an attempt to amend the Constitution to include the women's vote had been introduced in Congress, only to be squashed nine years later in the Senate. Six hundred thousand signatures had been presented at the New York State Constitutional Convention demanding recognition of the right of women to exercise the vote, and yet even that declaration of support failed to persuade the delegates to amend the state constitution. By the time representatives convened the 1903 federal Constitutional Convention, Sims continued, the push for gender equality and women's rights had entered the political mainstream. He would not let one more day pass, he said, without remedying all of these past injustices.

A proud southerner, Sims was a Democrat and a third-term Congressman when he arrived in Philadelphia. He was also part of a conservative Tennessee delegation, which made his apparently civil libertarian and radical egalitarian positions seemingly at odds with the views of many of his fellow southerners. And yet the Tennessee Congressman was, in practice, very much like his southern brethren. He was prejudiced, or more accurately, he was a traditionalist who believed that White males were morally and intellectually superior to all. Publicly, he declared the exact opposite. He acknowledged many similarities between the unfair treatment of Blacks and the unjust treatment of women. Both groups, he reminded the assembly, had been labelled "inferior" beings, less intelligent and less morally endowed than White men. He registered fear that many in the room still felt this way, and he wanted to make it clear that he did not see women, or Blacks for that matter, as inferior. He publicly affirmed his support for the Declaration of Sentiments, the statement adopted by the Seneca Falls Convention on women's rights more than a half century earlier. The Tennessee Volunteer even went so far as to publicly back women's rights advocates who had registered opposition to the 1863 constitutional section that mandated legal equality for freed slaves. During ratification, a number of women had argued that this section stopped far short of its promise because it didn't include women. It defined "citizenship" and "voting" as purely male privileges. Prominent women thus blasted the new Constitution for its sexist overtones. Forty years later, Sims announced his endorsement of such a position.

Sadly, though, it was all a sham—a ruse, or a ploy, aimed at achieving another objective altogether. The performance in front of his colleagues was a clever facade directed toward a completely separate goal, a more sinister ambition that involved further suppressing the Black vote. Sims was, ironically, interested in the advancement of women's rights *only* as a way to reclaim a southern heritage of racial oppression and subjugation. He hated what had become of the South. He advocated for women's rights because he believed it presented the straightest route to a past he so desperately wanted to restore.

You see, Thetus W. Sims subscribed to a clandestine "southern strategy" on women's suffrage intended to dilute the Black vote in the South. He had heard of the strategy from colleagues in Mississippi who recalled an argument by Henry Browne Blackwell that the South could lead the suffragist effort as a way of ensuring White supremacy. Desperate for real change, Blackwell was in essence suggesting that southerners could sacrifice gender for race. They could lose a small battle by yielding to the call for women's suffrage, he said, but still claim a major victory in the war against Black equality.

The southern strategy, as Sims remembered it, was straightforward. Allow educated women (most of whom would be White) access to the polls, and you mitigate or dilute the collective voting power of Black males. Simple enough. The more White votes cast, the more likely the electoral power of the White race will drown out the Black vote, and the less likely African Americans will win future elections. White women would follow their husbands to the polls and vote exactly as they were told, Sims reasoned, so there was little threat of them voting as a block in opposition to White men. But Blacks could not be controlled by the White male population, or at least not easily.

Sims was most frightened by the recent history of Black male suffrage. Blacks had begun voting after ratification of the 1863 U.S. Constitution. Over half a million Blacks voted in the 1870s; most voted for Republicans—the party of Lincoln, the party of the Great Emancipator.[14] The result? Power in collective action. African Americans probably delivered the presidency to Ulysses S. Grant in 1868 by voting *en masse* for the former Civil War General (who received a mere 311,000 votes more than his Democratic challenger, Horatio Seymour). African Americans also, and remarkably, won Congressional seats in former Confederate states: Joseph Rainey and Robert DeLarge in South Carolina; Benjamin Turner and James Rapier in Alabama, to name just a few. In all, over a dozen Black men served in the House of Representatives in the 1870s alone. There was even a moment in which Blacks actually constituted a majority in the South Carolina legislature. But then federal troops began to depart the South. Southern states, angered by the emancipation and anti-discrimination clauses of the 1863 Constitution, then set out to suppress the Black vote. State legislatures calculatedly introduced measures like poll taxes and literacy tests that did not apply to a particular race—*all* eligible males had to read and interpret passages from the state constitutions before being allowed to vote. And it did not end with legislative enactments. The 1890 Mississippi State Constitutional Convention was assembled specifically to "exclude the Negro" from any future ticket. All proposed constitutional changes were evaluated through the prism of discrimination.

These initiatives weren't enough for many southerners. Sims, for one, wanted even more insurance that the Black vote would never amount to much. He saw his opportunity in the lead up to the 1903 federal Constitutional Convention. The issue of women's rights, and especially enfranchisement, was gaining traction among political elites. This trend lit a fuse in Sims' head. He understood that he would have a receptive audience for the extension of women's rights at the constitutional convention. The educated men there did not have to know that he had an ulterior motive. If he acted properly and played the role flawlessly, his fellow delegates would never suspect that his advocacy was part of the southern strategy. He would promote civil rights for women as a way to preserve the South's social hierarchy.

Civil liberties sure make for strange bedfellows. Sims found himself arguing for a cause he didn't truly believe in, alongside some of the most vocal and outspoken civil rights activists of the period. Men like George Francis Train, Francis Minor, Blackwell, and Anthony railed against the inequities built into a male-dominated system. Sims was doing the exact same thing, even if his purpose was completely different. In many ways, these men would prove less efficacious than their female colleagues in championing the cause of gender equality, but ironically, they successfully leveraged the paternalism of the era to open doors and gain critical access. They used the unequal system to shoot for greater equality. Other men listened to them. Their leadership was, in fact, instrumental in helping to get the women's movement off the ground, and they had a number of allies at the constitutional convention.

Sims knew the battle over women's suffrage at the convention would be won or lost with political subtlety. He worried about carrying the four states that already permitted women to vote—Wyoming, Colorado, Utah, and Idaho—because their representatives were not fools.[15] They would not easily give up their individual states' marketing advantage to a federal constitutional provision that established universal female suffrage. He worried that they would partner with other state delegates (especially from the South) in opposition to the extension of the franchise.

It was the headline in the Philadelphia *Public Ledger* on Tuesday, June 2nd, 1903, that first outed Sims and his nefarious plan. It read: "'Southern Strategy' to Grant Women the Right to Vote at Constitutional Convention a Pretext for Suppressing the Negro Vote." A subhead mentioned Sims directly, identifying him as the "ringleader" of a "Convention cabal" that was using the work of gender rights activists as a cover, or smokescreen, for continued discrimination against African Americans. It all started to unravel for Sims when George W. Ochs, editor of the newspaper and brother of the publisher, came upon the rumor while sharing an ale with an "undisclosed" delegate. The anonymous source told Ochs about the "southern strategy." Ochs' source admitted to personally opposing any extension of the franchise beyond its current scope, so he had a personal reason to relay the damning information. Ochs, obviously excited about the scoop, promised confidentiality. He also promised fairness in crafting the piece. He quickly returned to his office to begin writing.

The story made a splash both locally and, with time, in the major metropolitan centers of the United States. Republicans immediately cried foul and argued that Sims' deception was just another example of the widespread corruption and scandal that plagued politics at the turn of the century. Initially, Sims refuted the story, claiming to friends and colleagues that he knew nothing of this "so-called southern strategy." He requested private audiences with as many prominent delegates as possible to relay his side of the story. Ultimately, however, the pressure was too much for him. He asked President Cannon for floor time on Thursday, June 18th, to address the damage to his reputation and to his good name. He delivered an emotional and fiery speech that morning in which he deliberately and systematically explicated his vision for a twentieth-century America. What he didn't do on that occasion was deny his motivation to suppress the Black vote by championing women's suffrage. Honesty and integrity, he said, would never yield to political expediency. The story was true and he held no regrets. He concluded the speech by tendering his resignation as a delegate to the 1903 federal Constitutional Convention. Convention media coverage had claimed its first victim.

Sims' abrupt departure would not interrupt the drive for women's rights. Other delegates were passionately supportive of a constitutional measure to ensure the vote, and they refused to let the measure die. Several delegates, in fact, had been working on a resolution to add specific language to the constitutional draft that looked a lot like the clause in the 1863 Constitution guaranteeing Black men the right to vote. That group sprang into action just as soon as Sims announced his resignation. Nicholas Murray Butler, the President of Columbia University, was part of that group, and he became the major spokesperson who took up the suffrage mantle. He found an unlikely partner in Julius Burrows, a United States Senator from Michigan who had a most interesting past.

While serving as a member of the U.S. House of Representatives, Burrows had become entangled in one of the most bizarre and petty episodes in congressional history. In 1876, he delivered a routine speech in the House on the civil rights of freed Black men. Immediately following that speech, Stephen B. Elkins, a Representative from the New Mexico Territory, turned to shake Burrows' hand. The problem was that Elkins' handshake was witnessed by a number of southern Congressmen who were bent on delivering payback for all the pain their region had suffered during the past fifteen years. At precisely that moment, New Mexico was applying for statehood, a process that required approval by Congress. Southern Representatives were quick to condemn Elkins for publicly backing any argument for equal rights, and they refused to endorse New Mexico's application for statehood. It was a devastating blow. New Mexico would not achieve statehood for another thirty-six years.

Now, Burrows proposed a resolution, co-sponsored by Butler, on the convention floor. Revise the provision in the 1863 Constitution that protects the right of all races to vote by simply adding "sex" to the list, he said. That was the easiest and cleanest way to achieve the objective. The Article I section could be slightly amended to read: "The right of citizens of the United States to vote shall not be denied or abridged by the United States or by any State on account of race, color, or sex." The language he and Burrows were proposing resembled the constitutional texts of states that were already protecting female franchise. Article VI, Section 1 of the 1889 Wyoming Constitution was one they cited.

That clause went even further, Butler announced. "Both male and female citizens of this State shall enjoy equally all civil, political and religious rights and privileges" was the very next sentence in the Wyoming Constitution. What is more, he continued, Article IV, Section 1 of the 1895 Utah Constitution had the same two sentences, verbatim. Butler and Burrows did not think it necessary to include the second sentence in the federal Constitution; but by mentioning it and then rejecting its inclusion, the two sponsors hoped to make skeptical delegates think their position was not so radical after all. The delegates were only extending the vote right now, they reminded the convention. Other rights and privileges could wait.

There was one more housekeeping chore that required attention. The addition of the word "sex," Burrows and Butler argued, should be accompanied by the simultaneous removal of the current conclusion to the sentence. What did that mean, some asked? Butler's response was swift. He said the voting provision in the 1863 Constitution tried to leave no doubt about who was being protected. It read: "the right of the citizens of the United States to vote shall not be denied or abridged by the United States or by any State on account of race, color, or previous condition of servitude." "Race" and "color" still obviously applied, but the other qualifier was somewhat outdated. Butler argued that almost forty years had passed since the demise of slavery and it was no longer imperative that any constitutional clause include language about a "previous condition of servitude." In fact, he asserted, wasn't the point of Jeffersonian constitutionalism to reflect each generation's *current* condition? Wasn't this generation—the generation they were supposed to be accommodating while drafting the 1903 Constitution—a full *two* generations removed from the period of slavery? The part of the 1863 constitutional provision that spoke of legal servitude, he argued, could easily be dropped. He and Burrows moved to do so.

In the end, the vote on the resolution was a bit closer than most expected. With a vote of 151 to 109 (and three abstentions), only 42 ballots separated passage from defeat, but the assembly ultimately endorsed the Butler-Burrows language. A majority of convention-goers agreed that the additional sentence that appeared in some state constitutions—the one that granted both male and female citizens other civil, religious, and political rights—could stay on the editing floor. It seemed a bit redundant, especially given that the clauses concerning religion that were still a part of the U.S. Constitution did not privilege any particular gender.

The 1903 constitutional draft would thus include a revised provision extending the vote to both male and female citizens. It was a major victory for suffragists. Applause was heard from both the convention hall floor and from the gallery. A few dozen women even witnessed the significant moment, having put down their protest signs in order to take spectator seats in the chamber. The press were also quick to jump on the story, recognizing how monumental this vote was. Their coverage was generous, but at least one editorial managed to acknowledge the peculiarity of the circumstance: "because women were not represented at the Convention," the writer pointed out, "no woman was able to experience the historical triumph in a truly tangible way. No woman, in short, was able to cast a vote in favor of her own personal liberty. The irony, like so many elements of America's political machine, is rich."

Booker T. Washington felt emboldened by the spirit of justice he had just experienced. Coming fresh on the heels of the successful effort to extend the franchise to women, his moment, Washington recognized, had arrived. He was ready.

Washington was an unflappable and contemplative man. An intelligent man. He thought he had to be. Indeed, he thought *all* Black men had to be. Survival for the Black race, he insisted, depends on patience, persistence, intelligence, and resilience. His approach to civil rights won him many followers, but it also managed to insulate him from certain power centers in the equality movement. The title of his most famous book, *Up from Slavery*, practically said it all. These words suggested that his personal narrative was one in which he was lifted from the horrors of slavery, sometimes by his own power and sometimes with the assistance of others.[16]

Washington was a methodical planner, and he arrived in Philadelphia with what can only be described as a meticulous plan. He wanted to see two things included in the proposed constitutional draft: first, a provision protecting the common laborer and businessman, especially from the exploitative actions of recently emerging monopolies;[17] and second, a statement, drawn from the Declaration of Independence, about the enduring freedom and inviolable dignity of *all* persons. The first goal developed out of the terrible economic conditions Americans had endured over the previous three decades and out of his personal conviction that Blacks were most likely to achieve success, and the begrudging acceptance of the powerful White community, if they contributed equally to the labor market. He had for some time focused on a "strategy for racial advancement through self-help and racial solidarity."[18] Individuals were responsible for their own condition, he argued, but the Black community as a whole could also play a significant part in advancing critical social causes.

The cornerstone of his civil rights activism was a belief in the transformative power of personal industry. In 1903, he wrote: "it has been necessary for the Negro to learn the difference between being worked and working—to learn that being worked meant degradation, that working means civilization; that all forms of labor are honorable, and all forms of idleness disgraceful."[19] He had founded the National Negro Business League (NNBL) three years before the 1903 Convention on precisely this principle. He stood witness to mighty organizations like the American Federation of Labor that were supposed to aid blue-collar laborers, but that sacrificed the moral high ground by implementing Jim Crow segregation policies instead. The AFL, quite simply, had succumbed to racial pressure. All around him was the injustice and discrimination that lingered from the Civil War and

Reconstruction, and that dated back centuries to the advent of American slavery. It was unfair, he knew. His response was not to promote agitation, but to work within the existing political and financial structures. The NNBL, combined with some constitutional fortification, Washington thought, was the most practical way to ensure upward social mobility for his race.

Washington's second wish for the convention was a bit more delicate. It flirted with issues of civil rights, and he knew his voice in that area was somewhat weaker. He watched with admiration as states increasingly experimented with more general, and more sweeping, constitutional language to open the Declaration (or Bill) of Rights portions of their texts. These statements didn't identify a specific right to be protected. Instead, they set a tone for the rest of the document, a tone steeped in the social contract theories of the seventeenth and eighteenth centuries. In most cases, these statements were borrowed directly from the language of the Declaration of Independence. Consider California's 1879 Constitution, for example. Article I, Section 1 reads: "All men are by nature free and independent, and have certain inalienable rights, among which are those of enjoying and defending life and liberty; acquiring, possessing, and protecting property; and pursuing and obtaining safety and happiness." Or the 1901 Alabama State Constitution, which opens with the following words: "That the great, general, and essential principles of liberty and free government may be recognized and established, we declare: that all men are free and independent, that they are endowed by their Creator with certain inalienable rights, that among these are life, liberty, and the pursuit of happiness." Or Virginia's 1902 Constitution: "That all men are by nature equally free and independent, and have certain inherent rights of which, when they enter into a state of society, they cannot, by any compact, deprive or divest their posterity, namely, the enjoyment of life and liberty, with the means of acquiring and possessing property, and pursuing and obtaining happiness and safety."

These proclamations, Washington concluded, amounted to statements defending the idea of a liberated, sovereign citizenry.

They were still a critical part of an Enlightenment lesson, he knew, that each person possesses an equal moral worth. People may be unequal in almost every other way, but their moral capacity—their moral value, if you will—is, according to God at least, equal. Washington traveled to Philadelphia wanting to reinforce that deeply held American ideal through the constitutional form. Of course, he also recognized the inherent discrimination in the state constitutional declarations. The Tuskegee leader thus sought a more expansive reading of the basic Enlightenment values. Indeed, he wished to expand the scope of the state constitutional statements so that the federal Constitution would protect the dignity, liberty, and autonomy of *all* humans. He saw his opportunity at the constitutional convention.[20]

Washington arrived in Philadelphia with language in hand, for this particular goal at least. He preferred a simple statement, one that borrowed directly from California's Constitution. He made a few minor alterations to the language and came to the federal convention prepared to offer the following resolution: "Be it resolved, that the following clause be included as Article I, Section 1 of the 1903 federal Constitution: 'All persons are by nature free and independent, and have certain inalienable rights, among which are enjoying and defending life and liberty; acquiring, possessing, and protecting property; and pursuing and obtaining safety and happiness.'" He thought his chances of persuading his colleagues were enhanced if he kept the language simple and straightforward.

He thus had two resolutions prepared to present: one related to the right to labor as free men, which Washington called "the most important privilege that was granted to Black men as a result of the Civil War,"[21] and a second related to basic humanity and natural rights. He was pleased that they seemed aligned with each other. Both, he insisted, were about individual dignity.

Ever the astute observer of the fragile racial climate, however, Washington knew he could not realize his ambitions alone. It was easy enough for him to prepare a series of resolutions or an argument in favor of each new constitutional clause. What was exponentially more difficult for Washington was to navigate the bigotry and pretentiousness that permeated the predominantly White constitutional convention. Many delegates, especially those from southern states, would simply refuse to give him the benefit of the doubt. He would thus have to rely on allies both inside and outside the assembly.

One of Washington's biggest benefactors at the time was Robert Curtis Ogden. A businessman and industrialist, Ogden was a mainstay in Philadelphia and New York business circles. He joined Andrew Carnegie, John D. Rockefeller, J. P. Morgan, and others in pledging significant dollars to support Washington's educational projects. For example, money from these philanthropists helped to fund the purchase of a plot of land that would become the permanent home of the Tuskegee Institute. As the constitutional convention approached, the relationship between the East Coast financier and the Alabama educator shifted ever so slightly. Washington communicated his plans for recommending the two constitutional clauses, and he and Ogden sat down to strategize about how best to advance both ideas. Ogden agreed that Washington needed partners. He was worried, though. He and Washington spoke at length about the impact the two resolutions would have on future support for the Tuskegee Institute. The civil rights provision, they both agreed, would do no harm and might even boost philanthropic activity to the school. The free labor recommendation, however, might be interpreted by industrialists as anti–big business. The most generous donations to the Tuskegee Institute had come from the exact individuals Washington intended to confront. Rockefeller, Morgan, Carnegie, and others had pledged a general commitment to the education of southern African Americans, and to Washington's school in particular. The plan to use constitutional means to alter the relationship between capital and labor might not endear Washington or his professional pursuits to these benefactors. It was a conundrum that set his self-interest against what he knew was the country's most critical need.

A month or so before the opening of the federal convention, Ogden had requested a roster of delegates. Though it was still incomplete, he studied the roster and determined that a handful of men could serve well in the role of Washington's collaborator. In particular, he had focused on Frederick Taylor Gates, a northern Baptist minister whose life journey had placed him in some of the wealthiest living rooms in all of America. Gates was born in upstate New York and educated first at the University of Rochester and then later at the Rochester Theological Seminary. In 1889, Gates had the good fortune to meet fellow Baptist and oil magnate, John D. Rockefeller Sr. They became fast friends. By 1892, Rockefeller had formed a four-person advisory board to manage his enormous wealth, and he placed Gates at its head. For a time, Gates was also charged with supervising Rockefeller's philanthropic interests. He invested primarily in education, medicine, and foundations.

Ogden and Gates were also well acquainted. Ogden saw Gates as a sympathetic and credible voice in the civil rights movement. Gates' interest in fostering greater educational opportunity, Ogden knew, aligned perfectly with Washington's professional passions. Indeed, Ogden was reasonably confident that Gates would help Booker T. Washington. But Ogden was not so sure about Gates' support for Washington's other proposed constitutional addition, the one focused on the plight of the laborer. Ogden reasoned—accurately, it turned out—that Gates would *not* be a willing partner on any constitutional language that took aim at the corporate trusts. Rockefeller's Standard Oil was, in many ways, the standard bearer for modern monopolies. Standard Oil was such a successful business in large part *because* it held a monopoly in oil. To be sure, Gates was not going to betray his employer, mentor, and friend by revealing the company's less than ethical practices. Ogden would thus have to recruit another colleague to partner with Washington on his plan to protect the common laborer. For that, he turned to John Brown Lennon.

John Brown Lennon lived in Bloomington, Illinois, and was, at the time of the federal constitutional convention, secretary of the Journeymen Tailors Union (JTU), a trade union founded in the 1870s to protect the interests of clothiers. Lennon himself was a tailor, having learned the trade by watching his father's artistry with fabric and thread. But he found little gratification in the actual shaping of garments. His greatest satisfaction came from steering the rank-and-file tailors to a better collective professional life. Collective bargaining, in other words, was his calling. He had a healthy disdain for the robber barons and super rich, who often cheated the workers out of fair wages in order to pad their pockets and the pockets of their shareholders. He distrusted John D. Rockefeller and J. P. Morgan for that reason. He often felt nauseated when recounting the experience of steel workers in Andrew Carnegie's Homestead plant, who had to endure horrible working conditions, lower wages, longer hours, and a ruthless company chairman in Henry Clay Frick. Disagreements between the rank and file and management at the plant reached a head in 1892, when workers began to lose their lives on the factory floor. A strike ensued, and Frick called in a mercenary army—the Pinkertons—to quell the uprising. That led to further bloodshed and more unwelcome publicity for the Carnegie Steel Company. Enter anarchists, who attempted to assassinate Frick, and the Pennsylvania militia, which tried to push back the striking workers. The event became a critical moment in the history of labor relations.

Lennon understood this moment in American history—he walked around with the confidence of an expert—for he knew that organized labor enjoyed some leverage. He recognized that the American public had grown restless about income disparities and anticompetitive actions. The Homestead strike was disruptive and deadly. So was the Pullman strike. The typical American worker, Lennon believed, was not seeing the benefits of an industrial boom. Lennon thus thought he had the popular winds at his back. He was not a socialist, but he was a true disciple of the good that can come to the masses by way of effective organized labor.

Lennon would prove an ideal helpmeet for Booker T. Washington.[22] Both cared about the worker, and both were comparatively moderate. Indeed, the Illinois legislature had chosen Lennon to be part of the state's constitutional convention delegation because of his kinship with blue-collar workers and because his stance on unionization and labor relations was far more temperate than that of the socialists, like Eugene V. Debs, who were gaining popularity. Lennon recognized that *state* constitutional clauses seeking to prohibit monopolies were essentially useless, because most goods produced by these monster companies crossed state lines. It was a matter of *inter*state commerce then, not *intra*state commerce. Only the federal government—through the federal Constitution— could give the relief that he and Washington desired. Lennon thus arrived in Philadelphia eager to seek out Washington and join forces on a constitutional resolution that would prohibit future business consolidations and, simultaneously, enshrine important protections for the common laborer.

For Lennon, the practice of pushing a constitutional clause through the drafting process seemed old hat. He saw it as a negotiation, plain and simple. He and Washington thus strategized about constitutional language and about building support among the delegates. They knew that if given the chance to speak openly on the convention floor, they could persuade others that the American financial and commercial markets were imperfect and that lower wages and less than ideal working conditions were the inevitable consequence. They worried that self-interest might prove a special hurdle for those in the convention hall who benefited from the laissez-faire economic policies of the past. A lot of delegates belonged to the upper class, after all. But they also had confidence that public sentiment was on their side. The financial Panic of 1873 was comfortably in the rearview mirror, but the depression of 1893 was fresh on the minds of most American citizens.

Employing federal legislation as a means to regulate the concentration of wealth was a relatively new policy strategy at the turn of the nineteenth century. The Interstate Commerce Act, which gave the federal government more power to regulate commercial activity, had been passed in 1887. The Sherman Antitrust Act had followed three years later. Its purpose was to prohibit agreements and mergers that would reduce competition in particular markets. Government, in other words, now had the possibility of actively preventing the consolidation of companies and the unconstrained price hikes and wage cuts that would inevitably follow. The political branches would take a more active role in ensuring free and open markets.

Republican Senator John Sherman of Ohio was the principal author of that bill. He invoked the principles of classical liberalism to strengthen his argument. He lumped together the classical liberal idea that government should not create or encourage monopolies with the contemporary notion that government can be a powerful force in preventing such developments. Supporters of the Sherman Antitrust Act relied on the country's long history of opposition to monopolies as fodder for passing that legislation: the protests against the East India Trading Company that led to the Boston Tea Party, the original Framers' refusal to grant Congress monopoly power in most areas, the anti-Federalist argument against the concentration of commercial power, the debate over incorporating a national bank, the Supreme Court decision in the famous *Charles River* case, and on and on.[23] The country was founded on some basic economic principles, they said: the protection of private property, the idea that the individual owns his own means of production, the inviolability of contracts, market capitalism, and free trade.

The U.S. Supreme Court, however, was a problem. Washington and Lennon agonized over two Court decisions, both announced in 1895, that contradicted the very purpose of Sherman's antitrust legislation. The first, *United States v. E. C. Knight Company*, involved the American Sugar Refining Company, which had slowly gained a 90 percent market share in the manufacturing of the sweet additive. Because the process of manufacturing occurred within the physical borders of a single state, the Supreme Court insisted Congress' power over *inter*state commerce did not apply.[24]

But it was the second case, *In re Debs*, that represented the more devastating blow to the American wage earner. In that case, the Supreme Court (this time unanimously) upheld an injunction against the American Railroad Union, whose members were striking in protest of a 25 percent wage cut by the Pullman Palace Car Company. Here, the Court reasoned that government had the power to use injunctions as a means to squash union protest activity. The decision proved to be an unexpected impediment to a growing movement in favor of labor, and it worried Washington and Lennon.[25]

Washington descended on Philadelphia with the plan to introduce a complex resolution that would reverse the two Supreme Court decisions and award Congress the specific authority to "outlaw any contract, merger, conspiracy, or combination in the form of trust or otherwise, in restraint of free trade." Washington would argue that the recommended clause should appear among the list of congressional powers in Article II, Section 8. He and Lennon were reasonably confident that the language, should it stay intact through debate and deliberation, would infuse Congress with power enough to prevent the rise of future monopolies and, simultaneously, enhance the relative muscle of America's growing labor interests. But it might not be enough.

The two sponsors ideally wanted to see a further section added to the draft Constitution's Declaration of Rights (in Article I) that *explicitly* protected the rights of laborers. They also wondered whether the constitutionally protected "freedom of association" could be expanded somehow to include language protecting workers. Washington, in particular, recognized that this might be viewed by other delegates as a bit radical, even socialist. A safer option might be to introduce more language into the Commerce Clause in order to clarify the employee-employer relationship. Washington and Lennon would leave it to the collective delegation to decide which avenue to pursue.

The moment finally arrived. Booker T. Washington took the floor on July 29th to officially introduce two resolutions into the minutes. First, he described how his two resolutions derived from the same basic philosophy—a progressive and natural commitment to improving the lives of those who have comparatively weaker voices in the political and economic marketplace. He then followed the exact plan he had discussed with Gates and Lennon.

The first resolution he introduced, the one taken from the California Constitution and expected to set the tone for the list of civil rights and liberties that followed, was intended to constitutionalize certain foundational principles of the American republic: the sanctity of life, liberty, property, security, and the pursuit of happiness. Why shouldn't America's Constitution also include the grand promises of liberalism, he wondered aloud. Wasn't it the responsibility of the delegation to promote those values that stirred America to independence? The second resolution, Washington continued, sprang directly from the first. Here, he insisted, the aim was to enshrine concrete protections for the working class, for those who are not always adequately represented in America's republican chambers. He was not asking the delegates to disrupt the carefully developed social and economic hierarchy. The wealthy and the White will still wield a disproportionate share of power, he insisted. What he was looking to do was take an incremental step toward greater equity and justice.

Washington continued by explaining why supporting the common laborer was in the country's best interest. He spoke of the value rural farmers and urban factory workers bring to America's economic machine. He reminded the convention of the message he delivered so frequently: that an industrious African American workforce profits all. He concluded his remarks by repeating a passage taken from his famous Atlanta speech, that true economic progress cannot be achieved with racial division. "There is no defense or security for any of us," he said, "except in the highest intelligence and development of all."[26]

All that remained was to formally introduce the resolutions. As Washington presented the first motion, Frederick Gates prepared to stand and second it. Gates had listened patiently to Washington's prepared remarks. He was deeply moved. Still, when it was his turn to speak, Gates found it difficult to restrain himself from commenting on the perils of any constitutional clause that threatened the status quo of both laborers and management. He had the floor, and he thought about crossing over into Lennon's territory. Ever the foot soldier for capital, he had to bite his tongue and not stray from his appointed task. He kept his point of view on this matter private.

Meanwhile, Lennon prepared to stand and support Washington's second proposal, the complex resolution that took direct aim at monopolies and that, ideally, also enshrined language supporting the common laborer. This proposal differed from the first in that Washington did not have all the constitutional language ready to present. Washington's strategy was to gauge the preference of the delegates on the placement of the new resolution: did they think the Declaration of Rights in Article I or the Commerce Clause in Article II was the appropriate place? He intended to come back at a later date to present the actual text. The particulars, he said, would depend on which location the convention favored.

In all, two resolutions were on the floor. Each had been seconded, so the convention could take them up separately or together. President Cannon chose the former. He would allow debate on each proposal to occur naturally, but separately. Conversation about Washington's proposal to add a clause at the beginning of the Constitution's Declaration of Rights that set a natural rights tone took precedence, in part because it was slightly easier for the assembly to comprehend. That didn't stop the opponents, though. Arguments for and against the constitutional clause were swift and animated. Some argued that including the proposed language, taken directly from the California Constitution, would significantly upgrade the breadth and scope of rights embedded in the constitutional text. To which others argued that the vagaries of the language—meant for a Declaration of Independence, *not* for a Constitution—would only muddy the law and confuse the courts. Opponents pointed to already existing vague language in the Constitution—the Necessary and Proper Clause, for instance—as reason to vote down the resolution. Chief Justice John Marshall's opinion in *McCulloch v. Maryland* still stung for some.

Opponents also resurrected an argument first enunciated by Federalists immediately following the release of the 1787 draft

Constitution. It was Alexander Hamilton, writing as Publius in *Federalist* 84, who most forcefully advised against including a Declaration of Rights as part of the constitutional text. He proffered two arguments against such a plan: the "redundancy" argument and the "dangerousness" argument. The redundancy argument was simple. Constitutions don't need bills of rights because the purpose of a Constitution of enumerated powers is to prohibit officials from interfering in the exercise of individual liberty. Similarly, the dangerousness argument states that it is even hazardous for a Constitution to include a bill of rights. Including such enumerated rights—especially vague ones like "enjoying and defending life and liberty; acquiring, possessing, and protecting property; and pursuing and obtaining safety and happiness"—will encourage shameless citizens to imagine even more rights, Hamilton warned. Rights that may belie American tradition could then be said to connect with ones explicitly mentioned in the constitutional instrument. How can courts then say no to claims of infringement?[27]

Over time, however, the yeas began to get the upper hand. Opponents eventually conceded that the proposed reference to life, liberty, property, security, and happiness would interestingly tie the 1903 Constitution to America's birth certificate. Gates even stood to remind the delegates that this Constitution would likely need as much help as possible to grow the necessary roots that would enable it to fully constitute the American polity. Look at the 1863 Constitution, he said. It did not adequately echo the values and principles of the late eighteenth-century American founding, and tragically, it could not withstand the pressures brought to bear on it by an industrialized nation. A bond to the eighteenth century provides important insurance. "Perhaps if the framers of the 1863 Constitution had just embraced the Declaration of Independence . . . ," the sentence's conclusion remained silently implied.

Others remarked that states had enjoyed some success from the inclusion of similar clauses in their constitutions. State courts were not having trouble interpreting the original meaning of the clauses, proponents argued. Supporters concluded with an appeal to equality and progress. A constitutional clause that protected the life, liberty, property, security, and happiness of *all persons* was a fitting companion to the provision, endorsed earlier, that extended the franchise to women. It made sense to change the entire tenor of the Constitution, to begin anew with the attitude that all individuals, and not just White men, were protected by the text's energy. Eventually, the nays gave up the fight and permitted the resolution to pass. The 1903 draft Constitution would include an important passage that expanded the very meaning of liberty and freedom. Booker T. Washington had won an important victory for civil rights. His second victory would be much longer in coming.

A few days after the passage of Washington's first resolution, the convention voted to table the second one. Here, too, debate was vigorous. The delegates simply were not prepared to cast ballots on a measure to protect labor against the dominance of corporate profits. Several factors likely derailed the initial push to vote on the resolution, including Washington's reluctance to bring the entire language package to the floor. He had the first part figured out. The provision taken directly from the Sherman antitrust legislation that forbade "restraint in free trade," he repeated, could occupy its own line in Article II, Section 8. But the part that involved a fundamental right to labor had not yet been fashioned. And that strategic error cost Washington and Lennon a chance to build on the success of the earlier victory. The misstep gave adversaries the opening to request a temporary delay. A motion to table the discussion was thus offered and seconded. It passed by a fairly comfortable margin.

Many of the men in the convention hall that year experienced some form of private tension or conflict: they were part of the wealthy elite, but they were also serious Progressives. Their social class placed them squarely on one side of the ideological dividing line, while their progressive impulses pulled them in exactly the opposite direction. They favored the *idea* of an elevated worker, but they also preferred that democratic majorities decide the workers' fate.[28] Such a dichotomy would become a common theme over the next several months as the convention limped forward. The delegates had yet to thoroughly explore the constitutional implications of issues related to foreign affairs, immigration, and Indian affairs, but the draft of the text was coming into view. And it was looking fairly reformist. The proposals and debates during the first three months of the 1903 federal Constitutional Convention aligned nicely with the Progressive agenda. The next three months would be different.

Quanah Parker observed with a touch of envy as Booker T. Washington masterfully navigated the complex terrain of the constitutional convention. The Comanche Chief enjoyed few of the social advantages that helped Washington in this setting. His network of allies and friends numbered only a fraction of those who were willing to support the Tuskegee educator. He had not had the foresight to identify White partners who could defend the presence of a person of color speaking on the convention floor. He was painfully aware that the federal government's attempts to suppress American Indian traditions had resulted in the repeated massacre of Indian tribespeople; indeed, the campaign to "tame" the Indian was a campaign that can only be described as genocidal. He also knew that officials subscribed to the principle of assimilation—"kill the Indian," they would say, "and save the man." He knew that his was an uphill climb at the convention—steep like Washington's, but even more treacherous. To his credit, he harbored no regrets about his level of preparation for the federal convention. He reasoned that Booker T. Washington was unique—exceptional, in fact—among the delegates. Quanah's exposure to the elements of a privileged class was comparatively lacking.

He was sickened by the development of American Indian policy during his lifetime. He had read books about U.S. government officials forcing Indians to sign the Treaty of Hopewell in 1785 and then removing the Native peoples from their sacred lands.

He was familiar with the attack on Tecumseh in 1811 and the Battle of Horseshoe Bend three years later. He understood that his ancestors were devastated by the Indian Removal Act in 1830, and that his people still suffered mightily from the consequences of that racist policy. He shared stories of death and hardship on the Trail of Tears with his children and grandchildren. He spoke with deep sadness of the 1851 Indian Appropriations Act, which prohibited Indians from leaving the Reservation without permission. His face turned red with anger when he recounted the many broken promises made by the White man. He reminded American Indians of Sitting Bull and of Crazy Horse's bravery at the Battle of the Little Bighorn.

But overall, he was deeply aware of the irredeemable loss of American Indian culture during the eighteenth and nineteenth centuries. Over the course of two centuries—a tiny blip of time in the history of Native peoples—entire tribes from Georgia to Montana had been wiped away at the hands of White European immigrants. With that loss of life came a corresponding loss of customs, traditions, and culture.

The systematic attempt to erase tribal customs and welcome Indians into a White world—but only on the White man's terms—contributed to Quanah's growing anger. The entire assimilationist strategy was a political effort to stifle one of the country's "threatening minorities." The courts were also involved. In case after case, the United States Supreme Court endorsed assimilation-era policies, referring to Indians as "wards of the state" or "subjects of federal guardianship." American Indians were not American citizens; they could not claim the same rights under the existing Constitution; they lived on rotten land, and now, under the Progressives, they were being forced to adopt the values of the majority White population. The consequence of this attempted assimilation, Quanah recognized, was a century-long war between the federal government and American Indian tribes. The once prevalent and proud Indian communities were relegated to barren landscapes on assigned reservations. Their independent ways of life tragically curtailed.

It was President Grover Cleveland's Dawes Severalty Act (officially the General Allotment Act of 1887) that most rankled Quanah. For decades, Indians had been allowed to manage the use of their lands (even when forcibly removed to reservations). Such allowance was critical to the Indians' sense of self-worth and sovereignty; indeed, it resonated with a traditionalist faith in communalism. The Dawes Act, however, permitted the President of the United States to divide reservation lands into individual parcels to be distributed separately to American Indian families. Up to 160 acres were deeded to each American Indian man and his family. In essence, the Dawes Act abolished the Indian principle of communal land management and replaced it with the Western notion of private property.

To add insult to injury, the Dawes legislation was just the first act of a multi-act play that eventually drained much of the emotional fight from indigenous peoples. The original Act was peculiar in that it applied to most Indian communities, but it exempted the "five civilized tribes"—the Cherokee, Chickasaw, Choctaw, Creek, and Seminole. However, eventually, the Curtis Act of 1898 completed the transfer of once-protected Indian lands to White administrative control.

Secretly, the Dawes Commission and the Dawes and Curtis Acts—known collectively as the Allotment Acts—were part of an orchestrated strategy by government officials to further two critical political objectives: assimilation and land acquisition. That is, the legislation was a clever stunt to claim millions of acres of land promised to American Indian tribes. In all, 86 million acres were seized and transferred to government officials. Those millions of acres were then sold to White settlers moving west.

Quanah was a realist. He knew that, with one prominent exception, delegates were not especially keen on reversing the particulars of the Allotment Acts. The overwhelming majority of convention-goers were convinced that the Acts benefited all parties involved in Indian affairs. The one exception was Henry Moore Teller, U.S. Senator from Colorado and outspoken critic of the federal government's attempt to assimilate Indian tribesmen.

Teller despised the Allotment Acts. He saw right through the government's deception. He famously said about the Dawes Act: "The real aim of this bill is to get at the Indian lands and open them up for settlement. The provisions for the apparent benefit of the Indians are but the pretext to get at his lands and occupy them. . . . If this were done in the name of greed, it would be bad enough; but to do it in the name of humanity, and under the cloak of an ardent desire to promote the Indian's welfare by making him like ourselves, whether he will or not, is infinitely worse."[29]

Quanah and Teller struck up a correspondence in the months leading up to the Philadelphia convention. Their letters are rich with emotion. In one, Quanah derides the federal government's attempts to market the land allotment policy as beneficial to Native peoples by calling officials "ratbags" and "foozlers"—nineteenth-century slang for idiots and cheats. Picking up his cue, Teller wrote back to Quanah and piled on. Those who back the Allotment Acts, he said, are nothing but "hornswogglers." Quanah thus knew he could depend on Teller to advocate for constitutional change that would roll back the assimilationist policies. The Comanche Chief wanted federal authorities to reverse the severalty policy and return sovereign control of reservation lands to the individual tribes. A constitutional clause could do that.

He would not get his wish. Conference delegates spent much of the first half of August debating the broad issues of American Indian rights, land acquisition, forced removal, treaties, citizenship, and the like. The questions floated were both basic and profound: is the Constitution even the appropriate vehicle for regulating Indian land ownership? Should the Constitution stipulate how state and federal governments relate to independent tribes? Should the clause in Article II, Section 8 that grants Congress the power to "regulate commerce with foreign nations and among the several states, *and with the Indian tribes*" (emphasis added), be somehow amended? Do the rights provisions that were added to the Constitution in the last half century—the Due Process, Equal Protection, Privileges and Immunities, and Right to Vote Clauses—even apply to Indians given that they are not

U.S. citizens?[30] The backlog of questions and discussion topics started to pile up. It seemed every time one issue was resolved, three fresh issues were raised.

Quanah and Teller tried repeatedly to persuade their fellow convention delegates that it would be wise to adopt something like a New York State law that protected Indian land rights. The purpose of that 1821 state action was to "protect against intrusions on Indian land," and to make it "unlawful for any person or persons, other than Indians, to settle or reside on any lands belonging to or occupied by any nation or tribe of Indians." The law also stated "that all leases, contracts and agreements . . . whereby any person or persons, other than Indians, shall be permitted to reside upon such lands, shall be absolutely void."[31]

Quanah and Teller determined that, with a few slight modifications, the New York law could be tailored to read more like a constitutional phrase. Its proper placement as a constitutional addition was a little less clear, but the two agreed that it could probably fit in Article VII between Section 2—which conferred supremacy on the Constitution and all treaties—and the current Section 3—which required most government officials to swear an oath of office. Their new Section 3, they reasoned, could make it illegal for "any person or persons, other than Indians, to settle or reside on any lands belonging to or occupied by any nation or tribe of Indians, and that all leases, contracts, allowing any person or persons, other than Indians, to reside upon such lands, shall be void." And if the delegates were not persuaded by that language, they could suggest terminology that more suited their tastes. If passed by the assembly, any constitutional provision like this would not only protect American Indian lands from further encroachment by White settlers, but also restore some dignity to the shattered tribes.

Opposition was swift. In fact, few in the assembly were prepared for the force of the backlash. The opposition to constitutional wording that would protect American Indian lands from further allotment (and confiscation) was evident right from the start. Many delegates subscribed to the same thinking as their President. Teddy Roosevelt had signaled his support for

the Allotment Acts repeatedly during his term as Vice President
and then President. In 1901, with an apparent twinkle in his eye,
Roosevelt informed Congress that the Dawes Act was "a mighty
pulverizing engine to break up the tribal mass." His position was
unambiguous. "In my judgment," he claimed, "the time has arrived when we should definitely make up our minds to recognize
the Indian as an individual and not as a member of a tribe. The
Indian should be treated as an individual—like the White man."[32]
Reversing decades of "progress" in favor of a single American
people, delegates argued, was imprudent when we were actually
making headway on the *United* States.

To be sure, the Progressive era was an assimilationist era. In
many instances, the most fortunate Americans wished that immigrants, American Indians, European Jews, the poor, and so
on, would accommodate the specific elements of their heritage
that set them apart from the White masses to White preferences.
Persons in power wanted the particular lifestyles and customs
of "aliens" to be erased in favor of a conventionally American
existence. Assimilation, for the majority White population, was
simply easier than the alternative, which was to respect differing
cultural values and accept groups on their own terms. Hence, in
this moment, the strategy of self-interest prevailed. Quanah and
Teller's proposal for a constitutional addition that would recover
for Indians a degree of self-rule over Indian lands was defeated
before it was even presented on the convention floor.

Only one other major issue remained for the delegates. It would
take months to untangle and consider, but in the end, it would
mark the high point of the 1903 federal Constitutional Convention. On September 4th, 1903, the delegates turned their attention to America's growing presence on the international stage.
Henry Cabot Lodge would lead that conversation.

America's foreign policy had whiplashed in the decades leading up to the 1903 Constitutional Convention. In the broadest of

terms, the country went from a mostly isolationist nation in the nineteenth century to a decidedly more imperialist or expansionist force by 1902. The shift toward a more aggressive presence in the international arena was championed by a number of key political and intellectual figures, including Presidents Benjamin Harrison, William McKinley, and Teddy Roosevelt; Secretary of War Elihu Root; publishing mavens William Randolph Hearst and Joseph Pulitzer; and Lodge himself. The anti-expansionist cabal consisted of an equally impressive list of characters. Individuals like William Jennings Bryan, Mark Twain, and Andrew Carnegie cried foul when government officials began to talk about annexation, expansionism, occupation, and aggression.

The country had been building up to this moment practically since its independence. First it was manifest destiny, the displacement of American Indians, the purchases of Louisiana and Alaska, and wars with Britain and Mexico. Then it was James Blaine and the country's increased influence in Latin America. Toward the end of America's first century of independence, there was the country's growing confidence at home and abroad. Eventually, small island chains in the Pacific and Caribbean found themselves in the crosshairs of international diplomacy. Indeed, territories such as Hawaii, the Philippines, Cuba, and Puerto Rico became the most prominent pawns (victims?) of America's shifting foreign policy. Soon, though, other countries around the world would be implicated as well. By the time the delegates reached Philadelphia, most had participated in some heated discussion about annexation, tariffs, protectionism, and global control.

Three main factors combined to accentuate American imperialism in the late nineteenth century. First, rapid industrialization in the United States created a need for new commercial outlets. American companies began to look increasingly beyond the borders of the United States for new and different buyers. Second, political and cultural leaders adopted the idea that America has an inherent responsibility—a duty even—to spread the ideals of democracy, liberty, equality, and Christianity to other parts of the world. This attitude came to be defined as "American exceptionalism," and it was based on the egoist principle that America is somehow distinct, unique, and blessed. Finally, there emerged a movement to apply social Darwinist principles to foreign policy decisions. This belief was related to American exceptionalism in that it was grounded in a conviction that the United States is unmatched in its moral and material superiority. As such, the country should claim its rightful place as a world leader.

Nineteenth-century religious fervor led to acts of intolerance and discrimination. But it also led to acts of compassion, service, selflessness, and humanity. Both the righteousness and the power of Christianity in the United States ushered in a sense that American missionaries could civilize the uncivilized world. Famous Protestant clergyman Josiah Strong captured the sentiment most succinctly when he wrote, "civilize and Christianize."[33] Strong preached that Christianity in the United States was somehow purer, deeper, and more profound than religious teachings in other parts of the world.

The country's recent experiences in the Pacific and the Caribbean also informed opinions. Most delegates were convinced that the American imperialism of the late nineteenth century began when the United States decided to raise tariffs on sugar imports. That policy occurred in 1890, and it caused a significant strain on Cuba's already fragile economy. Spain, Cuba's colonial overseer, refused to help the small island territory, prompting Cuban nationalist guerillas to launch an independence movement, attacking the Spanish forces on the island. A war with Spain erupted, and America refused to pick a side. But by 1896, shifting electoral victories and the emergence of pro-Cuba Democrats in Congress signaled a substantial change in America's foreign policy, especially toward Spain. The country waded into the Cuban War for Independence, initially by offering assistance to Cuban Americans and condemning the many atrocities brought on by the actions of Spanish military leaders.[34]

The sinking of the USS Maine in Havana Harbor was a signal moment in the history of American imperialism. The powerful warship had arrived in Havana on January 28th, 1898, as a show of "good will and American strength." It was a bold and unmistakable message. Three weeks after the *Maine*'s arrival though, an explosion sank it, killing over 70 percent of its crew. The Spanish were immediately blamed for the tragedy. Powerful newspaper reporters in the United States relentlessly accused the Spanish authorities of causing the explosion. By April 25th, 1898, the United States was in a full-scale war with the powerful Iberian country. It was America's first declared war in over fifty years.[35] The war would not last long.

A mere ten weeks after the declaration of war, the battles were over. Much occurred in that short period though. Military campaigns were conducted in the Caribbean south of the United States and in the Spanish-occupied Philippines, thousands of miles to the west. American ships annihilated the Spanish fleet in Manila Bay and chased down Spanish ships retreating from Havana Harbor. The United States subsequently staked its claim to parts of Cuba, the Philippines, Guam, and Puerto Rico. Ironically, the United States defeated Spain's attempt to expand its authority across the globe as a necessary part of its *own* campaign to enlarge America's geopolitical footprint. The United States had formally and officially signaled to the world its fondness for aggression.

While U.S. forces were battling the Spanish in remote waters across the globe, U.S. political leaders were maneuvering for an even greater imperial prize: Hawaii. The islands in the Pacific held strategic military advantages for the United States and that fact, combined with increasing business interests on the islands, raised the stakes on Hawaiian annexation. The eventual takeover of Hawaii started, like the Cuban crisis, with that same piece of legislation that raised import prices on sugar. Like Cuba, Hawaii relied on its sugar exports to float its overall economy. When the McKinley Tariff Act of 1890 was passed, powerful business and political interests kicked into high gear. They started calling for the immediate annexation of Hawaii. Annexing Hawaii, they said, would change its status from a foreign country to an American territory, thereby eliminating the hefty import tax. The battle over annexation eventually led to the overthrow of Hawaii's ruling monarch, Queen Liliuokalani; the dissolution of the Hawaiian kingdom; and a major swing in America's attitude toward the island chain. The end for an independent Hawaii, though, more or less came with the transition in White House residents. The staunch anti-imperialists of the Cleveland administration gave way to the more hawkish instincts of the McKinley presidency. The die was cast. President McKinley signed Congress' joint resolution to annex Hawaii in July 1898, and by mid-August, mainland Americans were celebrating "Annexation Day," the official end to Hawaiian independent rule and the start of Hawaii as an official U.S. territory.

Delegates to the 1903 Constitutional Convention witnessed these events firsthand. Nevada Congressman Francis G. Newlands, author of the joint resolution to annex Hawaii, and Illinois Senator Shelby M. Cullom, a member of the five-man commission on the annexation, were prominent convention attendees. So was retired Major General Wesley Merritt, the first Military Governor of the Philippine Islands. Of course, most of the delegates had an opinion on American imperialism even if they had not yet been intimately involved in the affairs of the past decade. Few, however, held the same passion on the subject as did Henry Cabot Lodge. Lodge was a student of international warfare and diplomacy. As a member of the Senate, the Massachusetts native supported American military intervention in Venezuela, the annexation of Hawaii, the Spanish-American War, and President Roosevelt's hardline foreign policy. His singular goal in attending the constitutional convention was to fundamentally change the world order.

Lodge had a giant partner too. President Roosevelt would emerge as the most active President since Lincoln, first in domestic affairs and then later in the foreign policy arena. Lodge wanted to capture some of Roosevelt's energy in the draft constitutional document. He thought he could take advantage of the relative paucity of constraints on the President's power in Article III of the 1863 Constitution—a legacy of the brevity of Article

II in the original 1787 text. The extent of constitutional powers granted the President, he thought, can be difficult to gauge. It is not always easy to determine whether the Constitution authorizes certain presidential actions like military interventions, strategic alliances, or outright annexations. The President is Commander in Chief, Lodge knew, but that did not guarantee that his command could legally extend to deploying troops abroad. If anything, Lodge thought, the bulk of foreign policy power resided with Congress, not the President. The jurisdiction to declare war, raise armies, maintain navies, suppress insurrections, repel invasions—in short, to respond to national and international emergencies—is located among Congress' powers in Article II, Section 8. Even so, he surmised, it is not always clear that the Constitution *prohibits* broad presidential authority either, especially in foreign affairs. Lodge was convinced that we were in a gray area. He wanted to change that.

He wished to propose to the constitutional assembly that they enhance the President's decision-making power in situations involving international affairs. A complex world order requires a greater capacity for swift and aggressive action, he said. Lodge was not interested in transferring Congress' already enumerated powers to the President. Rather, his interest lay in *augmenting* Article III so that the President controlled more of the foreign policy agenda. He wanted greater influence to be placed in the hands of the chief executive. His reasoning was logical. The President alone has access to classified information and specific resources that could invariably aid in quick and decisive action. In the modern whirl of twentieth-century international politics, Lodge insisted, a single executive is better equipped, and better informed, to act on America's interests. Congress, by its very nature, is incapable of such swift action.

His proposal was inspired by language he discovered in the 1902 Virginia State Constitution. Article V, Section 73 was of particular interest to Lodge. It read, in part: "The Governor shall be commander-in-chief of the land and naval forces of the State; have power to embody the militia to repel invasion, suppress insurrection and enforce the execution of the laws; conduct, either in person or in such manner as shall be prescribed by law, all intercourse with foreign or other States. . . ."

That final clause intrigued Lodge the most. He thought it could be massaged to apply to the U.S. President. What if Article III, Section 2 of the 1903 U.S. Constitution included a provision granting the President the ability to "embody the military to repel invasion, suppress insurrection, execute the laws, and pursue strategic national interests abroad"? A separate clause could also empower the President to "conduct affairs with foreign nations and execute all necessary and proper policies to protect the country's vital global interests." Adding these clauses to the U.S. Constitution would remove some of the ambiguity of Article III. It would also shore up the President's increasing dominion over foreign policy. Future involvement in territories within America's global sphere, Lodge reasoned, would be sanctioned by such a grant of constitutional power. It was the exact thing a President like Teddy Roosevelt needed to further America's expansionist agenda.

Lodge was a snob and a racist—insisting that certain cultures could never be fully assimilated because they could never produce proper Englishmen—but he was powerful and fearless. He knew when he had victory in his grasp. And so, on the third day of November, 1903, Henry Cabot Lodge formally introduced a motion to strengthen the power of the executive branch in matters of global affairs. The slightly altered language of the Virginia Constitution was presented to the assembly in the morning, and by the afternoon, it looked likely that Lodge would get his way. Debate ensued for another two days, but the writing was on the wall: the delegates were going to approve the measure. The President of the United States would receive an unequivocal endorsement from the federal convention. He was now officially the captain of America's foreign policy engine.

Like the landslide Republican victories that ushered in a party realignment around the turn of the twentieth century (and every subsequent party realignment), Lodge's successful motion fundamentally altered the balance of institutional power among the coordinate federal branches. For only the second time in the history of summoning generational constitutional conventions, delegates designed a Constitution that tinkered with Madison's core vision for three coequal branches (the first occurred in 1825, when the framers altered the selection process for federal judges). Henry Cabot Lodge and his many allies wanted more power in the executive branch, and their timing was impeccable. It is remarkable what a few clauses in a Constitution can do. The passage of the Lodge motion turned out to be a major moment in the development of American politics.

The Convention Adjourns
The final five weeks of the 1903 Constitutional Convention were spent debating several issues that had circled around the seven-month gathering. One looked like it might have traction among delegates. Ultimately, though, it failed to garner the level of interest and enthusiasm required to see it through. It was the issue of senatorial selection. The current process, as articulated in Article II, Section 3, Clause 1, allowed state legislatures to choose their U.S. Senators. This process seemed to work reasonably well—until it didn't. The delegates to the 1903 Constitutional Convention were quite familiar with the argument in favor of change.[36] They were not, however, eager to act on that argument. Few wanted to alter the constitutionally mandated design for senatorial selection. Many delegates in Philadelphia were Senators themselves and they were understandably reluctant to dismantle the precise system that assured (most of) them of reelection. It's a basic rule of incumbency: don't mess with the process that got you there in the first place, and then kept you there. As a result, nothing happened with the issue.

Not to be forgotten, toward the very end of the convention Booker T. Washington reminded the delegation of his proposed and then tabled motion on monopolies and workers' rights. Nothing had occurred in the intervening months between his introducing the resolution and this moment to suggest that constitution-makers had a greater appetite for such an addition to the text. And yet even a delegation of 266 souls can surprise. Interest in anti-competition was evident in the assembly. It had always been so. Many were just not sure that the constitutional document was the proper place for such regulatory activity—preferring the democratic process as the mechanism to control trusts instead. But these delegates wanted to rein in the power of the monopolistic corporations. Several spoke of pressure they felt from their home constituencies to harness the monopolies' economic influence. Others agreed with Washington and Lennon that some provision or clause related to workers' rights was needed. The Progressive agenda was, at least outwardly, a worker-friendly agenda, they said. In the end, the delegation agreed to include only the language derived from the Sherman Antitrust Act in the new constitutional draft. From ratification forward, Congress would retain the constitutional authority to "outlaw any contract, merger, conspiracy, or combination in the form of trust or otherwise, in restraint of free trade." It was a victory for Washington and Lennon, though not a complete one. The idea that one could conceive of an individual constitutional right to do an honest day's work and earn an honest day's pay without harassment from management would have to wait.

The 1903 federal Constitutional Convention witnessed many firsts. It was the first constitutional convention in U.S. history to welcome people of color. It was also the first to be illuminated by the awesome power of electricity. It was the first at which a few delegates arrived by automobile. The mass-produced and affordable Model T was still a few years off, but the Studebaker was available for use. A handful of delegates arrived in, and departed from, Philadelphia in these new and fascinating machines. This convention was also the first to allow outsiders, including the press, to witness the deliberations. It was the first to employ the use of a telephone, and the typewriter, and the paperclip.

And yet in many ways the 1903 federal Constitutional Convention in Philadelphia resembled all the others. It was influenced by a political landscape that was not level. Partisanship reigned. Republicans (especially northern Republicans) seemed to have the upper hand in deliberations with southern Democrats. Progressive Republicans controlled Congress and the White House, and that control translated into Progressive triumphs at the constitutional convention. Those who were aligned with the sitting President were more likely to taste victory than those who weren't. Efforts to raze the prior Constitution altogether and take a fresh look at what a twentieth-century generation might desire failed because of expediency and because of a belief that the basic architecture of the American political system still functioned reasonably well. Politicians at the convention were still influenced by their reputations. Too few of the delegates came from professions outside of politics.

Still, the draft Constitution produced in Philadelphia that year was laudable. The prepared text responded to the needs of the time, as far as Constitutions are able, that is. It enhanced the government's ability to ensure commercial competition beyond the Sherman antitrust legislation. It empowered the President to make aggressive and proactive moves in the foreign policy domain. It continued the systems of federalism, separate branches, checks and balances, and local authority over police powers. And in the single largest democratic shot in the arm since the country's founding, more than 25 million voters—*women* voters—were added to the electoral register. And not just White women. All women, including women of color, were enfranchised.

The tone of the Constitution changed too, from one that was unmistakably patriarchal and masculine to one that was slightly more just and inclusive. That's not to say that the shift in constitutional tone would translate into greater social and personal freedoms for women in the years ahead. Far from it. Women's equality in areas such as employment, pay, admissions, property, inheritance, housing, and the like, still lagged far behind the promises embedded in the new constitutional document. But some progress was made that year. A small leap was realized in the simple act of extending the franchise and refining the Constitution's Declaration of Rights. Suffragists had secured a significant achievement, one they (and others) had been demanding for some time.

The story of civil rights under the 1903 U.S. Constitution would include many chapters. Most obviously, it would be a story of African Americans trying to overcome the systemic obstacles to racial freedom and equal status. The narrative would also include the plight of women in this country, as they too tried to establish a collective voice in America's power centers. It would prove difficult. Constitutional language notwithstanding, the country in 1903 was about as prepared to welcome women's equality as it was to welcome the equality of African Americans, Irish immigrants, Native peoples, Hispanic speakers, European Jews, and so on. The drafting and ratification of the 1903 Constitution was, therefore, only the latest chapter in the story of America's slow and painful creep toward its promised values. The next Constitution—the 1953 U.S. Constitution—would extend the tale.

1953

IF CONSTITUTION-MAKING was a game of chance, and thank goodness it is not, two wagers laid down in 1903 would almost certainly break the house today: first, that constitutions through-out time would get longer in page and word counts; and second, that constitutional conventions would begin to include significant interest group representation and not simply politicians and pol-icymakers energized by the public good.

The first guaranteed wager is a product of the development and evolution of constitutions worldwide—they have come to be seen as a panacea for every political ill or social squabble faced by a polity. Their increased length, in words and pages, has fully reflected the belief that constitutions can solve almost any prob-lem or dispute. The contrast between America's first two federal Constitutions (the Articles of Confederation and the 1787 U.S. Constitution) and state constitutions of today is notable. Most state constitutions are dozens of pages in length, with more than a hundred articles, sections, and clauses. America's early federal Constitutions were less than ten pages and included fewer than fifty articles and clauses.[1] Superficially, this difference can be felt when sitting down to read these swelling documents. What is less well understood is that expanding the scope, language, and detail of modern constitutional documents has real implications for governance.

The second guaranteed wager is a manifestation of Madison's most cynical warning. He wrote in *Federalist* 51: "If men were angels, no government would be necessary. If angels were to govern men, neither external nor internal controls on government would be necessary." Angels would no doubt approach the constitution-making project with humility and deference, he suggested. But since we are not governed by angels, we must set up our processes as if we will forever be governed by demons. For many, lobbyists and special interest groups are the political equivalent of those evildoers. Madison, in fact, designed the early American polity precisely to contain the power of special interests, or "factions," as he called them. By definition, interest groups are focused primarily on their particular cause, and often those priorities do not reflect the greater good.

The 1953 Constitution of the United States, and the convention that brought that document to life, showed clear signs of this new constitution-making reality. After fifty years, framers were summoned again to Philadelphia to prepare a constitutional draft that would represent the ideas and priorities of a generation bookended by two World Wars. The federal Constitution they fabricated was longer than any produced before, and the evidence of interest group activity was obvious. The discerning observer doubtless would have noticed the subtle correlation between the two newest features of modern constitutionalism, for the presence of special interests at any constitutional founding so often means the inclusion of portions of their platforms in the constitutional text. The more interest groups, the more platforms. The more platforms, the more pages in the text.

That discerning observer surely would have also noted the irony, for a longer text does not always mean a sharper text. The more provisions in a federal Constitution, the more challenging it is to interpret its enumerations. A higher degree of detail can all but extinguish the flexibility a constitution requires for it to be applicable. This was Supreme Court Chief Justice John Marshall's biggest concern when he spoke of "the minor ingredients which compose" the great outlines in a constitutional text.[2] Do not get too specific, he seems to warn: don't ever forget it is a constitution and not a "legal code" you are fashioning.[3]

History has demonstrated, with national constitutions at least, that ambiguity and vagueness can be assets to good government, at least with regard to democratic republics. If the "great outlines" are discernible, the institutions of government can handle the necessary interpretive moments. Sure, sometimes judges take advantage of the ambiguities and insert their personal predilections into their interpretations. But an effective constitution, Marshall contends, is a constitution whose disposition bends toward faith in the interpretive process. Craft a constitution that allows the branches of government some flexibility in applying the text, and you'll enjoy a healthier polity. The delegates to the 1953 Constitutional Convention would have done well to heed that advice. Unfortunately, they didn't always take it.

Much had changed in the half century between the 1903 Convention and the 1953 constitutional gathering. Human nature felt roughly the same, but the world felt very different. It seemingly began with a world war the size of which was unknown at the time. Even after World War I concluded, Americans still faced crippling domestic and international pressures. The country's worst economic depression in the late 1920s and early '30s produced fear among the masses, while the terror of World War II helped develop America's "greatest generation." African Americans fought two wars with only minimal help: one at home and one alongside fellow military men in Europe and the Pacific. The battle at home was expansive. Race riots in Detroit, Beaumont, Mobile, Los Angeles, and New York City raised awareness of the fight for jobs, housing, equal pay, and social justice. The civil rights movement was starting to take shape. Jim Crow laws, the segregated South, and northern racism were a constant reminder of American hypocrisy and injustice.

Millions of Americans had a hard time making ends meet during much of the first half of the twentieth century. Industrial growth, assembly-line manufacturing, and mass production were the period's signature corporate achievements. Some benefited from this revolution in production; many did not. Unions became more popular. Americans experienced a series of economic recessions, one after the other. Much of the population suffered from such economic maladies as hyperinflation, deflation, bank failures, unemployment, declining GDP, weakening purchasing power, and so on. It is true that the economic downturns were often followed by periods of recovery, but those moments of boom often sidestepped the working class.

Then there was the Great Depression. The 1929 crash of the stock market and the crisis in economic confidence that followed so thoroughly exhausted most Americans of that generation that their lives changed forever. The long-term effect was probably more an attitude shift than anything else. Americans became more jaded about their economic future. Government bodies tried to respond to the crisis by introducing programs aimed at providing important services and safety nets. And those public initiatives mostly worked. By the early 1950s, the American economy was booming; the country's military strength was evident; and most citizens were feeling pretty confident.

American politics of the period also evolved in strange and curious ways. The blatant corruption that plagued politics at the start of the twentieth century gave way to another style of influence peddling: interest group politics. The importance of civic virtue in elections receded a bit as the presence of money and name recognition, and the strength of well-funded lobbyists, increased. The 1946 Congress passed the most comprehensive lobbying legislation to date. The Federal Regulation of Lobbying Act required all individuals spending at least half of their time walking the halls of political power to register with the Secretary of the U.S. Senate and the Clerk of the House of

Representatives. The Act regulated "any person who shall engage himself for pay or for any consideration for the purpose
of attempting to influence passage or defeat of any legislation
by the Congress of the United States." The goal was to reduce
interest group potency.

Meanwhile, Joseph McCarthy had captured America's attention. Hysteria over the "Red Scare" and the fear that political
leaders, entertainment icons, and one's neighbors were dabbling
in treasonous endeavors and subversive activities gripped the
American public. McCarthyism attacked civil liberties from a new
flank. It was perhaps the most visible public display of intolerance
ever perpetrated against White power elites this country had
ever witnessed. The right to association and free expression were
trampled in the political frenzy. It was a period of intellectual
tyranny for most. It was a period of physical tyranny for a few.[4]

To be sure, the period immediately preceding the 1953 Constitutional Convention was one of contrasts. On display was the
incredible commitment of American soldiers, as well as the sacrifices made by those who aided the war effort from home. But this
was also a time when the principles of individualism, isolation,
and rebelliousness began to gain currency. The Marlboro Man,
riding alone in the rugged West, emerged as a symbol of strength
and heroism. Over time, Americans witnessed the gradual atro-
phy of community.[5]

The contrasts were also evident in the area of civil rights. The
first half of the twentieth century witnessed an expansion of civil
rights and liberties, especially for women. The New Deal added
much-needed protections for middle- and lower-class workers.
The National Association for the Advancement of Colored People
(NAACP) won several early discrimination cases, ones that would
eventually lead to *Brown v. Board of Education* (1954) and the dismantling of legal segregation. A. Philip Randolph successfully
caught the attention of Franklin Delano Roosevelt (FDR) and
influenced real change in several social justice movements. Still,
the hard struggle for civil rights in most minority communities
continued.

When a nation abridges the civil rights and liberties of its people, the abridgments are often a means to different ends. Some ends are just plain evil: racism and terror with lynchings, Jim Crow laws, and segregation. Other ends are supposedly more defensible: apparent national security with the internment of Japanese Americans, stopping the spread of communism with the McCarthy hearings, preventing a "clear and present danger" with the post–World War I free speech cases. But the story of America's relationship with civil rights and freedoms is so often a story of regret. And of contrast. Exposure to these contrasts, and many others, would be the major animating feature of the 1953 Philadelphia Convention.

There was genuine anticipation across the country for the 1953 Convention. The year had already begun quite eventfully, highlighted by the inauguration on January 20th of Dwight D. Eisenhower, the first Republican President in more than two decades. The Korean War was reaching something of a head after President Eisenhower threatened to use atomic weapons in the region. Jonas Salk boldly, and successfully, tested the polio vaccine on himself and his family. On March 5th, 1953, Josef Stalin died, ending his almost three decades of autocratic reign over the Soviet Union. In the days before the convention opened, Sir Edmund Hillary and Tenzing Norgay commenced their epic climb of Mount Everest. In the days after, Elizabeth II was crowned the Queen of England, a title she still holds.

Closer to Philadelphia, state legislatures were putting the final touches on the delegate send-offs. Some treated the moment in a celebratory way, with fireworks, parades, banners, and tributes. Other state legislatures were more subdued or modest in their fanfare. But celebration was in the air. News media outlets followed the progress of delegate selection with great interest. The convention would be the first in American history to intersect with the use of television as a form of information dissemination. The major broadcast channels devoted time in the weeks and months prior to the convention to educating the population about what to expect. There was no talk at the time of televising the proceedings, though some would come to regret that decision. Indeed, one reason the decision was made to televise the McCarthy hearings a year later was that some networks believed the constitutional convention had been a golden opportunity that got away. They weren't going to make that mistake again.

An interesting marker of human progress is the time it now took for delegates to travel to Philadelphia. In 1953, travel time could be measured in hours, whereas in 1787 it would have been weeks. Planes and automobiles replaced the trains of earlier convention periods, which had replaced the horses and buggies of the first few meetings. Many delegates were not present for the entire 1953 proceedings, preferring to shuffle in and out of Philadelphia at various times, depending on their other professional and personal responsibilities. Communication was also vastly improved. Instead of letters recounting the specifics of the deliberations, telephone calls were the preferred choice of those participating in 1953.

Almost everything about this federal convention was different from what had occurred in 1787. The pledge of secrecy among the delegates in 1787 had been violated, admittedly through mutual agreement, by the 1903 assembly. There was no way to get that genie back in the bottle in 1953. Official notetakers were hired and assigned the duties that informally fell to James Madison in 1787.

The 1953 delegation itself would look very different as well. The demographic profile of the conclave was unlike that of any prior federal convention. Women were selected to be delegates for the first time, and they were reasonably well represented. Among those females representing their respective states at the convention were Jeannette Rankin (the first woman elected to Congress), Frances Perkins (who served as Labor Secretary under FDR and was the first woman appointed to a Cabinet post), Hattie Caraway (the first woman elected to the U.S. Senate), Martha Griffiths (a future Congresswoman from Michigan), and Mary McLeod Bethune (head of FDR's "Black cabinet" and Vice President of the NAACP). Other African Americans and members of other minority racial groups were also included. Famous social activist and publisher W.E.B. Du Bois was there. So was Arthur Mitchell, the first African American Congressman from the Democratic Party. Poet and playwright Langston Hughes secured an invitation to Philadelphia, as did the great Thurgood Marshall. Antonio Fernós-Isern, the Resident Commissioner from Puerto Rico, served as a nonvoting member of the U.S. Congress. He got a vote in the 1953 Constitutional Convention.

It was by far the most diverse collection of federal convention delegates ever assembled. But while it could boast of diversity, it was lacking in one important respect: constitution-making experience. Few in the delegation had ever acted as a constitutional framer, primarily because the frequency of assembling state constitutional conventions had dropped off considerably. Only ten states undertook the process of fashioning new constitutional texts in the fifty years between the 1903 and 1953 federal Conventions.[6] Contrast that to the period between the 1863 and 1903 federal Conventions when fifty-four new state constitutions were drafted.

States had become reticent about the power and appeal of a new constitution. They worried that certain hot-button topics would simply derail any proceedings and their efforts at bringing about genuine change would go unrealized. Several states, in fact (New York in 1915 and 1938 and Rhode Island in 1944, among others), set out to convene a wholesale constitutional convention only to have the draft scrapped partway through or rejected during ratification. Political officials in various states often floated the idea of organizing a drafting convention, only to be talked out of it or rebuffed by opponents.

Constitutional amendments were a different story, though. The number of amendments to state constitutions in the first fifty years of the twentieth century increased dramatically. According to the Maryland State Constitutions Project, more than 12,000 amendments have been added to state constitutions in the two centuries between 1800 and 2000. The majority of these amendments were introduced in the twentieth century.[7] That activity had provided some in the delegation with a modest amount of practice in shaping constitutions. At least one member of the delegation had valuable drafting experience, however. Alfred Driscoll of New Jersey was a keen defender of periodic constitutional renewal. He had also enjoyed a storied political career. He served in a number of local capacities before he took a turn as a New Jersey State Senator. At the time of the 1953 Convention, Driscoll was concluding his second term as New Jersey's Governor. Under his watch, the state ramped up plans to complete the Garden State Parkway and the New Jersey Turnpike. He was also famous for elevating future Supreme Court Justice William Brennan to his state's highest court.

After receiving his law degree at Harvard, Driscoll had gone to work at a prominent Camden, New Jersey, law firm. Soon, though, the political bug bit him. He joined a small faction of the Republican Party—the "Clean Government" wing—and set out on a life in politics. The "clean government" mantra stayed with him throughout his days. He was named to New Jersey's Commission on State Administrative Reorganization because he was seen as such an effective watchdog. His stated goal was to tamp down administrative waste. In 1947, Driscoll defeated his Democratic challenger for Governor. He then proceeded to do something highly unusual, something that would come in handy six years later at the federal constitutional convention: he spent the three-month transition period before he took office studying the details of a possible new state constitution. He even used his inauguration speech as an opportunity to pledge his backing for a state constitutional convention. He agreed with state officials that a limited state constitutional convention—one that did not touch such thorny issues as reapportionment—would be the wisest route to take. He also agreed that his office would handle most of the logistics of the convention, including the development of materials for delegates, the establishment of rules for deliberation, and the ratification referendum that would come later.

Remarkably, the resulting draft state constitution achieved many of the objectives Driscoll sought. He had fought for a stronger executive and a "streamlined" judiciary. He got those. He had also advocated for the reorganization of the state bureaucracy and the protection of collective bargaining for certain employees. Those too were in the draft text. Perhaps the most memorable feature of New Jersey's 1947 Constitution was its stand on segregation. It was, in fact, the first state constitution in the nation to outlaw segregation across the state. Alfred Driscoll concluded his term as Governor in 1953, just in time to take part in the federal constitutional convention with considerable confidence and with real experience in constitutional draftsmanship.

Driscoll was not the only delegate with gubernatorial practice invited to the meeting. Percival Baxter, former Governor of the state of Maine, was selected by the legislature in Augusta to represent his state in Philadelphia. Baxter was probably the most famous Mainer of his day, so his appointment was met with little criticism. He was also one of the most eccentric politicians around. A states' rights Republican, Baxter is probably best known for tales that have little to do with his political acumen. He was fiercely loyal to his dog, Garry, even posing for official portraits with the pooch and ordering the state flag to be flown at half-mast when Garry died. He made it his personal crusade to conserve lands in and around Mount Katahdin (eventually the area would be designated a state park, bearing his name). He fought the Ku Klux Klan in Maine, and after his political career was over, he traveled extensively in the Soviet Union, acting as an informal ambassador for his state and country. When he entered a room, he made quite an impression.[8]

Driscoll and Baxter represented two distinct points on a wide spectrum of states' rights advocates. Driscoll was not as extreme as Baxter, but he, too, believed the federal government had grown too powerful and that states were losing a portion of their sovereign police powers. World War II was the most obvious recent example of a situation in which the federal government's authority outshone that of the states. That was perhaps logical; a solid case could be made for federal government oversight of any foreign military campaign (especially given the changes made to presidential authority in the 1903 Constitution). But Franklin Roosevelt's New Deal and Harry S. Truman's Fair Deal were something altogether different. It concerned folks like Driscoll and Baxter that Congress and the President could take such an active role in protecting the health, safety, and welfare of the individual citizens. That was traditionally the states' job. The clause taken from the original Tenth Amendment, and still embedded in the 1903 Constitution's Article I Declaration of Rights, that reminded politicians that states "reserved" the constitutional powers not "delegated" or "prohibited" seemed to carry less authority during FDR's and Truman's presidential terms.

Republicans worried that such comprehensive programs challenged the fundamental tenets of federalism. They asked questions to that effect: Were states now too passive to reclaim some control over local police powers? Were the crises that Americans faced during the Great Depression and World War II so monumental that only a unitary President (with the help of Congress and the bureaucracy) could solve them? What role do states have in a modern American polity? These questions were asked increasingly in the months leading up to the constitutional convention.[9]

The 1953 Constitutional Convention would thus be a referendum on the power and persuasion of the American presidency. Though FDR would not live to witness this federal convention, his legacy was continually on display. The convention met a full two Presidents and almost a decade removed from FDR's death, but his impact on the proceedings was profound. America during the period between conventions had been molded in FDR's image. The convention delegates, and the citizens at large, were now living in FDR's world. Some liked that world; others most assuredly did not.

President Roosevelt's first one hundred days in office had been remarkable. His actions inevitably had constitutional ramifications. In response to the calamitous effects of the Great Depression, the President closed banks, advocated for the lifting of Prohibition, and signed the Tennessee Valley Authority Act into law. The TVA Act created an organization that invested in infrastructure—rebuilding bridges and roads, constructing dams and waterways. It was job creation at its finest. The President also paid out farm subsidies to boost prices and earnings for American farmers. He implemented the National Industrial Recovery Act to assist factory workers struggling with low wages and poor working conditions. And he did all of this in his first three months in office.

A few years later, with the Great Depression still crippling the lives of most Americans, FDR launched a follow-up attack on domestic poverty. His Second New Deal, which had similar constitutional implications, established the Works Progress Administration, the Social Security Act, and a number of other initiatives all aimed at ending the financial crisis. Harry Truman assumed the presidency upon Roosevelt's death in April 1945, and he, too, took up the Democratic mantle. Truman's Fair Deal consisted of additional measures to aid the less fortunate. His 21-Point Program, delivered to Congress in September 1945, included more money for unemployment insurance, a permanent Fair Employment Practice Committee, an increase in the minimum wage, additional aid to farmers, a revised tax code, an expansion of public works projects, and so on. The former Vice President saw his role as continuing many of the New Deal policies of his predecessor.

But FDR and Truman certainly had their critics. Many of Truman's proposals were eventually stalled by an unfriendly Congress. His woes with an antagonistic legislature were reminiscent of FDR's trouble with a willful judiciary. Both Congress and the Supreme Court cited federalism as grounds to oppose several New Deal programs.[10] Many Republican politicians were also unenthused with the mere idea of an activist presidency. Herbert Hoover was an outspoken critic. Even prominent Governors, like Driscoll and Baxter, had their doubts about the constitutionality of FDR's projects. Federalism, they claimed, was in peril. Hence, many delegates eventually arrived in Philadelphia with an agenda, an agenda that revolved around reducing the lingering shadow of FDR's New Deal initiatives.

Once in Philadelphia, Driscoll and Baxter began to hold secret meetings with delegates who, they knew, held some reservations about the vestiges of FDR's New Deal. The participants in these secret meetings—which included Rush Holt and Robert Taft (shortly before his untimely death in late July 1953)—were careful to distinguish their animosity toward the New Deal initiatives from their concern about the shift in power that accompanied the comprehensive plan. One was symptomatic of a much larger issue, but both were a problem. For many prominent Republicans of the period, the New Deal felt a lot like socialism. *Collectivism* was the term of the day, but it still smelled like *socialism*.

In addition, the secret group deliberated about the power of the federal government. They believed in a constitutional structure best described by Donald Lutz: "American history has, as its center, a federal design, an 'indestructible Union, composed of indestructible states,' a federal design that serves as the tightly coiled mainspring of American history that drives institutional development and political processes, generates the major political controversies, tests its best leaders, [and] defies definition."[11] The supposed indestructibility of the federal system, and of the individual states, is what made these states' righters uneasy now. The secret cabal was singularly focused on remedying that problem; it would prove to be the undercurrent of the entire meeting.

The Constitutional Convention Opens
After four tries, the process of drafting a constitutional text in an organized federal convention now seemed to follow a fairly standard and precise routine. The delegates respected certain customs that had begun in 1787 and were reinforced in each of the subsequent conventions. The formal part of the selection process was set: state legislatures discussed a list of possible delegates, chose a few, sent invitations, and waited for responses. The fortunate few would then prepare for the convention.

Once in place, the delegates obeyed certain procedural rules. There are the standard procedures, of course: parliamentary rules of order, the reading of minutes from the prior day's discussion, verbal vote tallies, formal motions, and the like. But there are unwritten rules, too, and many of those have passed down from the original 1787 Constitutional Convention. Madison's notes of May 28th and 29th give us a glimpse into the world of constitutional convention protocols: motions that are seconded can be withdrawn by the original presenter prior to the vote; when speaking, delegates address their remarks to the President of the convention and no one else; others are not permitted to interrupt the speaker, nor engage in any other activity—reading, whispering, sleeping—while the individual has the floor; no delegate can speak more than twice on a motion or resolution before all others have an opportunity to speak; committees are not allowed to convene while the entire delegation is in session; straw polls are an effective way of taking the pulse of the delegation. Madison described other protocols as well, of course. Almost all of these formal and informal procedures, in one form or another, still govern federal constitution-making conventions more than 230 years after the Virginian and his colleagues imagined and agreed upon them.

It's worth remembering these important procedural threads that ran through the first four constitutional conventions, because so much of what everyone had grown accustomed to went out the window during the 1953 Convention. Sure, the delegates still played by the rules, but the tone of the entire meeting— the mood of the assembly—began to change in 1953 (it would worsen in 2022). Jockeying and horse-trading became more pronounced. Bargains were made between delegates. To be sure, these political strategies and practices were present at all previous federal conventions, but they were not flaunted. When delegates looked to cut bargains and advance particular interests, it was done with a sort of gentlemanly creed that assumed special interest politics was a dirty concept. No more. In many respects, the 1953 Constitutional Convention marks America's entrée into modern constitution-making, when interests—self and otherwise—eclipsed the long-standing tradition favoring civic virtue and public righteousness.

It started with the selection of a convention president. Leading up to the convention, Sam Rayburn was probably the most obvious choice, or at least the odds-on favorite to get the job. A popular member of the U.S. House of Representatives from Texas, he would go on to become one of the longest serving Congressmen in U.S. history. And it wasn't a typical political career. He was an extremely effective lawmaker.[12] And he was a character. He was well-known for his rhetorical quips. Rayburn was famous for saying things like, "if you want to get along, go along," and "when two men always think alike, only one of them is doing any thinking." He was the quintessential elected official—scrupulously honest, a forceful leader, and an asset both to his state and to the country.

Now in the minority, though, Rayburn took stock of his political future. He was disappointed that the Democrats had lost the majority in the House and Senate in 1946, and he placed much of the blame directly on himself. He recognized that President Truman was highly unpopular and that midterm elections were often referenda on the President's approval rating. Even still, Rayburn could not shake the idea that *he* was responsible for the partisan shift in power. Despite the loss, he remained popular among his colleagues. As such, Rayburn surprised his fellow Democratic Members of Congress when he refused the post of House Minority Leader. He did not think he was worthy. This display of humility only endeared him further to his Democratic colleagues, and after much cajoling and persuading, he was eventually elected Minority Leader and would go on to spend more than two decades as the House leader of the Democratic Party.

He was almost as popular with Republicans as he was with fellow Democrats. Many of the actions he took as Speaker of the House and Minority Leader were successful precisely because he worked at forging relationships with Representatives from the opposite party. Republicans appreciated his open style, making him a beloved member not just of his party but of the House of Representatives.[13] For that reason, it seemed likely that he would ascend to the presidency of the constitutional convention. His Democratic Party was in the minority, both in the legislative chamber and in the White House, but Rayburn's popularity could overcome partisan politics. Or so he thought.

The man ultimately elected to preside over the 1953 federal Constitutional Convention would eventually rise to occupy the highest political office in the land, but at the time, he was a barely known figure in national politics. Gerald R. Ford was a two-term Congressman from Michigan, whose major claim to fame was a successful career as a center for the University of Michigan football team and a notable stint in the U.S. Navy. His political career to that point was thoroughly unremarkable. That said, he certainly had an impressive intellect and a sharp sense of humor. And he was ambitious. At the time of the convention, he was maneuvering within Republican political circles to be a more consequential player on the national stage. He managed to secure a plum committee assignment—to the House Appropriations Committee—and he became a charter member (along with a young Congressman from California named Richard Nixon) of the Chowder and Marching Club, a group of like-minded, young congressional Republicans who would act as a voting bloc.[14] Ford wanted to be recognized; he wanted a career similar to Sam Rayburn's.

He did not seek out the presidency of the constitutional convention, but he did not protest when his friend and colleague from Michigan, John R. Dethmers, put his name forward for consideration. Dethmers was a stalwart in the Republican Party, a leading figure at both the state and the national levels. In 1953, when he was appointed by the state legislature to represent Michigan in Philadelphia, Dethmers was the Chief Justice of the Michigan Supreme Court. He was also quite familiar with Gerald Ford. The jurist had come to know Ford through a variety of professional and social interactions, enough to develop a respect for the way Ford thought about politics and the Constitution. He was convinced Ford would make a marvelous presiding officer at the convention.

The problem was how to convince others. It would take more than just Dethmers' considerable skills at persuasion to get a majority of delegates to sign on to the idea that young Gerald Ford should follow in George Washington's and Thomas Jefferson's footsteps. Ford was not yet of that caliber; not even close. Dethmers would begin by polling the Michigan delegation and the delegations from neighboring states. If he could build a cohort of Midwestern supporters, he thought he could seize the momentum and carry Ford to the convention chair. Whispers of support for Sam Rayburn were everywhere, so Dethmers knew that he had to find a way, honorably and discreetly, to attack Rayburn's candidacy. That would be tough.

Dethmers had one thing going for him: a fairly significant shift in partisan power at the national level. The Republicans had managed to turn fifty-five Democratic seats in the 1946 midterm election and twenty-eight seats in the 1950 midterm election. The once-formidable Democratic majority in Washington was showing signs in the late 1940s and early 1950s of cracking. By 1953, Americans had elected a Republican to the White House. Dethmers could cite the dismal career of Truman as a rationale for inserting the Republican Ford as President of the convention.

Or he could focus on Rayburn's 1951 blunder with the twenty-one day rule. In 1949, Rayburn supported legislation that essentially made it possible for any committee chair to bring an action to the House floor if the Rules Committee neglected to act within a three-week period. Rayburn, frustrated with the stodgy Rules Committee, voted in favor of the measure, only to reverse himself two years later when it was repealed. The flip-flop was embarrassing to Rayburn. But it was not significant enough to render him unfit for leading the convention. Dethmers would have to look elsewhere.

Perhaps Rayburn's extremely short and highly secretive marriage to Metze Jones was something Dethmers could exploit.

Jones was the sister of Rayburn's fellow Texas Congressman Marvin Jones. After a long courtship, she agreed to marry Rayburn in 1927 and move to Washington. That didn't last long. Jones was miserable in the nation's capital. She hated the city. She also hated Rayburn's long work schedule and his fondness for whiskey and poker. The two quietly divorced only three months after professing their wedding vows. Could Dethmers leverage that embarrassment to wobble Rayburn's candidacy? Probably not. Dethmers had run out of options. He could not uncover information that would impugn the former Speaker of the House, so he had to turn to good old-fashioned politics to do the trick. He would make promises; some of which he'd keep.

Promises were the currency of the realm in mid-century American politics. The cliché of politicians making deals in smoky backrooms was popular precisely because it was accurate. Though Dethmers had not fully participated in such fraternal gatherings, he was savvy enough to know how to employ them. During the weeks prior to the start of the convention proceedings, therefore, Dethmers met with as many Midwestern Republicans as he could. He told fellow delegates that Ford was the right choice, that he would be sympathetic to a moderate Republican agenda, and that southern Democrats, like Rayburn, could not be trusted to do the same. Sure, Rayburn had impeccable credentials, but he fell short in one area: he was a Democrat at a time when being so was not fashionable.

Amazingly, it worked! It took five ballots to decide a winner, as no candidate received a majority on any of the first four. Sam Rayburn quietly withdrew from consideration after the second ballot. Much later, he would confess to some surprise that he was not chosen, but he understood the importance of the moment, and he refused to get caught up in the political posturing that so often accompanies these decisions. Slowly, other potential candidates also withdrew until Ford was declared the winner. Gerald Ford, two-term Congressman from Grand Rapids, Michigan, and eventual U.S. President, had his first national victory. He would seize the moment.

-+>-<+-

Thurgood Marshall was more famous than most of the delegates in the convention hall. He came to Philadelphia riding high after successfully arguing several crucial discrimination cases before the Supreme Court. That success elevated his reputation within the legal community. It solidified his place in the pantheon of legal minds, and it gave him a degree of confidence that his place at the constitutional drafting table was merited. Most of the lawyers who participated in the 1953 Constitutional Convention had heard of Marshall, and several had even engaged him in debate about the importance of social justice. A few had experienced firsthand Marshall's legendary skills as a rhetorical powerhouse.

Marshall would debate anyone, at any time. For him, it was sport, introduced and honed around the dinner table when he was a youth in Baltimore. He loved to play with words and ideas, seeking to force his opponent to concede even the most trivial point. His debating skills were most on display in America's courtrooms, but they were also evident at dinner parties, boardrooms, and in casual conversation. And he had the personality to match that skill set, at least early in his career. He was a gregarious soul—friendly, outgoing, and personable. His booming laugh invariably lifted the spirits of those around him. Later in his life, he would gain a reputation as a cantankerous and irascible man, but at the time of the convention he lived a bit wildly. He famously said that he intended to "live life as a loose garment."[15] He did just that, enjoying parlor games and hard liquor. Still, those who knew him best always understood that the jurist's infectious personality should never be confused with nonchalance. Marshall was a serious man, a passionate advocate for the cause of equality. He joined the NAACP in 1936 and was leading that organization's Legal Defense and Educational Fund only four years later. His impact on American law is immense.

Thurgood Marshall had a complicated relationship with the U.S. Constitution. He chose to see that document as the cornerstone of America's commitment to the rule of law, but he also recognized its many defects, especially those that were not erased by prior conventions and that continued to perpetuate America's version of a caste system. He was thus excited to receive an invitation from the legislature of New York (his adopted home state) to represent the Empire State in Philadelphia. Marshall was keen to learn from others and to contribute to the conversation in areas where he had expertise. His greatest contribution would come when the discussion turned to civil rights and the judiciary. The NAACP Legal Defense and Educational Fund, with Marshall at the helm, had employed an innovative legal strategy to dismantle the foundation of segregation in public education. The idea was simple, but effective. Marshall would use the judiciary to combat discrimination. He would not rely on the elected officials at the state or federal level, because they had no incentive to make fundamental racial change. African Americans delivered only a small percentage of the vote, and thus it was easy for most politicians to ignore their interests. Doing so would not jeopardize a candidate's electoral chances. Federal judges, however, were immune from the pressures of reelection and thus they had more freedom to enforce the Constitution's Equal Protection Clause. Marshall's strategy, therefore, was to exploit the independence of the federal (and state) judiciary. It turned out to be a winning strategy.

In the five years before the constitutional convention, Marshall argued a number of successful education cases that would culminate in the elimination of the practice of "separate but equal" education in America's public schools. The class action suit *Brown v. Board of Education of Topeka, Kansas* was originally argued before the U.S. Supreme Court in 1952, but the Justices requested re-argument. They scheduled the second oral argument for December 1953, a full seven months *after* the opening of the convention. Marshall would argue the case, of course. He was enough of a realist to know that the case must continue because there was no guarantee that the 1953 constitutional framers assembled in Philadelphia would accept his argument that the Equal Protection Clause, added to the U.S. Constitution ninety years earlier, lacked sufficient force. He intended to try to persuade fellow delegates to reinforce the Equal Protection Clause in some way, but he was not optimistic that he would be successful.

His uncertainty was warranted. Shortly after the opening of the 1953 Constitutional Convention, the leader of the NAACP Legal Defense and Educational Fund and eventual Associate Justice of the U.S. Supreme Court stood to address his fellow constitution-makers about the enduring racism and discrimination that was destroying contemporary American society. He spoke with great passion and deliberateness. He insisted that the existing constitutional provision guaranteeing the "equal protection of the laws" did not apply equitably and that segregation was simply another method used by Whites to "enslave the descendants of slavery."

He resurrected arguments made in court that segregated schools (and facilities, restaurants, hotels, and on and on) perpetuated a belief that Blacks are inferior, that their race is somehow lesser or subhuman. "We all know what is occurring," he said. "The argument that 'separate but equal' is somehow just, fair, and constitutional because it ensures supposed equal treatment misses the crucial point that stigmatization is a devastating weapon intended to keep an entire race down. It is only different in kind from the scourge of slavery." Both his emotions and his booming voice filled the assembly hall. He spoke for twenty minutes as if he was in America's appellate courtroom. He concluded by asking his fellow delegates to conceive of some way to lend greater power or weight to a largely impotent Equal Protection Clause.

That was a tall task. Never before had federal constitution-makers attempted to strengthen an existing constitutional right or provision. They added and subtracted clauses at each convention, and they even modified the text through the amendment process between conventions. But this was different. How would one change the language of the Equal Protection Clause to make it more potent? Add more adjectives or adverbs to the sentence? Or an interjection? "No state or federal entity shall deny to any person within its jurisdiction the equal protection of the laws. Truly!"? Delegates were genuinely confused about what Marshall was asking. His attempt to clarify spurred another round of intense debate.

Few recognized that Marshall was as interested in drawing attention to the work of courts as he was to the wording of constitutions. The responsibility to determine the comparative force or power of an individual constitutional clause typically falls to the judiciary, not to the constitutional framer. Jurists consider how a clause applies to a particular set of facts and the influence of that clause is more or less dependent on a number of variables—the details of the case, the circumstances of the moment, the political ideology of the judge, how she reads the entire Constitution, her moral compass, her political leanings, precedent, even the social climate at the time of the decision. Over time, the strength and intensity of a constitutional clause will wax and wane. That was the natural order of things, according to most delegates listening to Marshall's line of reasoning. They were missing Marshall's primary point that objectivity in constitutional interpretation is elusive, particularly when the language of the constitutional text reveals few clues as to the strength and force of a specific clause.[16]

It was not to be. To try to tinker with the language of a constitutional clause in order to do a judge's job was too much for the majority of delegates to embrace. Though moved by Marshall's words and passion—and by his cause—a majority of federal convention delegates (led primarily by a southern Democratic caucus) refused to modify the existing equality provisions in the 1953 draft Constitution. These provisions were sufficient to protect individuals and groups on the margins, they thought. In fact, the string of successful cases brought forth by Marshall and the NAACP Legal Defense and Educational Fund was evidence of the power of the Equal Protection Clause. He was winning the battle. The Equal Protection Clause was evolving in exactly the ways intended.

Looking back on Marshall's quest to find a way, through the constitution-making process, to eradicate the practice of segregation, it is clear that his success as a litigator was a major factor in his inability to muster support in Philadelphia. Victories in cases like *Shelley v. Kraemer* (1948) and *Sweatt v. Painter* (1950) provided cover for those delegates who were reluctant to alter the language or meaning of the Equal Protection Clause. A group of northern liberals, fearing backlash from southerners whose support they would need in future votes during the convention, were quite vocal in claiming that the judiciary, in its interpretive capacity, was chipping away at the edges of America's segregated society. Marshall's litigation strategy was working, they insisted. Give the courts more time, and segregation would be a thing of the past. Sit tight while cases like *Brown v. Board of Education* are decided, this group conveniently argued. The federal judiciary could do the bidding of Congress and ensure enforcement of the equal protection provision. That way, the delegates to the 1953 Constitutional Convention wouldn't have to. A motion to alter the language of the Equal Protection Clause never even came to the convention floor.

Marshall was disappointed in the outcome of the debate over equal protection. But he was not surprised. He was used to displays of political expediency—or was it weakness?—by public officials. Even the most progressive of White leaders on the subject of race were often unwilling to stick their necks out for African Americans. Marshall's experience with this type of timidity, after all, had helped to form his legal strategy. Were it not for the absence of true political leadership on issues of race, Marshall and the NAACP might have looked to Congress' enforcement power for relief. The convention's refusal to consider modified language for the Equal Protection Clause was just another in a series of political disappointments experienced by Marshall. He would not stick around these proceedings much longer.

The thought provoked by Marshall's powerful speeches in the convention hall, however, would persist. One speech in particular, would influence fellow delegates. It was about the influence of the

judiciary on constitutional draftsmanship. The speech was a theo-
retical blockbuster for many in the room that day. Politics—party
and otherwise—Marshall began, is always the primary driver in
constitutional convention debate. Framers are most frequently
steered by the political winds of the moment when they sit down
to discuss the details of new constitutional texts; they really can't
help themselves. Most framers are politicians in one form or
another, and they are most comfortable trading in the currency
familiar to them. They are used to thinking politically and that
comes through during the debates. Before we judge too quickly,
though, let's just say that's not necessarily a bad thing. Often, the
political gusts that draw framers' attention produce interesting
and effective constitutional texts, he said. Constitutions manufac-
tured mainly by politicians have certainly ordered stable polities
at the state and national level—foreign and domestic—ever since
the late eighteenth century. The lesson might be that the politics
of elections, laws, and executive actions is a major influence in
the conversations that occur at constitutional conventions. Surely,
Marshall argued, that must be logically true.

Even so, he continued, convention participants are also influenced by other variables. The judiciary, especially in the twentieth
century, is probably as responsible for the direction of convention
debate as any other political phenomenon or institution. That is
to say, framers are as much focused on how the *courts* interpret
the existing Constitution as they are on the ways in which a new
Constitution might advance their own political goals. That wasn't
necessarily the case in the early nineteenth century, and certainly
it was not so in 1787. But the thousands of court cases decided
in the last hundred-plus years have exposed the many fissures in
America's constitutional document. Constitutional conventions,
in interesting ways, are intended to seal those fractures.

Marshall reminded the delegates to the federal convention
that they had a plethora of judicial rulings and opinions to consider. The NAACP's attempts to desegregate public education
were just a small sampling of these decisions. On the issue of free
speech alone, the Supreme Court had adjudicated such contests

as *Terminiello v. Chicago* (1949) on breaches of the peace, *American Communications Association v. Douds* (1950) on anti-communist oaths, *Dennis v. United States* (1951) on incitement, *Feiner v. New York* (1951) again on breaches of the peace, and *Beauharnais v. Illinois* (1952) on group libel, all within a five-year period leading up to the constitutional convention.

The constitution-makers were also focused on federal court decisions in other areas: the separation of church and state in *Cantwell v. Connecticut* (1940) and *Everson v. Board of Education of the Township of Ewing* (1947), patriotism and the pledge of allegiance in *Minersville School District v. Gobitis* (1940) and *West Virginia State Board of Education v. Barnette* (1943), equal protection and the internment of Japanese Americans in *Hirabayashi v. United States* (1943) and *Korematsu v. United States* (1944), and the expanding power of the federal government in *United States v. Darby* (1941), *Wickard v. Filburn* (1942), *United States v. Causby* (1946), and *United Public Workers v. Mitchell* (1947).

At the time of the 1953 Constitutional Convention, these decisions were fresh and polemical. Marshall wanted delegates to remember them. They stirred debate in political and judicial circles, and he believed they should spark action among the ranks in the convention hall. Instead, they caused mostly hand-wringing. Several delegates—Ohio Senator John W. Bricker and New Jersey Representative William Widnall (both Republicans) and John Shenk (Associate Justice of the California Supreme Court) among them—regularly cited the liberal priorities of a New Deal court as grounds for anxiety. Bricker, in particular, tried to convince his fellow delegates that the constitutional convention was a good venue for correcting some of the "ill-advised" decisions coming out of the federal and state courts. He and like-minded colleagues would have some success over the five-month convention, introducing several provisions and clauses meant to stall the liberal push from the Supreme Court. Their success at introducing ideas, however, would not translate into any meaningful change in the draft Constitution. Thurgood Marshall was not the only delegate disappointed in the cowardice of his colleagues.

➤✕◀

The time had come for the delegation, led by Driscoll, Baxter, and their informal caucus of states' rights Republicans, to consider the issue of presidential term limits. For some time, members of this group had known the question of including a presidential term limit provision in the 1953 constitutional text would arise. In fact, the issue of presidential term limits was, in some ways, low-hanging fruit for these delegates. FDR's successful 1940 campaign for a third term as America's chief executive had thrust the question into the spotlight. His successful election to a fourth term in 1944 just upped the ante. The delegates' concerns were primarily about the decline of federalism, but they thought their best chance of controlling the rise in federal governmental power would come from limiting Presidents to two consecutive terms.[17]

No prior President had sought a third consecutive term in office (much less a fourth), in large part out of respect for George Washington, who entered into the job reluctantly and left wearily.[18] Other U.S. Presidents had followed his example. Jefferson probably could have secured a third term in office, but he chose not to stray from the precedent set down by his hero. One could surmise that Abraham Lincoln might have won a third term, but here, too, it seems likely that he would have considered retirement as well. By the time FDR emerged on the national scene, thirty-one men had occupied the office, but none had won a third term. FDR's decision to ignore the unwritten custom had struck some as wise and others as arrogant.

The 1953 delegates had a lot of information to work with. George Washington's decision to step down after two terms in office had temporarily silenced a debate about presidential term limits that began during the 1787 Constitutional Convention. Several proposals regarding presidential terms had been floated in Philadelphia that summer. Alexander Hamilton and James Madison occupied one end of the spectrum, arguing that lifetime appointments by Congress were the way to go. George Mason and others were puzzled by the idea of a lifetime term for a supposedly "elected" President. How is that setup any different from a monarchy, they wondered. Doesn't it violate a central purpose of the American Revolution? To throw off the chains on the executive, making him unaccountable, is an affront to those who gave their lives in the Revolutionary War to avoid that very thing. During the 1787 Constitutional Convention, Mason argued vociferously against any proposal that would curb the regular elections of Presidents. His arguments proved persuasive. When put to a vote, the Madison-Hamilton proposal in favor of lifetime presidential appointments was narrowly defeated. Four state delegations voted for the measure; six voted against it.

That didn't end the debate about presidential terms, however. The next proposal to gain traction during the 1787 Convention would have allowed Congress to appoint Presidents for renewable seven-year terms. This proposal actually made it into an early draft of the constitutional text. It was ultimately abandoned because delegates like Gouverneur Morris cried foul. Why should Congress select the President, he asked? Wouldn't that encourage corruption, as potential Presidents would be tempted to bribe Members of Congress to secure the post? Wouldn't popular election be a better mechanism? Let the people have their say in whom they want as chief executive. The answer turned out to be a compromise of sorts—a complex "Electoral College" would possess the responsibility of choosing each President. Proponents of congressional selection were satisfied because members of this Electoral College would be sophisticated enough to select wise and virtuous citizens. Opponents of congressional selection were also satisfied because the everyday voter was indirectly responsible for choosing the electors who would populate the Electoral College. Both sides of the argument won meaningful victories.

Finally, the 1787 assembly settled on a renewable four-year term for each President. But the issue of the length of the term was different from the question of the *number* of terms—successive or otherwise—a President could secure. Most delegates to America's first constitutional convention remained opposed to any term limits at all. Hamilton famously wrote in *Federalist* 69 that "the Magistrate is to be elected for four years; and is to be re-eligible as often as the people of the United States shall think him worthy of their confidence." In the end, the members of the 1787 Constitutional Convention agreed that no mention of term limits would be included in the Constitution.

Subsequent Constitutions were also silent on presidential term limits. The question arose from time to time, as if consideration of presidential term limits was a necessary component for completing an exhaustive drafting process. And yet it did not seem necessary to attack a problem that did not exist. No President had overstayed his welcome in the years between the first constitutional convention and the fourth. FDR's ambitions, and the ambitions of the Democratic Party, however, put the issue squarely back into America's consciousness. For a time, it looked as if Roosevelt would abide by the Washingtonian convention. He was a bit coy in seeking a third term, but he was more vocal about his desire to win a fourth. His opponent in 1944, Republican Thomas E. Dewey, made presidential term limits part of his campaign platform. He famously claimed, "four terms, or sixteen years, is the most dangerous threat to our freedom ever proposed."[19]

That platform did not earn Dewey the White House, but it did help to place the issue of presidential term limits squarely in the spotlight. At that point, the major question was really about timing. The year was 1944, and the next constitutional convention was almost a decade away. Could term limits proponents wait until 1953 to tackle the issue, or should they commence the complicated and laborious amendment process? Most Members of Congress favored the immediate approach: let's amend the current Constitution right now, they said, because there is no evidence to suggest that FDR won't just keep running for President. But some preferred to wait. A constitutional convention, this group argued, is precisely the place to thoroughly debate the merits of presidential term limits within the context of other structural issues.

FDR's untimely death eighty-two days into his fourth term more or less resolved the question of timing. The urgency to amend the Constitution so that FDR did not get a fifth term as President was now gone. The precedent had been set, though, and other chief executives could follow FDR (and not Washington) into seemingly endless terms. But commentators also knew that the country was facing only two more presidential elections between FDR's sudden passing and the 1953 constitutional gathering (1948 and 1952). That suggested they could hold off on any amendment. Baxter, Holt, and other opponents of a strong federal executive felt they could wait until the 1953 Convention to tackle the thorny issue. They would be ready when that time came.

There were other concerns besides FDR's ambitions that fueled the advocates of presidential term limits. One in particular stood out. A year before the start of the 1953 Philadelphia Convention, the U.S. Supreme Court issued a withering rebuke of Truman's executive order that sought to seize privately owned steel mills. The case was *Youngstown Sheet and Tube Company v. Sawyer* (1952), and it arose because the President tried to take control of private steel mills in order to reinforce supplies needed for the Korean War effort. The mills were threatening a strike, and Truman worried about the potential drop in steel production.

Truman attempted in this moment to expand the power of the President, and he had reason to be confident that the Supreme Court would decide in his favor. For one thing, the Justices (many of whom had been appointed under the FDR-Truman regime) were sympathetic to expanding executive authority under the New Deal and Fair Deal. Furthermore, Truman cited the importance of national security as justification for the action. Indeed, he was quite certain the Supreme Court would defer to him on issues involving national security. And finally, he had witnessed President Roosevelt successfully taking this same step when he assumed control of the powerful retailer Montgomery Ward in December 1944, after that company's management refused to follow the orders of the National Wage Labor Board. Again, the impetus for FDR's actions was war. Truman thought he was simply following in FDR's footsteps.

The Court was unimpressed. Presidents cannot seize private property without express authorization from Congress, the majority argued. Even a compelling state interest, like national security, requires certain conditions and/or approvals for the expansion of executive authority beyond what is expressly granted in the Constitution. Justice Hugo Black, writing for a divided Court, maintained that "in the framework of our Constitution, the President's power to see that the laws are faithfully executed refutes the idea that he is to be a lawmaker." It was Justice Robert H. Jackson's opinion that rose to the pragmatic top. He insisted that the President's power is at its height when he "acts pursuant to an express or implied authorization of Congress" and is at its lowest when "the President takes measures incompatible with the expressed or implied will of Congress."[20] President Truman's actions were unconstitutional because they were in defiance of Congress' wishes; they fell under Jackson's "lowest ebb" category. Defeated, Truman would return the mills to their private owners.

Truman's unsuccessful attempt to nationalize the steel mills added fodder for the advocates of presidential term limits. And so on Tuesday, June 16th, Percival Baxter rose to address his fellow convention colleagues. Ever the professional, he had prepared remarks ahead of time for the occasion; he was not the type to wing anything, especially a speech in front of some of the most prominent American figures of the period. The central thread of his comments was the "runaway" presidency, a term he had used in other contexts to receptive audiences. He said he was concerned that comprehensive programs like the New Deal and the Fair Deal were undermining the power of the states, and that part of the reason for the weakening of state power could be traced back to FDR's stronghold on the presidency. He said he was interested in strengthening state jurisdiction over police powers—a conversation he looked forward to having with the delegation—but for now, he insisted that imposing term limits on the presidency was an appropriate response and one that would bring balance back to America's coordinated system of separate powers and federalism. He concluded by offering a motion to add the following clause to the 1953 draft Constitution: "No person shall be elected to the office of the President more than twice." The clause, he suggested, should be inserted into Article III—the article that described the powers, requirements, and processes of the executive branch.

The clandestine states' rights group of delegates had decided that Rush Holt would rise to second Baxter's motion. Once a Democrat, Holt had switched his party affiliation to the Republican side in 1949, and now he was a staunch critic of unilateral federal power. His second carried some weight. Driscoll was then quick to announce *his* support for the measure, adding comments on the virtues of a strong federalist structure. In all, close to a dozen delegates voiced some form of endorsement for the motion proposed by Percival Baxter. He was feeling positive about its prospects.

There was a problem with the proposal, however: the status of President Truman himself. Truman's experience in first assuming the presidency was comparatively unusual, and it highlighted the potential oversight in Baxter's proposed resolution. Specifically, Truman was thrust into office on April 12th, 1945, because of FDR's unexpected death. Truman was not elected to the office in 1944, but he served as President for all but eighty-two days of that particular term. How should a constitutional provision limiting the number of terms a President can remain in office deal with situations where a Vice President, like Truman, assumes the office because of the death or disability of his predecessor? Does the partial term count toward the two described by Baxter in his convention proposal? Or does someone like Truman get a third term because of the unusual circumstances of his initial elevation? Truman, himself, had ordered a report from a commission, headed by former President Herbert Hoover, that called for some type of presidential term limit. The Hoover Commission report was followed by a group of congressional members, led by the new

Republican majority, floating the idea of a ten-year limit on the presidency. The ten-year limit represented a precise calculation that a President could rise to the position for two full years and then be elected twice more. Truman's situation, therefore, would permit him to run for reelection only once. A second elected term would exceed the ten-year maximum.

A first-term Senator from Illinois, Everett Dirksen, was quick to point out the inherent difficulty in Baxter's resolution. Dirksen argued that there had to be language that accounts for a Vice President stepping into the job and leading over a partial term. The resolution would cause confusion if it were to stand as is, he insisted. The solution he proposed mirrored the work of the Hoover Commission: allow a President to serve no more than ten years in office—two full terms plus two years of another term. He thus offered an amendment to the earlier proposal. The revised proposal read: "No person shall be elected to the office of the President more than twice and no person who has held the office of President for more than two years of a term to which another person was elected President shall be elected to the office of President more than once." It was clear and to the point. Dirksen thought it was the correct approach to the term limit problem.

Both the original proposal and Dirksen's amendment enjoyed wide support among the delegates; this would prove one of the least contentious parts of the 1953 Convention gathering. Most Republicans and Democrats in Congress and in the statehouses across the country had already signaled that this new constitutional rule would be good for the nation. The vote in favor of adopting the complete resolution was not even close. The 1953 draft Constitution would include the provision. More interestingly and unexpectedly, the conversation about presidential term limits led directly to candid talks about other recommendations for government efficiency, specifically those that came out of the Hoover Commission. Roughly 70 percent of the commission's recommended reforms were implemented by legislative or executive action. But could the Constitution do more to consolidate departments and streamline governance? Some delegates were in favor of exploring possibilities, while others felt the Constitution was not the proper vehicle to address purely administrative matters. It was a debate that would emerge at various times throughout the proceedings.

By mid-summer, the delegates to the 1953 Constitutional Convention had managed to expand the draft text so much that it now weighed in as the longest U.S. Constitution ever written. Added were details that are quite common in state Constitutions, but were not yet a part of any federal charter. Take "exemptions from taxation" as an example. There had been no mention of institutions and organizations being exempt from federal tax rules in any prior national Constitution. The original 1787 clause allowing Congress the power to "lay and collect taxes" had remained untouched through each of the three previous constitutional iterations. In addition, a tax amendment, introduced immediately after the 1903 Constitutional Convention and ratified in 1913, had made its way into the body of the 1953 Constitution. That clause empowered the federal government to collect income tax. Finally, the several mentions of taxes in the less obvious corners of the Constitution also remained: the apportionment of Representatives and taxes based on population in Article II, Section 2, Clause 2; the ban on taxes laid in the absence of a census in Article II, Section 9, Clause 4; and the prohibition against imposing taxes on the importation of goods from other states in the very next clause.[21] But that was it. The word *tax* did not appear in any other section of any generational Constitution. In all, a mere 103 words constituted the entirety of the clauses mentioning taxation in the 1903 Constitution.

Delegates in 1953 wanted greater specification of tax burdens and responsibilities. So, resolutions were introduced that clarified certain areas of the law. Some passed; others did not. One resolution borrowed directly from Georgia's 1945 State Constitution.

It identified those situations and organizations that would be exempt from federal tax burdens. Its first sentence read: "Congress may, by law, exempt from taxation all public property, places of religious worship or burial, all institutions of purely public charity, and all property owned by or irrevocably held in trust for the exclusive benefit of religious, educational, and charitable institutions." The clause that eventually made it into Article II (the legislative article) was almost 400 words in length and included details that smacked of a standard legal code. Delegates, nonetheless, preferred this level of specification.

They did so as well with other components of the draft Constitution. The delegates to the 1953 Philadelphia Convention included provisions for the salaries of many federal employees, the rights and obligations of "corporations," the process of employing public referenda during national elections, and even, in Article II, Section 7, Clause 3, the particulars of "reading" joint resolutions in each house of Congress. These provisions were inspired by the state constitutions of the time; there was a logic of sorts to their inclusion in the federal text. To the citizens who grew up revering the short U.S. Constitutions of the past because they held a certain magisterial quality, however, the insertion of relatively mundane provisions like the ones added to the 1953 draft represented a substantial loss. Gone was the brevity of prior charters, and with it the sense that only the most fundamental provisions for ordering an entire polity should be included in such instruments. Gone was the Constitution's simple elegance.

Perhaps the greatest insult to fans of the simpler Constitution came in early August when E. James Winslow, a delegate from Keene, New Hampshire, moved that the federal Constitution include a provision that officials be reimbursed for mileage while conducting the business of government. In particular, Winslow thought that Members of Congress should be compensated for their out-of-pocket expenses while in both regular and special legislative sessions. He had proposed a similar measure in 1948 when he represented his town at the New Hampshire Constitutional Convention. The Granite Stater now claimed that this was standard in contemporary constitutions; all the states have provisions like this, he insisted. Nevertheless, the proposal could not gain any traction. Some delegates thought it frivolous, unnecessary in the extreme. Others thought it cheapened the legitimacy and credibility of the draft text. Still others worried about ratification, fearing that securing the necessary support of the states would be more difficult if the draft Constitution included provisions as mundane as the one Winslow suggested. In the end, his motion was never seriously considered, but it was symbolic and representative of the approach taken by this round of constitutional delegates.

It can be said that the impact of Winslow's proposal went well beyond a mere mention in the minutes of the 1953 Convention. Somewhat circuitously, it brought to the foreground a potential defect in each of America's four prior Constitutions: the threshold for ratification. As delegates began to question whether banal provisions might jeopardize the entire ratification effort, they turned their attention to the philosophical underpinnings of the ratification process itself. They dissected its various stages and contemplated each portion of the process. In the end, no one in Philadelphia suggested replacing ratification with another route to public endorsement, but they did home in on one awkward piece. For the first time, the delegates seriously contemplated altering the ratio of states needed to endorse the draft charter.

Here's the problem: the 1787 Framers went public with a draft Constitution that required only *nine* of the thirteen states to ratify it—a mere 69 percent. If nine states ratified, Article VII stipulated, the Constitution would become authoritative; it would replace the Articles of Confederation and become the law of the land. But authoritative for whom? All the states? Or only those that ratified the text? The language of Article VII suggests the latter. It reads: "The Ratification of the Conventions of nine States shall be sufficient for the Establishment of this Constitution *between the states so ratifying the Same*" (emphasis added). The Constitution would only apply to those states that certified it.

Ratification was a state's admission ticket into the Union; it was a requirement for inclusion. The 1787 Framers were clearly not willing to subject *non*-ratifying states to the particulars of their new Constitution. Of course, we now know that any concerns about those resistant states became moot on May 29th, 1790, when Rhode Island became the thirteenth and final state to endorse the new Constitution. Still, questions were raised. Why not require all thirteen states to ratify the text in the first place? Why stop at only nine? And why nine? How about ten? Or eight? Or just a majority?

The answers to these questions are fairly simple, and they have everything to do with one of the most underappreciated (and radical) plans set in motion by the 1787 Framers: to achieve in the citizenry a universal and self-conscious shift in allegiance from their state governments to the national, unified polity. In the late eighteenth century, the concept of a nation of *united* states was both new and untested. Citizens did not consider themselves, first and foremost, Americans. Their primary allegiance was to their independent state. As Jefferson once remarked, "Virginia, Sir, is my country." Almost all at that time would have related to Jefferson's view: individuals were citizens of the state in which they lived and only distantly participants in this new experiment in national unification. "The states were Free and Independent not only from Britain but also from each other," write Cynthia and Sanford Levinson. "Thirteen disjointed minirepublics were strung along the Atlantic seaboard, not really part of a cohesive country under a single government. Each state had its own political system, money, and constitution."[22] In short, people understood their country to be the state in which they resided; there was little conception of being an "*American* citizen."

It was thus easy for the Framers to imagine a scenario in which one or more states would refuse to ratify a fundamental law that shifted large swaths of power from the states to an unknown federal government. The Framers feared the tyranny of this minority. They worried that perhaps a single state would not sign onto the new Constitution and, instead, would choose to remain an independent nation. The whole constitutional project would thus hinge on the inclinations of that single state. Publius said as much in *Federalist* 40: "Instead of reporting a plan requiring the confirmation of the legislatures of all the states, they have reported a plan which is to be confirmed by the people, and may be carried into effect by nine states only. It is worthy of remark that [any] objection [to this number], though the most plausible, has been the least urged in the publications which have swarmed against the Convention. The forbearance can only have proceeded from an irresistible conviction of the absurdity of subjecting the fate of twelve states to the perverseness or corruption of a thirteenth." The wishes of a supermajority of states (and people) were therefore not going to be held hostage by the disapproval of a single state.

There was more to it, of course. Mark Graber has suggested that the 1787 Framers took a calculated risk—a high-stakes gamble—in requiring only nine endorsements. In a sense, the Framers intended to play states off of each other. The threshold of nine, Graber says, encouraged states to get out in front and ratify early. "Nine encouraged early ratification while preventing holdout states from extracting favorable concessions."[23] In other words, the 1787 constitutional drafters understood that if nine states ratified early—a prospect that seemed likely—the hesitant states would have no leverage to demand compromises.[24] All incentives to stay out of the Union would be diminished, and these hesitant states would presumably fall into line. The Framers were gambling on the momentum of early state ratification. And it worked. Eventually, the Framers got what they wanted: citizens of the newly formed United States emerged from the ratification debates with a constitutional document *unanimously* certified.

Furthermore, as Graber also points out, there was no debate about what would happen to the holdout states if they refused to ratify. This was because the Federalists did not want to suggest to the state Ratifying Conventions that the Framers would be satisfied with a couple of resisters, that they would give the disapproving states a free pass. The Constitution, Graber essentially says, speaks of "We the People," not of "We the *Ratifying* People." Nowhere in the text, aside from Article VII itself, was it anticipated that some states would choose to remain on the ratification sidelines, and so the implicit message was to get on board with this particular Constitution. In Graber's words, "the point of nine was to get to thirteen."[25]

The insistence that only a subsection of states was enough to trigger consent, and that the federal government would not necessarily go away, was an interesting moment in the history of pragmatic government. The gamble paid off once, but would it again? The complex issue of the ratifying threshold lingered into the next federal convention, though again there was little formal discussion about changing the basic formula.[26] Convention-goers in 1825 thought it was appropriate to follow the spirit of the original Philadelphia Framers. It was then that they did something radical: they dropped the last part of the original Article VII sentence. The new constitutional article read, "The Ratification of the Conventions of eighteen States shall be sufficient for the Establishment and Authority of this Constitution." Missing was any mention in the 1825 Constitution that the new text applied only to the states "so ratifying the Same." The words were simply dropped. The result was a kind of benign ignorance. Without the qualifying (and clarifying) language, the union of ratifying states could simply continue its business while the small group of non-ratifying states sat around puzzled.

In preparing for the possibility that certain states might reject ratification, the framers of the 1825 Constitution pointed to Article V's amendment process for reinforcement. To amend the Constitution, several cumbersome steps are required, including passage of two-thirds of both Houses of Congress followed by ratification of three-fourths of all the states. The process does not call for unanimity. Several 1825 delegates consequently asked the logical question: If Madison and his colleagues were satisfied with less than unanimity for constitutional amendments— including the Bill of Rights, arguably the most important part of the Constitution we have inherited—why are we so worried about unanimity in the ratification of the entire text? Any amendment to any U.S. Constitution applies to the 25 percent of states that refuse to ratify the amendment (or never bring it to a vote) just as it applies to the 75 percent of states that successfully ratify it. Put another way, a state that chooses *not* to ratify an amendment cannot escape that amendment's provisions if three-fourths of the other states agree that it should be added to the Constitution. There is no equivalent "so ratifying the same" clause in Article V. Consequently, the 1825 delegation argued, a less than unanimous ratification of the entire text is perfectly acceptable.

As more and more states joined the Union, the number of states needed to ratify simply increased, but the percentage—roughly 70 percent—stayed the same. In 1825, the Constitution required eighteen out of the twenty-four states to endorse the text, while in 1903 the number was thirty-four out of forty-five. (The 1863 Constitution was an anomaly in that the draft text required only a simple majority—eighteen out of thirty-five—because the Confederate states were absent from the proceedings and the framers did not know what to expect once these territories rejoined the Union.)

Throughout the decades, the same concerns plagued delegates to the constitutional convention. Earlier delegates remained a bit anxious about the problem of the tyranny of a small minority. Most were also not yet fully confident that members of state Ratifying Conventions would completely identify with the nation over their individual states. Delegates understood that no one was still uttering their own version of the words Jefferson spoke—"Virginia, Sir, is my country"—but many citizens still held some allegiance to their home states. That worried framers through the years, so that no constitutional framer prior to 1953 had been willing to abandon the supermajority requirement for a rule of unanimity.

Things began to shift in the late 1940s and early '50s. Americans trusted their government in record numbers during this period. There was a shared optimism about the future; Americans were not disillusioned about the path they were on. The

Pew Research Center found that, in the decade of the 1950s, 80 percent of all Americans believed that government would "do what is right just about always or most of the time." (Compare that period to today, where the figure stands at less than 20%.)[27] Delegates to the 1953 Constitutional Convention could feel that pervasive sense of trust, that optimism, even as they criticized the actions of various politicians. Republicans, for example, disagreed with Truman's positions on a number of issues, but they rarely questioned his motivations. They had faith that he was moved not by his own private interests but by those of his party and of the nation. They wanted him out of office, to be sure, but not because they believed he was acting outside of some powerful commitment to advancing the interests of the nation. They just disagreed with his agenda.

The faith that eight in ten Americans had in the motivations and instincts of the federal government bolstered the delegates' opinion that now was the time to consider a higher threshold for ratification. Additionally, the way in which World War II had unfolded—Pearl Harbor, D-Day, VE Day—infused most Americans with a sense of national pride, a confidence that together we were striving toward a common future. Perhaps now, 166 years removed from the time when the Framers of the original Constitution were scared to test the national identity of the people and almost 90 years removed from a civil war based on states' rights and regionalism, the time had come to test the strength of a nation of truly *united* states.

For that reason, Harold Patten, Democratic Congressman from Arizona, moved on August 3rd that Article VIII, describing the process of ratification, include a requirement that all forty-eight states endorse the draft text. There are many advantages to requiring unanimity, he argued. To begin with, it erases the awkwardness of rationalizing decisions by states that ultimately refuse to ratify. Patten then gave a brief history lesson. Ever since the 1787 Constitution was ratified by all thirteen states, he said, subsequent Constitutions have been ratified by most, but not all, state Ratifying Conventions. Inevitably, then, the editorial

244 — A Constitution for the Living

pages are filled for a short time with comments about what that means for those states that rejected the new plan of government. Are they not subject to the endorsed Constitution, he asked? Do they enjoy some special relationship with the Constitution and/ or with those states that ratified the text? Do citizens across the country simply ignore the fact that certain states were never really on board with the fresh text?

These questions were always present, he insisted, but inevitably they were inconsequential. Sweeping the awkwardness under the rug was the preferred choice of all past ratification efforts. Once the wording from the 1787 Constitution was altered to remove the section binding only those states that ratify the text, the national government (aside from 1863) simply treated the metaphorically Federalist and anti-Federalist states alike. Whether you supported the Constitution or not, all was forgiven after a time. No more, he thought. The time has come for the framers to display the courage to mandate unanimity. It would be good for the country to stand together in support of this Constitution. It would be patriotic.

Shortly after Patten concluded his remarks, Hazel Baker Denton, a Democratic Assemblywoman from Nevada, stood to second the motion. Denton had been a grade school teacher all her adult life until she retired in 1952. She decided then that she would run for the State Assembly on the Democratic ticket. She won on a platform of enhancing public schools, libraries, and state parks. She was, at the time, one of only two women elected to statewide office. Her interest in altering the threshold for ratification derived from her steadfast patriotic fervor. She was a true pioneer, in both the literal sense (her family was among the first to settle in rural Utah and then in rural Nevada) and the metaphorical sense (she was a gender trailblazer). In her mind, she was the epitome of American ingenuity and independence. She, more so than most, felt a powerful devotion to the United States of America. The country had been good to her.

Patten and Denton felt righteous about the resolution. They immediately moved that the Constitution include the following article: "The Ratification of the Conventions of all 48 States shall be necessary for the Establishment of this Constitution." The wording was purposefully lean. Let there be no confusion, they argued. They were, in essence, reinserting a qualifier in this formulation. The threshold was now unanimity. Never satisfied with the first iteration, the delegation fiddled with the word "necessary" for a time. Some suggested that "required" represented a sturdier word choice. Several straw polls were taken. But in the end the assembly circled around to Patten's original expression. The final vote on August 10th was overwhelmingly in favor of approval. Patten and Denton left the convention that day feeling triumphant, though the interesting irony of that moment was completely lost on them. The new ratification article, at eighteen words, was now the shortest article ever drafted for a federal Constitution. Ironically, it was embedded in the longest federal Constitution ever presented for ratification.

Shortly before Labor Day, the delegation prepared to charge the Committee of Detail with the important task of placing all the convention's work—all the agreed-upon resolutions—into a single constitutional draft. This moment always marked the beginning of the end of the entire convention session. The Committee of Detail would then take the disassembled clauses and order them into a coherent whole. The prior federal Constitutions provided ample guides for the Committee's primary task, but there was still plenty of work to do, especially in this year when the length of the Constitution expanded so significantly. It would take some time to check the precise language and organize the entire document. The 1787 Committee of Detail took two weeks to complete its task; the 1953 Committee could expect to do the same.

In 1953, the Committee of Detail consisted of thirteen convention delegates selected by the entire assembly (the number was chosen in honor of the thirteen original states). The only rule for selection was that each committee member had to come

246 - A Constitution for the Living

from a different region of the United States, a clear nod to the 1787 Committee of Detail, which consisted of five members, all representing different parts of the country. Robert Clothier, the fourteenth President of Rutgers University, was chosen to be the chair. Clothier was an inspired choice, not because he was Princeton educated or a war veteran, or even because he was once a *Wall Street Journal* reporter or currently the leader of a major state university. The decision to place him in charge of the Committee of Detail made perfect sense because he had served so effectively as President of the 1947 New Jersey Constitutional Convention, the exact same one that Governor Alfred Driscoll thought so critical to the future of his state. Clothier's experience in crafting a constitutional document, albeit a state one, prepared him nicely for the responsibility of overseeing the construction of the 1953 federal text. He was honored to lead such a vital committee.

A Committee of Detail was assembled for every constitutional convention, beginning with the first in 1787. It has always been an important committee for several reasons: first, it is responsible for organizing the final constitutional draft; second, it is expected that the committee will incorporate provisions and clauses never considered or debated during the convention; and third, it enjoys a certain liberty to modify language already agreed upon so as to maximize consistency throughout the document. Consider the latter two jobs of the committee. They are impressively large in scope and power. A tiny subgroup of the larger collective is empowered to introduce language into the text and to take the language passed by the convention delegates and alter it to fit the committee's image of the ideal Constitution. Though no minutes have ever been taken during any of the committee meetings through the years, we have some sense of the scale of its influence by comparing the minutes of the full convention to the report of the committee. They are often quite different, suggesting that the committee adds and subtracts with impunity.

In terms of its first responsibility, that is clearly marked. Whenever a Committee of Detail is established, its formal charge is to finalize the document for ultimate consideration by the full assembly. The committee's second and third responsibilities are a bit less obvious. Beginning in 1787, members of the committee saw it as their duty to include constitutional clauses and provisions that might not have received the same attention as others. Further, they maintained that they had the authority to modify language already passed.[28] One example of a clause added to the 1787 Constitution by the Committee of Detail is the one that exempts members of the House and Senate from arrest when engaging in "speech or debate" in either chamber. Another, interestingly, is the Necessary and Proper Clause.[29]

The most famous liberty taken by a Committee of Detail occurred in 1787 when the members wrestled with the precise language of the Preamble. They had little guidance from the full convention on the exact nature of the sovereign. Was the Constitution derived from the people or from the states, they wondered? Perhaps it was the people from the individual states? Either way, it seemed this was a crucial question to have answered, and one that the framers had neglected for most of the proceedings. The committee's report eventually took a sort of middle ground on the issue; it mentioned both the people and the states. The first proposed Preamble, which came from the Committee of Detail and was inspired by the Preamble to the Articles of Confederation, read, "We the people of the States of New Hampshire, Massachusetts, Rhode Island and Providence Plantations, Connecticut, New-York, New-Jersey, Pennsylvania, Delaware, Maryland, Virginia, North-Carolina, South-Carolina, and Georgia, do ordain, declare, and establish the following Constitution for the Government of Ourselves and our Posterity." That didn't sound right. Borrowing from the Preamble to the Articles set the wrong tone. Disappointed with the compromise taken by the committee and with the lack of aspirational language, therefore, several members of the full delegation drafted an alternative that dropped the state list and inserted the now famous phrase, "We the People of the United States," and included all the aspirations the Constitution was intended to realize.

Dropping the list of states and identifying the People of the United States as authorizing the Constitution made all the difference. Ever since then, federal Constitutions have been generated by the People and not the states, and by a citizenry with allegiance primarily to some national entity called the "United States of America." The work of the 1787 Committee of Detail, and the subsequent discussion about its report, contributed to a recognition of the true sovereign in America.

One other interesting liberty taken by a prior Committee of Detail deserves mention. In 1825, the framers handed over their disassembled set of clauses, resolutions, and provisions to the Committee of Detail without giving much thought to the exact wording of the Preamble. Enamored with the majesty of the existing aspirational language, they had just transferred the existing Preamble in its entirety to the new text. The Committee of Detail, however, noticed an inconsistency with the Jeffersonian ideal for generational constitutional change: the application of any future federal Constitution to "our Posterity."

The Preamble listed the various goals of the Constitution, those goals with which Americans have become so familiar. Included in this list is a pledge that the Constitution will "form a more perfect Union, establish Justice, insure domestic tranquility, provide for the common defense, promote the general welfare, and secure the blessings of liberty." It then identified two constituents who, hopefully, will benefit from this Constitution: the current people ("Ourselves") and a future people ("our Posterity"). The reference to current people makes sense. It is quite reasonable for the Constitution to try to achieve these aspirational goals for the living population that crafted and ratified the document. The members of the 1825 Committee of Detail noticed, however, that the Constitution's goal of protecting a *future* people is, under the Jeffersonian theory of generational constitutional change, both unnecessary and dangerous. Why mention the Constitution's application to "our Posterity" if each generation has the power to write its own Constitution? It makes no sense. Seeing that important point, the 1825 Committee of

Detail erased any reference to posterity in the Constitution's Pre-amble.[30] It has never been reinserted.

Turning back to 1953, the Committee of Detail issued its re-port to the full assembly on Friday, September 18th. The report was ready for delivery the day before, but convention delegates took the 17th off to celebrate the anniversary of the signing of America's original Constitution. This report was different from those in the past. Clothier's committee was apparently less willing to add or subtract clauses and less likely to fiddle with the work of the full convention. The completely constructed Constitution that came back resembled pretty closely the one most delegates had imagined. Commentators have speculated that the deference shown by the committee was tied to the increasing attention paid to the general proceedings. Fearing a public backlash from add-ing, subtracting, or modifying language previously accepted by the full convention, the members of the committee chose to stick close to the agreed-upon material. Other observers have conjec-tured that Clothier was a different type of leader and that he approached the work in a unique way. He didn't follow the theory that the Committee of Detail maintains independent authority to substantively alter the text. His prior stint as President of the New Jersey Constitutional Convention, where he barely uttered a word, supports this inference. Either way, the Committee of Detail produced a handsome constitutional text, one that reflected the priorities of the World War II generation. It came as a relief to the full assembly that they would not have to battle the Committee on the particulars. The stage was set for the 1953 Convention to rise and submit its composition to the people for ratification.

The Convention Adjourns

By 1953, the romantic image of delegates lining up on the final day of the convention to place their signatures at the bottom of the text, an image imprinted on American minds by the pop-ularity of Howard Chandler Christy's 1940 oil painting depict-ing the 1787 signing, deviated substantially from the reality. Fewer than half the delegates were still present on Thursday,

October 22nd, when the 1953 Convention formally adjourned. The other half were absent because of prior commitments or, in a small handful of cases, because they chose to abandon the project altogether. Most of the absentees would travel to Philadelphia in the weeks that followed to officially, and ceremonially, sign the draft Constitution, but the Assembly Hall was noticeably empty that morning when Gerald Ford called the convention to order for the final time.

Conversation ensued while delegates awaited their turn at the signing station, a table at the front of the room where Ford regularly sat. One conversation among four delegates was particularly interesting. It was started when Dr. Ernest Irons turned to his benchmate and asked a simple question: Is James Madison getting the last laugh in the debate about constitutional endurance? Dr. Irons, past President of the American Medical Association and outspoken critic of Truman's plan for a national health care program, had been contemplating the temporal distance between federal conventions, and he was beginning to worry that too much time was allowed to elapse, that the number of decades between conventions was beginning to put stress on Jefferson's fundamental principle that "the world belongs in usufruct to the living." The periods between the first few gatherings were less than forty years. The distance between the last two was fifty. And now, based on actuarial tables that clearly indicated the average American was living a considerably longer life, it appeared that the next federal constitutional convention would not occur until well into the twenty-first century. Irons had done some rough calculations and he determined that the next convention would happen sometime around 2020. It turned out that he was off by a mere two years.

The question he posed to his fellow delegates was a good one. Could it be said that Madison lost the battle with Jefferson, but over time, he was winning the war? By mandating constitutional conventions on a generational cycle, were Americans creating the conditions for a more or less enduring constitutional text? The average national constitution around the world, after all, lasts only fifteen years.[31] Irons was predicting that the one he and his fellow delegates were about to sign was going to constitute the American republic for more than *four times* that average. There was a part of him that was troubled by such a realization. He counted himself among the vast majority of Americans who had grown up in a Jeffersonian world. Drafting new constitutional charters every generation was both expected and routine. It was now built into the very essence of the American tale.

He went on. If enough time passed between constitutional conventions, he wondered, could Americans really claim that these freshly designed plans for government effectively captured the social, political, and economic trends of a particular generation? Should we even care about trends and fads, which can happen in political organization just as easily as they can happen in fashion or culture? Though not concerned about the possible emergence of fascism in the United States, he cited the examples of interwar Germany and Italy to help prove his point. The authoritarian regimes of Hitler and Mussolini rose and fell—began and ended—in between the two twentieth-century Constitutions produced in the United States. Could something like that happen in the United States? It seemed unlikely and maybe even absurd. Even so, a generational cycle of constitutional reform was not an ideal mechanism to forestall such erratic changes in the political landscape. The mechanism of drafting new constitutional texts would not, for instance, have caught such a disaster as the rise of authoritarianism because the expanse of years between Constitutions was so large, and getting larger.

Consider the span of time between the last two conventions, he continued. The entire fabric of American society changed in those five decades. What was acceptable socially and politically in 1903 was thoroughly outdated by 1953. Even the mass consumerism and rebelliousness of the roaring twenties eventually gave way to a more prudish and restrained style in the 1950s. Irons was brash and arrogant, but even he admitted to utter ignorance about what would come from innovators during the next stretch of time: advancements and creativity or movement in some unexpected direction. Human progress, he concluded, is not linear.

Dr. Irons walked away from the constitutional convention deeply conflicted about what the collective had accomplished. He had no answers to the questions in his mind. To be sure, like so many delegates that year, he was exceptionally proud of the Constitution they had produced. He was convinced that the document denoted many of the current generation's priorities. But he also understood that forces were working against the draft's success. The longer the period between constitutional conventions, the more flexible a constitutional charter needed to be; and the more detailed a constitutional text is, the less flexible it is capable of being. He worried that the delegation had drafted the wrong kind of Constitution for the current circumstances.

And so, the fundamental question for Irons and for an America that had grown comfortable with rapid constitutional change, was whether the extraordinarily long Constitution produced in 1953 could withstand the massive upheaval likely in almost every corner of American culture over the next sixty-nine years. Was it pliable enough—broad enough in its language and meaning—to weather the revolutions in technology, communication, finance, politics, social connectedness, climate, justice, and authority that could be about to come? Or would it leave institutions and citizens alike confused and frustrated by its inflexibility? Time was both the adversary and the redeemer, the enemy and the savior. Time could prove too much for the 1953 Constitution, or the text could surprise the public and survive into a totally different world. James Madison, Irons thought, would have enjoyed watching this play out. Thomas Jefferson too.

2022 ——

THEY SAY THAT DISRUPTION is the key to innovation. There is, in fact, an entire business model that insists on the incomparable value of product and market displacement. Consider just a few examples: Uber and Lyft have fundamentally disrupted the traditional taxicab market; similarly, Airbnb is now challenging the established hotel chains for market dominance.[1]

To be sure, disruption can be thrilling. It can also be frightening, especially for the traditionalist who refuses to acknowledge the fresh paradigm. The stakes get even higher for the traditionalist when we add other, subjective variables, beyond simple market share and profits, into the equation: variables like values, ideology, politics, justice, equity, morality, and faith. One cannot record them on a simple ledger sheet or easily measure them with existing statistical instruments. As such, their presence tends to exacerbate the inevitable divide between the traditionalist's status quo and the disrupter's modernization and change.

Historically, the constitution-making enterprise has favored the traditionalist. Even now, most constitutions are still forged with traditional tools (conventions, deliberations, debates, resolutions, articles, and so forth) and traditional characters (mainly lawyers and politicians). But when we apply the disrupter model to constitution-making, some fascinating insights emerge. Constitutions change and so can the process of drafting them. One is right to ask, then, what are the chances that the paradigmatic approach to constitution-making will be replaced by an altogether different drafting model?

Thankfully, some of the answers to our most pressing questions are beginning to emerge. Indeed, an innovative and fresh approach to constitution-writing surfaced in the early twenty-first century and it holds genuine disruptive possibilities. It was practically the first new idea in constitutional formation—the first real disrupter—since the American Framers decided to lend pen to paper in the late eighteenth century. If successful, the idea could fundamentally change the entire paradigm for constitutional formation. *If* successful. That would be the looming question. To its immense credit, the small island nation of Iceland was the first to summon the courage to give it a go. Sadly, that courage was not fully rewarded. "Crowdsourcing" a nation's constitutional text would prove far more difficult than originally thought.[2]

Iceland's 2011 effort to crowdsource its new constitutional text was bold and inventive. The idea made a lot of sense. In their democratic country, with a proud tradition of popular sovereignty, Icelanders have come to expect a certain participatory role in the political process. Rather than follow the customary rules of constitution-making, the small North Atlantic nation decided to try something altogether different: encourage as many voices as possible to participate in the framing process and use contemporary technology and social media to lure all interested citizens to the drafting table. Iceland's 2009 elections helped. When word came down that the coalition government led by the Social Democrats was considering a major constitutional overhaul, citizens began to ask: why not invite all Icelanders to play constitutional framer? Iceland could be a maverick nation, nonconformist in its approach to constitution-making. It could reside at the vanguard of a whole new movement to push back the curtain on the secretive world of constitutional drafting. The result of the process was not quite revolutionary, but it surely was creative.

The story is worth recounting. It all began with the devastating, worldwide financial crisis in 2008.[3] The sentiment among most Icelanders was that their country's Constitution significantly contributed to the country's economic collapse. The original text was written in 1944, as Iceland gained independence from Denmark, and it seemed to work reasonably well until 2008, when the country's three major private banks suddenly defaulted. The financial devastation left most Icelanders reeling.

Not surprisingly, calls for reform started immediately, and included in those calls was a proposal to reimagine the country's fundamental law. Advocates for constitutional reform pushed for two outcomes: first, drafting a constitutional text that would prevent a recurrence of the financial crisis; and second, regaining the trust of citizens by emphasizing "accountability" in constitution-making and government action. These advocates organized massive public protests, the largest in the country's history. Thousands showed up at the Parliament building in Reykjavík on January 20th, 2009, to demand the resignation of Iceland's leaders.

Iceland's overall plan to crowdsource portions of its constitutional-drafting process materialized shortly thereafter. That process would occur in a few distinct stages. It began in 2009 with the random selection of roughly 1,200 private citizens and 300 representatives from industries, institutions, and other organizations. What was fascinating about this National Assembly (as its members called themselves) was that it was formed privately, from grassroots organizations. The responsibility of this National Assembly was to identify the country's "core values" by surveying the population. Over time, the National Assembly determined that "honesty and integrity" were the country's premier values. These were followed by "respect, justice, love, equal rights, sustainability, democracy, responsibility, freedom, family, equality, and trust." There was conversation about other values, including economic stability and freedom, but those did not rise to the very top. Meanwhile, government officials convened another group, this time made up of only about 950 citizens. This government-sponsored National Assembly was given the same assignment as the private operation, and it identified the same core values.

The next stage of the process was for the Constitutional Assembly, an elected group of twenty-five, to translate the core values into specific constitutional language.[4] The Constitutional Assembly was given sixty days to complete a brand-new constitutional draft. But even before the group started, complaints emerged about the entire election process, eventually leading the country's highest court to rule the election "null and void." This came as a relief to a small traditionalist segment of the population that thought the whole process of constitutional revision was silly and fraught. Not to be deterred, the Icelandic Parliament then pulled an end run and voted to appoint members to the Constitutional Assembly, managing to appoint almost every individual who had previously been elected.

Over the next several months, the twenty-five (now appointed) members of the Constitutional Assembly took to the task of constructing a draft Constitution. This is where the crowdsourcing really occurred. More than 3,600 Icelanders from across the country offered commentary. The Constitutional Assembly incorporated their ideas and delivered a completed draft Constitution to the Parliament in late July 2011.

The constitutional text and all the crowdsourcing data were now in Parliament's hands. The Constitution never came to a parliamentary vote, however. On the eve of such a vote, it was decided that any pronouncement about the future of the draft Constitution should wait until after the 2013 parliamentary elections. Those elections were held, and the result was a majority coalition that was largely opposed to any new Constitution. The traditionalists had reasserted their power. All the work of the National Assembly, the Constitutional Assembly, the past Parliament, and most importantly, the crowdsourcing population would be tabled. The complicated process of inviting all to the drafting table had yielded no tangible outcome. And yet the legacy of Iceland's crowdsourcing experiment would endure.

The United States and the world were watching. As the 2022 U.S. Constitutional Convention approached, talk of including more voices in the process intensified. Inspired by Iceland's attempt to crowdsource portions of its constitution-making process, various groups, including many watchdog organizations focused on greater government accountability, called for a similar model in the United States. In a rare convergence of corporate minds, the Heritage Foundation, Brookings Institution, and Cato Institute spoke in unison about the need for broader public participation. Congress, which retains the supervisory power to call constitutional conventions, listened. It formed a Joint Committee of the House and Senate in 2015 and charged it with figuring out the logistics of the event, including what role the general population would play in the document's eventual drafting.[5] To be sure, the task of pulling together a legitimate and credible constitutional convention was complicated. No one could claim that the environment for constitution-making resembled anything like that which predated the 1953 Convention. Almost everything was different now.

Three public suggestions generated the most excitement in the years leading up to the convention. First, the Joint Congressional Committee on the 2022 Constitutional Convention considered a direct crowdsourcing approach in which citizens would be encouraged to engage in the drafting process itself. As with the editing of Wikipedia, this method would permit everyday citizens to go online and add, subtract, and alter an evolving constitutional draft. The procedure was intended to be organic and inclusive. The problem was that it favored those with the technological skill to make the changes, not to mention the will and the time to do the work. Those with enough (leisure) time to monitor ongoing changes to the constitutional draft and participate in the process would have the most input. Further, there was serious concern that those with little or no access to computers would find themselves on the outside of the process. Economic privilege would thus favor certain citizen-framers. Skeptics were quick to register their disappointment. All prior constitutional conventions, they said, have favored the wealthy. How is this any different? The Joint Committee then quickly rejected the direct crowdsourcing idea, on the grounds that too many were likely to be shut out of the process for it to be worthwhile.

The second tactic involved a simple Google app. The tech giant had recently introduced Constitute, an app designed to compare Constitutions throughout the world. It was geared mostly to constitutional scholars and members of constitutional conventions who were drafting new texts around the world. But it could easily be adapted to permit anyone with the app to play, video-game style, the part of a framer. Participants could be expected to design constitutions, or portions thereof, and then be asked if they wanted their ideas to be deposited in a database to help inform members of the 2022 Constitutional Convention. Doubtless, most would say yes. Unsurprisingly, Google was game to partner with the convention planning committee.

The third, and final, option was a hybrid of many methods, including a variation on the caucus style of electing officials, a national referendum, a series of discussion forums, an app, a string of polls, and even a version of so-called constitutional cafés. The hybrid method was popular because it seemed to leverage a number of mechanisms for broad public participation. Individual citizens could enter the discussion through the means that most suited them. The use of a caucus-style meeting was perhaps the most intriguing. The caucus approach is always appealing because it resembles the old New England town hall meetings we've come to romanticize. And yet our caucuses are very different from the town hall meetings in our colonial past. Caucuses, in the United States at least, are always partisan. By definition, they include individuals with similar interests. And indeed, in the constitution-making process, dividing citizen-framers along such party or ideological lines, at least during the initial stages, can be helpful. Such a plan avoids the threat of complete political stalemate. Party colleagues are capable of fighting, of course, but the chances of inertia are minimized in one-party dialogue.

Constitutional cafés also garnered some enthusiasm. They represented the development of a project begun by Christopher Phillips, who embarked on a cross-country tour to see what ordinary citizens thought of the Constitution and what reforms were needed to bring it in line with contemporary society.[6] He called the resulting conversations "constitutional cafés," and they revealed both bizarre and poignant solutions to the defects of America's experiment in constitutional government. Several advocates backed continuing the constitutional cafés in preparation for the upcoming Philadelphia convention, even going so far as to suggest that public service organizations like AmeriCorps could deploy their volunteers to facilitate the conversations and gather the data.

Over the course of seven years, the Joint Congressional Committee charged with setting the agenda for the 2022 Constitutional Convention contemplated all these suggestions. After extensive hearings and briefings, the Joint Committee settled the question of the public's involvement in the process. It was no longer acceptable, the committee concluded, to allow only political elites access to so much of the constitution-making (and ratifying) project. If countries like South Africa can invite hundreds of representative voices to the constitution-making table, and countries like Iceland can adopt technological tools for the modern constitution-making age, the United States can certainly embrace a new drafting model. The members of the congressional committee finally settled on the plan to use a variety of formats—from caucuses to apps to constitutional cafés—in order to solicit public opinion on the core priorities of a twenty-first-century constitutional generation. The COVID-19 pandemic derailed some of the plans, but others went on as scheduled. The sentiment among congressional leaders was that it is always healthier to offer more rather than fewer avenues for citizens to project their individual voices. That sentiment was widely applauded.

The crowdsourcing process yielded very interesting results. Perhaps the most striking outcome involved the occasional unorthodox proposal that surfaced. "Establish a new six-year presidential term," one thread suggested, "including a fifth-year extension referendum—that is, an up-or-down confirmation election—which could result in an additional two years in office for the President. In the event of a no-confidence vote from the American public, a new national election featuring candidates from both political parties would be held."[7] Another thread argued that federal court judges ought to remain on the bench for a "single, non-renewable term of fifteen years."[8] Still another proposed that Americans scrap the lengthy presidential primary process in favor of a four-month period, with a lottery to determine the order of state primaries.[9]

Other suggestions were more in line with what the Joint Congressional Committee expected. "An automatic voter registration system," for example, was a popular request. So were the presidential line-item veto and the balanced budget mandate. There were hundreds of suggestions for reforming the "unrepresentative Senate." Some called for a simple increase in the number of Senators apportioned to the more populous states; others called for the abolition of the institution altogether.

One suggestion, in particular, generated a lot of traction. "Create a constitutional requirement that all able-bodied young Americans devote at least two years of their lives to the service [military and otherwise] of their nation. This universal civic duty would be, in essence, a Declaration of Responsibilities to accompany the Declaration of Rights."[10]

It turned out that crowdsourcing the drafting process was just one of many logistical challenges faced by the Joint Committee of Congress. The American Bar Association immediately raised a concern about the scope of the convention's work.[11] The ABA warned against placing every possible article and clause on the table for reconsideration. Some provisions of the Constitution (the Declaration of Rights in Article I, for example) should be sacrosanct and untouchable. Regime stability, grounded in part by linking present values to the past, requires that certain constitutional principles remain intact. The 1953 Constitution retained many of the articles and sections of the original 1787 Constitution, and the ABA, among others, wanted that tradition to continue.

The Joint Committee also considered a proposal, first introduced by Larry Sabato, that delegates to the 2022 Convention should be elected rather than appointed. Sabato was adamant about the idea. "Just about everyone who has examined the subject [of delegate selection]," he wrote, "agrees that the delegates to a twenty-first-century convention should be elected by the people."[12] This proposal the Joint Committee did *not* ignore—in a way. The lawmakers decided that 81 percent of the 535-member delegation (corresponding to the total number of Representatives and Senators in Congress) would be popularly elected. The other 19 percent—100 delegates, or two from each state—would be selected by the state legislatures. The Joint Committee wanted not only to preserve some connection to the traditional delegate selection process but also to ensure that genuine expertise was available during the convention. Experts like Sabato himself should be in Philadelphia, the Joint Committee reasoned, and there was no guarantee that such experts would be chosen through an electoral process. Each state legislature could thus extend two "special" invitations as they saw fit.

The Joint Congressional Committee also considered a proposal to bar federal lawmakers from participating as delegates. This suggestion was awkward to say the least, as it involved Members of Congress barring themselves from participating. The motivation for this suggestion came from a group of activists passionate about accountability in public office who worried that federal legislators would try to influence debate in order to enhance their individual or institutional positions. The Joint Committee rejected that suggestion too, citing the presence of congressional colleagues at every federal convention over the past 230-plus years.[13] Lawmakers with experience are invaluable, they said, to a constitutional drafting convention.

Trepidation also came from the political right. Before his death in 2020, Tom Coburn, a Republican and former U.S. Senator from Oklahoma, voiced concerns from his perch as senior adviser to the Convention of States, an organization advocating for state-driven constitutional reform.[14] Coburn had long been a critic of the current Constitution. He had repeatedly and publicly assailed any effort to modify the Constitution that did *not* include the following conservative mainstays: control of the public debt, congressional term limits, restrictions on federal government overreach, repeal of the federal income tax, and greater power in the states. Other conservative thinkers have placed abortion restrictions, gun rights, immigration reform, and a complete overhaul of the health care system on that same list. Conservative leaders like Coburn were quick to get their opinions on record. They wanted the public to hear their platform early and often, for they were generally apprehensive about the overall membership of the convention. They feared that mainstream conservative opinions would likely be drowned out by more liberal voices.

Planning the 2022 Convention took almost seven years and involved thousands of volunteers. It cost American taxpayers tens of millions of dollars (and that did not include the outlay of funds from private organizations seeking to influence the deliberations). It was an entirely new process for most. Fewer than 10 percent of the current U.S. population were even alive during the previous constitutional convention in 1953. The principal achievement for most Americans this time around was the inclusion of their voices in the process and the establishment of specific means to capture the people's ideas and thoughts prior to the opening of the Philadelphia convention. The delegates thus had access to mounds of data.

In addition to certain structural adjustments, the collective data showed that Americans wanted to see greater attention to natural resources and the environment, congressional term limits, a discussion about rights such as privacy, a consideration of marriage equality, more forceful protection of democracy and the electoral process from foreign interference, an end to racial injustice and discrimination, and some gun control measures taken up. Most delegates were prepared to consider all of these issues and more. Of course, a smooth convention could not be guaranteed, but crowdsourcing was a fresh approach to modern constitution-making. The country collectively held its breath in anticipation.

It held its breath for another reason as well. The biggest shadow looming over the 2022 Constitutional Convention was the deep divide—political and otherwise—facing the country. Spurred in large part by the election of Donald Trump as President in 2016, social, racial, economic, and political divisions stood in sharper relief than at practically any other time in recent memory.[15] There could be no mistaking the fact that President Trump's actions, and the responses they generated, had dramatically altered the entire political landscape. Everything from partisan entrenchment to a rekindling of the culture wars to the country's racial reckoning following the George Floyd murder accompanied his presidency. Even the tragic COVID-19 pandemic and the election of Joe Biden as the 46th president couldn't release the country from the grip of partisanship and strife. And yet such are precisely the sparks that often energize the constitution-making process. It is difficult to put aside differences and come together when the stakes are as high as they were in 2022. The Trump presidency would, in many ways, dominate the proceedings.

The city of Brotherly Love was again the setting for America's Constitutional Convention. It would be the fifth time delegates were summoned to Philadelphia to contemplate a new constitutional document. Almost nothing else was the same. The intimacy of Independence Hall was replaced in large part by the remoteness of Skype, Zoom, and Webex. There was an official meeting place, of course—the Philadelphia Convention Hall and Civic Center—but delegates could also connect through the latest technology. Many did. Additionally, most of the proceedings were recorded in real time. C-Span devoted a channel to continuous coverage of the entire event and scores of delegates, observers, and media outlets engaged in real-time commentary. Twitter and Eventbase were the preferred methods for disseminating one's thoughts quickly. A huge amount of information traveled in and out of the Philadelphia Convention Hall that summer.

The 2022 federal Convention was also the first to welcome a person of color as its President. On May 18th, 2021, exactly one year to the day before the constitutional convention opened, the Joint Congressional Committee selected W. Douglas Banks to lead the gathering. Banks' calling was the ministry—he was Senior Pastor at Mount Zion Baptist Church of Germantown, in Philadelphia—but that's not what drew the attention of the selection committee. Banks was a fifth-generation descendant of Thomas Jefferson and Sally Hemings.[16] He was nominated by members of his congregation, and the Joint Congressional Committee thought he was an inspired choice. Coming full circle and elevating a Jefferson to the convention presidency sent a definite message. Elevating a descendant of America's most famous enslaved person sent an even more powerful statement.

Banks eagerly accepted the appointment. For him, this was an opportunity. He was unafraid to deal with the tough issues that characterize every constitutional convention. He was also an amateur historian of sorts. He understood that race had been the common thread that ran through all prior conventions—from the 1825 gathering that had made a conscious decision to punt the issue of slavery to the 1953 Convention where Thurgood Marshall left his indelible mark. Banks' goal was to use his platform to remind delegates that the experience of Black and Brown people was different from the experience of any other group in American history. He knew that the constitutional questions about racial discrimination, inequality, and injustice had been asked in prior conventions, but too often they had remained unanswered. Delegates, he thought, must always remember that the privileged have a four-century head start. Our job is thus to scrutinize the constitutional designs and structures that have perpetuated that staggered start. "None of us is responsible for the past," he was known to say, "but all of us are most assuredly responsible for what we do from here."

The Constitutional Convention Opens

On May 18th, 2022, President Banks struck his gavel to signal the start of the convention. The rules of order, he said, would remain largely intact from previous conventions, but it was still important to remind the conclave of their details. He relayed the various expectations for the gathering. As always, committees were then formed, and a few loose ends tied up.

The procedural and logistical work of the convention now complete, debate turned to more substantive topics. For the first time, really, since the 1787 Philadelphia Convention, delegates began with a reconsideration of the basic architecture of American government. Again, few convention-goers were prepared to discard the entire system of federalism, separation of powers, and/or checks and balances, but a number of the principles and components that undergird America's republican composition were ripe for review. Proponents of fundamental change had come with data to back their cause. Only two in ten citizens, they announced, claimed that "democracy was working very well," while a full 61 percent of Americans insisted that "significant changes" are needed to the "design and structure" of the American polity.[17] Congress was particularly hard hit, these reformers noted, both for deferring regularly to the President and for its partisan bickering.[18] But the judiciary and the President fared little better, they said.

As delegates arrived in Philadelphia for the federal convention, most were not only aware of the institutions' declining reputations, but they, themselves, were fed up with Washington's partisan squabbling and political futility. The country elected a President in 2016 who many claimed was a racist and misogynist and whose rhetoric often divided the country in unprecedented ways. For this group, the President's negative silhouette hung over the proceedings. That same President, though, was seen by his many supporters as an effective steward of America's fragile economy, a strong and uncompromising champion for American exceptionalism, a decisive leader during the pandemic tragedy, and a true voice for the "forgotten masses." He enjoyed the backing of a base made up mostly of White, working-class, conservative men, a powerful electoral constituency in recent years. His approval rating continuously hovered around 40 percent.

To most elected convention delegates, the legislative branch had become largely a bystander in the game of American politics. It had been so for some time now, dating back several presidencies. Many assumed that part of the reason for Congress' poor reputation and comparative impotency was the extremely high reelection rate among incumbents, and they also perceived that lawmakers in Washington had become complacent in their positions. Enter the debate about term limits.

The issue itself has stumped American citizens for as long as the nation has elected lawmakers. Early on, several states prevented legislators and Governors from seeking unlimited terms in office. The 1776 Virginia Constitution, for example, term limited state officials with a subtle and somewhat ornamental admonition: "[T]hat the members of the [legislature] first may be restrained from oppression, by feeling and participating [in] the burdens of the people, they should, at fixed periods, be reduced to a private station, [and] return into that body from which they were taken."[19] Go back to private life, Article V of the Virginia Constitution clearly states. The work of lawmaking is hard. Take a much-needed break.

The Articles of Confederation similarly prevented any individual from serving too many terms in a row. It allowed a federal lawmaker to occupy his position for only three out of any six consecutive calendar years. Members of the Confederation Congress were thus forced to return home after a short stay in office.[20] The Constitutional Convention in 1787 also considered the possibility of congressional term limits, deciding at the last minute to pass over the language in the Virginia and New Jersey plans that mentioned it. In that setting, the sentiments of Roger Sherman won the day. "Nothing renders government more unstable," he quipped, "than a frequent change of the persons that administer it."[21] The 1787 U.S. Constitution thus made no mention of term limits at all.

The issue periodically resurfaced over the next two centuries, mostly at the local level. Many states, in fact, took up the term limits mantle and implemented legislative limits of their own. Presently, fifteen states bar their own state lawmakers from seeking unlimited terms in office.[22] The majority of these states cap the number of terms for members of the state House at four and the state Senate at two. Almost all of them implemented these restrictions during a ten-year stretch in the 1990s. It was at this point that the movement to contain legislative incumbency shifted from mainly the state level to the federal level. Twenty-three states tried to pass legislation in the 1990s that restricted the number of terms their own federal Representatives and Senators could serve. Knowing the consequences of entrenched lawmakers (and frequent turnover), these states believed they had the authority to limit congressional terms. That door, though, was completely shut in 1995, when the U.S. Supreme Court ruled in *U.S. Term Limits, Inc.,* v. *Thornton* (1995) that Arkansas could not increase the qualifications for federal office beyond what the Constitution mandates (age and residency, and in the case of the Senate, duration of citizenship). A state cannot add previous elected service, the Justices said, as an indicator of whether an individual can or cannot run for public office. A constitutional amendment is the only mechanism that can alter the qualifications clauses.

The arguments for and against congressional term limits are familiar. For proof that they are needed, proponents point to government inefficiency, the unpopularity of the institution, the prevalence of special interests, Congress' willingness to defer to the other institutions of government, and the general sense that politicians these days are largely alienated from their constituents. In contrast, in 2018, the Brookings Institution released a study outlining the reasons Americans should *oppose* congressional term limits.[23] It found that term limits would reduce voter choice, eliminate the experience needed to wade through complicated legislative matters, reduce policy expertise, arbitrarily bar skilled lawmakers, and do little to diminish the influence of special interests.

It was the democratic argument that most concerned the 2022 convention delegates. Folks in Philadelphia still assumed that the principle of free and open elections was a central feature of a functioning American polity. A major tenet of American democracy, they argued, is that anyone with the minimal constitutional qualifications enjoys the freedom to run for public office. Additionally, there are some serious advantages to seniority, especially for the lawmaker's home district. Senior members of the House and Senate tend to have more power, and more power in the legislative body tends to mean more dollars, aid, and programs flowing back to their districts.

All this spawned a serious philosophical clash between reformers who favored government effectiveness and purists who refused to sacrifice one of the foundational pillars of American government. That philosophical debate spilled out onto the convention floor on Thursday, June 2nd, when Philip Blumel, a delegate from Florida, addressed the audience and called for the revision of the qualifications clauses in Article II. Blumel, a financier who was also the President of U.S. Term Limits, a single-issue 501(c)3 based in Washington, DC, had been at the forefront of the term limits debate for most of his adult life. U.S. Term Limits was the nonprofit that had lost the *Thornton* case at the Supreme Court. This was its chance to push a constitutional reform agenda that almost eight in ten Americans favored. Blumel had plenty of ammunition at his disposal, including overwhelming support from the public.[24] What is more, that support crossed party lines. As many Democrats favored term limits as did Republicans and Independents.

Blumel was a sophisticated student of the Constitution. He could converse effortlessly with anyone on topics ranging from the theory of American constitutional development to the history of America's awkward waltz with incumbency. He was particularly enamored with Jeffersonian ideas for limited government, and hence he started his petition for reform with an appeal to common sense. How is it possible, he asked his fellow convention delegates, that Americans should tolerate a system where federal lawmakers were initially chosen by voters twenty, thirty, and forty years ago *when we don't even allow our Constitution to be drafted by a prior generation?* We allow Members of Congress to stay in office for, sometimes, a full half century, but until this convention, we haven't allowed the United States Constitution to exist that long.

He continued by rehearsing the statistics. Close to 95 percent of all Members of Congress—both in the House and the Senate—could expect to remain in their jobs for as long as they wished. Whether through direct mailing, corporate and special interest support, or just the visibility they obtained from television interviews and other media appearances, incumbent Members of the House and Senate received an almost insurmountable advantage, an advantage that belied the principle of competitive elections. The fear that democratic principles would be damaged by barring incumbents from running would be more than offset by the gains that would come from diminishing the incumbency advantage. The benefits of more competitive elections, he reminded the convention, are that lawmakers would be more accountable to a public that cares deeply about representation; fresh faces in politics would be less likely to be complacent; and connections to special interests would not be as deep. He suggested that ten to twelve consecutive years in office is about the outer limit; after that, elected officials begin to take the job for granted.

He had a proposal to address this. Three consecutive terms in the House of Representatives and two consecutive terms in the Senate, he said, should be the limit. Members of the lower chamber, in other words, should be restricted to six consecutive years in office, while members of the upper chamber should be limited to twelve. Ever the political strategist, Blumel knew full well that suggesting only three consecutive House terms would be a problem. Many at the Philadelphia convention would argue that such a spell in office was too short. Six years (unlike the twelve he proposed for Senators) was not enough time to get one's bearings or accomplish important constituent goals. The Florida delegate recognized that the states turning to term limits overwhelmingly favored *eight* consecutive years for their legislators. He could certainly live with that number for federal lawmakers, which is why he didn't start there. He would wait and see how the deliberations unfolded.

The delegates had logistical questions. Would the current crop of federal legislators, who entered politics without a term limit, be "grandfathered" in under his proposal? Yes, he replied. Any proposal to limit the number of terms in office would not start immediately, but would take effect at a designated future moment. If the convention agreed that members of the House were limited to six years in office, those currently in office could (assuming they won reelection) stay in place for the next six years. Prior service, in short, would not count.

If the clock started at ratification and, for current members, ended six, eight, or twelve years later, wouldn't that result in the wholesale renewal of Congress? Wouldn't that cause instability in the people's branch? Not necessarily, Blumel said. Even currently, with a 94 percent incumbency rate among those willing to stand for reelection,[25] there was still quite a bit of turnover through retirements and other means, and that had not crippled the institution. In other words, the institution could absorb significant turnover in its first cycle because, on average, thirty-two seats turn over every election and close to one hundred new members enter Congress every six years. Finally, did Blumel's proposal allow for former lawmakers to return to Congress after sitting out a term or two? The answer, he said, was unequivocally yes. His problem was not with the individuals in office; it was with a system that was so one-sidedly in favor of the incumbent that any real hope of competitive elections was tenuous.

Blumel had expected these questions. What he had not anticipated was the intensity of a parallel conversation about extending the length of congressional terms. Some delegates asked whether it made sense to change the "antiquated" (as they described it) two-year term for a U.S. Representative and/or the six-year term for a Senator. What about a four-year term for Representatives and an eight-year term for Senators? Members of Congress could then spend less time campaigning at home (especially members of the House), and they would also gain focus and experience for the more critical policymaking side of the job. Lawmakers could spend more energy on the very responsibility they were elected to do: legislating.

James Madison had an opinion about the length of congressional terms. He had favored the two-year term because it ensured a recurring connection to a Representative's local constituency. He called it "essential to liberty" that the House have an "immediate dependence on, and intimate sympathy with, the people. Frequent elections are unquestionably the only policy by which this dependence and sympathy can be effectually secured."[26] It is critical to note, however, that Madison's preference was in direct response to the anti-Federalist critique that sought *even more frequent elections*—the call by constitutional opponents for elections "daily, weekly, monthly, [or] annually." Madison, too, was a political operator. He believed the two-year term was the longest he could get without seriously jeopardizing ratification.

The 2022 Constitutional Convention debate about term limits and longer congressional terms lasted six days. In all, dozens of delegates spoke on the related topics, and as anticipated, the details evolved over the course of the proceedings. Opponents of the measure, especially those already in Congress, were often accused of self-interest. In the end, though, it was Blumel's original proposal to limit the number of consecutive terms for both House members and Senators that passed, with one mostly expected modification. Instead of the initial proposal to limit House members to three terms, the assembly decided that four terms was more fitting. Interestingly, a majority of delegates also voted in favor of an amendment to the final constitutional language that prohibited former lawmakers from registering as lobbyists for four years after completing a term in office. At long last, the defenders of congressional term limits could claim an important victory.

A. E. Dick Howard once remarked: "it is inherent in Americans' attitudes toward their constitutional system that when a sufficient number of them care enough about a problem they seek to give it constitutional dimensions."[27] When enough people are pissed off, in other words, they will try to link their position to the Constitution itself. A constitutional imprimatur, the thinking goes, adds weight and legitimacy.

In 2022, that inciting problem was the environment. Damage to the environment, both in the United States and around the world, represents the single greatest existential threat to the future of humanity. And yet in no prior federal constitutional convention has concern for environmental protection reached such a level that it has triggered a constitutional conversation. That would change in 2022, and it was a somewhat unlikely voice that would lead the discussion.

At first, Michael Brune felt like a fish out of water. As the executive director of the Sierra Club, America's oldest and most established environmental action organization, he was used to intimidating boardrooms, difficult negotiations, and not-so-subtle political agendas. That wasn't the problem. What concerned him was being on the other side of the political process. Nothing in his career had prepared him for the role of constitution-maker. This didn't feel like a congressional hearing or an environmental summit. It felt more monumental.

He and a handful of fellow environmental activist-leaders had been invited to be convention delegates. They immediately recognized that there was pressure on the assembly to insert specific constitutional language that in some way protected the environment. Brune understood that this was his chance to chart a constitutional path that would send the country in an entirely new environmental direction—one that recognized the peril of climate change, the importance of conservation and resource management, and the critical necessity of environmental justice.

If he could embed a provision in the draft Constitution that defended the environment against further degradation, it might be a game changer.

Brune and his colleagues knew that they could be constitutional pioneers—at least at the federal level. Several earlier attempts to amend the U.S. Constitution to enforce environmental protection measures had ended in failure. The proposal of Democratic Wisconsin Senator Gaylord Nelson in the early 1970s was perhaps the most straightforward. Nelson had encouraged Congress to endorse a constitutional amendment that simply said: "Every person has the inalienable right to a decent environment. The United States and every state shall guarantee this right." It failed passage. Twenty years later, a second proposed addition to the U.S. Constitution surfaced. It read: "The natural resources of the nation are the heritage of present and future generations. The right of each person to clean and healthful air and water, and to the protection of the other natural resources of the nation, shall not be infringed upon by any person." That one didn't gain any traction either. While efforts were made to amend the constitutional text, battles waged elsewhere, too. The federal and state courts issued opinion after opinion on environmental issues, but they had limited impact beyond their particular jurisdictions.[28]

States, though, *were* enjoying success in amending their constitutional charters. As of 2020, more than a dozen U.S. state constitutions now include some protection for the environment. Most of these constitutional articles start out with a "statement of public policy," usually focused on conservation efforts.[29] Article XIV, Section 4 of the New York State Constitution, for instance, begins: "The policy of the state shall be to conserve and protect its natural resources and scenic beauty and encourage the development and improvement of its agricultural lands for the production of food and other agricultural products." Similarly, Article XI, Section 1 of the Virginia Constitution states: "To the end that the people have clean air, pure water, and the use and enjoyment for recreation of adequate public lands, waters, and other natural resources, it shall be the policy of the Commonwealth to conserve, develop, and utilize its natural resources, its public lands, and its historical sites and buildings." These broad policy statements are then followed by more specific clauses and provisions aimed at detailing the expectations for conservation and resource management.[30] Such detail is not at all surprising. State constitutions are always exhaustive and descriptive because state governments are typically responsible for specific social policy.[31] Constitutions often help with the crafting and administration of that policy.

Brune understood that dynamic, though he figured any attempt to match such level of detail in the federal constitutional instrument was likely to go nowhere. Most convention delegates, while claiming to be stationed on the environmental front lines, were conservative in temperament. They were not inclined to endorse constitutional language that differed so dramatically from the other protections in the federal text. If an addition to the draft Constitution's Declaration of Rights was going to make it through the convention, it had to resemble the negative rights already present in the text. It had to be written in a particular way. Brune thus recognized that a broadly written, general policy statement about conservation and resource management, much like those found in state texts, might just fly. He was prepared to offer just such a statement.

Brune spoke slowly and confidently when recognized by the convention president. "Americans today face urgent national (and global) environmental challenges that would have been unimaginable to previous constitutional framers," he began. "Past leaders worked tirelessly to improve our environmental station, but they didn't fully connect their ambitions to the *constitutional* project. They didn't see that America's organic law holds the possibility of real reform." Brune continued by citing the data. He had reams of information that revealed the environmental threat facing us all. By now, he was speaking as forcefully as he had ever done in public. "Our task," he implored, "is to leverage the power of the constitutional text for the future of our planet. . . . It is time to end our nation's long and shameful history of allowing unscrupulous politicians and avaricious corporations to exploit and despoil our public lands and natural resources—often to the detriment of the public's health, welfare, and security. . . . We will not enjoy this chance again."[32] His position clear, he then tried to convince enough fellow delegates that constitutional renewal could make a difference.

Brune's intent was to deliver enough data—and enough fire—to compel his colleagues to action. He was prepared to propose a single motion, one that he believed would significantly, and permanently, solidify a constitutional protection for the environment. Its inspiration derived from those state constitutions that already safeguarded natural resources and he intended to advocate for its inclusion in the federal Constitution's Article I Declaration of Rights. Environmental rights, he insisted, are *natural* rights—human rights that all can, and should, enjoy. The language of his draft provision began: "The right of the people to clean air and water, and to the preservation of a safe and healthy environment, shall not be infringed." The second sentence was even more forceful: "The public natural resources of the United States of America are the common property of all the people, including future generations, and shall be preserved and maintained for the benefit of all."

This was not an intellectual exercise for Brune or for those environmental leaders standing by his side in spirit. It was, in every way possible, a call to arms. He was particularly interested in the delegation's reaction to the inclusion of "future generations" in his draft language, for he was familiar with the theory of Jeffersonian constitutionalism and the 1825 decision to eliminate the word "Posterity" from the Constitution's Preamble. He thought this was different. The constitutional protection of clean air, fresh water, and natural resources was intended precisely *to* ensure future generations. The country could no longer afford to be negligent and careless when it came to the environment, and it certainly could not afford to think only of the current generation. That kind of thinking is what got us into trouble in the first place.

Brune's last words before yielding the floor were especially sharp: "If we do not enshrine the right to live in a safe and healthy environment, a right that is surely fundamental to promoting the 'General Welfare' of the American people," he said, "that right will forever be sacrificed at the altar of commercial and political expediency. And those who will suffer most greatly? The most vulnerable among us."

He nodded to President Banks, signaling the end of his formal remarks. Brune's motion was immediately seconded and entered into the record. The floor was open for discussion. At first, the naysayers rose. Several delegates commented on the data, indicating their general skepticism by attempting to poke holes in Brune's variables and his methodology. Big data, they insisted, can be misleading, and the conclusions should not be trusted. Other opponents argued that the draft constitutional clause would have serious, and quite negative, implications for America's core manufacturing industries. The litigation alone would bury the courts and cripple the sector. Constitutionalizing a right to clean air and water could lead to more and more injunctions, which would slow production, stall wages, and increase unemployment. The country's economic recovery after the COVID-19 pandemic would come to a screeching halt. It was a zero-sum game in their eyes: either we protect the environment and sacrifice jobs or we prioritize the working men and women of the country and let the environmental chips fall where they may. Business-first opponents could not be convinced otherwise. Several explicitly announced their intention to vote against Brune's proposal.

Of course, Brune had plenty of allies too. A cohort of delegates from traditionally progressive western states like California, Oregon, and Washington sounded off on the cynics by reinforcing the economic and societal benefits associated with environmental protection. They also conjured up the words of America's greatest political heroes. Jefferson, they reminded the delegation, understood the fragility of the ecosystem and the importance of vigilance. "In the environment," Jefferson remarked, "every victory is temporary, every defeat permanent." Similarly, Abraham

Lincoln was an early proponent of alternative energy: "As yet," the sixteenth President noted, "the wind is an untamed and un-harnessed force; and quite possibly one of the greatest discoveries hereafter to be made, will be the taming and harnessing of it." And Teddy Roosevelt, of course, is the great environmentalist. His quotable remarks are too numerous to count, as one female delegate argued, but here are a few for contemplation: "Of all the questions which can come before this nation, short of the actual preservation of its existence in a great war, there is none which compares in importance with the great central task of leaving this land even a better land for our descendants than it is for us." She read another, this one penetrating to the heart of the environmental justice movement: "this country will not be a permanently good place for any of us to live in unless we make it a reasonably good place for all of us to live in." She concluded with a timely, but gentle, condemnation, in Roosevelt's words: "The United States at this moment occupies a lamentable position as being perhaps the chief offender among . . . nations in permitting the destruction and pollution of nature. Our whole modern civilization is at fault in the matter. But we in America are probably most at fault."

Debate ensued until, eventually, the question was called. The time had come to vote. Michael Brune expected to be nervous at this moment, but he was not. He sat calmly as delegates registered their support or opposition to the measure. The vote was tallied electronically, so he didn't have to wait long before the results were in. In the end, the motion passed, 57 percent to 40 percent, with 3 percent of the delegation either abstaining or unable to vote. America's new Constitution would include a fundamental right to a clean and healthy environment. It was a major victory for Brune and his fellow environmentalists. For the first time in history, the federal Constitution unequivocally declared the nation's commitment to a better and more healthful environment.

→><←

By mid-July, the delegation had explored a number of critical topics. The discussions surrounding congressional term limits and environmental resource management were more or less complete, needing just a tweak or two from the Committee of Detail. Other questions about the new draft were asked and answered. The document was beginning to take shape. Still, several additional debates had commenced at various points and, for one reason or another, had been tabled. Many of those reappeared in the waning weeks of summer and the early fall. Concerns over the Electoral College, equal representation in the U.S. Senate, the presidential impeachment process, and the difficulty of amending the text were just a few of the major items removed from the table and placed back on the floor. These issues represented the defects of the current U.S. Constitution most frequently cited during the crowdsourcing process.

Each issue was led by a different champion at the convention. Whether they realized it or not, though, each champion was influenced by the work of a single delegate: Sanford Levinson, a famous and outspoken constitutional scholar who, in many respects, had been waiting for this moment all his professional life. An astute observer might deduce that Levinson consciously channeled both Benjamin Franklin and John Adams while in Philadelphia. He was Franklin insofar as he privately used the city's informal gathering spots—the hotel lobbies, the local taverns, the frequented restaurants—as extensions of the convention itself; Levinson gladly engaged in dialogue during the event's off-hours as a means to levy influence on others. He was Adams in that he was also willing to be publicly vocal—brash, even—to inspire delegates to his point of view.[33] This combination would serve him well. He was most effective in moving the conversation forward and illuminating, as he saw it, several basic structural flaws with the current constitutional text. Three flaws in particular captured Levinson's attention: the illegitimacy of the Senate, the inability of the people to vote that they had "no confidence" in their President, and the absurdly difficult method for amending or reforming the constitutional document.

Over the course of four months, Levinson managed to get the convention delegates to consider each flaw. He began in mid-July by promoting a radical change to the United States Congress. He began by addressing the "illegitimacy" of the contemporary Senate, a chamber where the notion of "equal representation" is at best a hollow promise. Levinson has long derided the Senate because states like Wyoming, Alaska, Delaware, Montana, South Dakota, North Dakota, and Vermont—states that have "twice the number of Senators as they do Representatives in the House"—enjoy disproportionate influence in relation to their rather small populations.[34] California, Texas, and New York— three of the most populous states—elect the exact same number of Senators. How is that democratic, asked Levinson and other famous political pundits?

Levinson and others were keen on reforming the Senate so it would be more in accordance with democratic principles. So, what to do? Allocating the number of Senators by state population was not the answer; the Senate would then simply resemble a mini-House of Representatives. Some sort of weighted ballot whereby Senators from more populous states were awarded more "weight" in their voting preferences wouldn't work either; it was too complicated to make much sense. Doing away with the Senate altogether was too radical an option. With no obvious choice, Levinson and his allies settled on a plan of action that limited the scope of Senatorial power while, simultaneously, creating a new legislative branch that would carry out many of the policymaking duties currently housed in the Senate. Levinson was convinced that this was the best option for twenty-first-century America.

The proposal for reform looked like this: "The United States Senate will be limited in its authority to confirming presidential nominations for office. Its members will be elected by the populace in each state for a term of six years, as at present. In addition, a new House of Congress shall be created, titled the National Assembly, to consist of 200 members. One hundred and fifty of them will be elected by ten regions of the United States, which have equal populations. Each region will elect fifteen members through a system of proportional representation designed to ensure the representation of a full range of views held by significant numbers of the American public. Of the remaining members of the National Assembly, thirty-five will be ex officio, consisting of all former Presidents, Vice Presidents, Secretaries of State, retired Justices of the Supreme Court, former Chairs of the Federal Reserve, retired Chairs of the Joint Chiefs of Staff, and a group of retired Governors chosen at random. The remaining fifteen members will be citizens selected at random, by region, by the public at large."[35]

Levinson knew that such a proposed design modification was a long shot to pass the assembly. He felt he had to at least throw it out there. And so he did. Debate was robust, and it extended into the following day. Opponents quickly pounced on the radical change, claiming ignorance as to how this new branch of the legislature would even work. Proponents volleyed back, insisting that the central tenets of the upper chamber—extended terms, geographical representation, fewer legislators than the House of Representatives—remained mostly intact. Moreover, supporters argued, the collective knowledge and insight of the ex officio members was invaluable. They could help to steer policy debates in reasonable directions because they had lived through similar negotiations and had foresight derived from the equivalent of centuries of practical experience. It would work, these sponsors insisted. When all was said and done, though, the idea did not prevail. It was too unconventional for a delegation that inevitably preferred to gravitate to the ideological center.

Levinson would have more success five weeks later when he took the floor again to propose another significant change to the existing fundamental law. This time the target was Article VI of the 1953 Constitution—the Amendment article. Article VI was a holdover from the original 1787 document; it had never been modified in any of the previous constitutional conventions. Indeed, for many, it had worked relatively well throughout American history. Amendments were passing. The threshold for altering the text—a vote of two-thirds in each House of Congress, followed by ratification from three-fourths of the several states—was not seen as overly daunting. But in recent years, that process of amendment was beginning to feel too ambitious. "Article [VI] constitutes what may be the most important bars of our constitutional iron cage precisely because it works to make practically impossible needed changes in our polity."[36] No proposed constitutional amendment had successfully run the gauntlet since 1992. The process for amendment had not changed; but the political landscape certainly had. The country felt more divided than ever, and one consequence was the diminished possibility of constitutional reform.

The high bar for amending the text was even more concerning because of the Jeffersonian constitutional principle that each generation ought to write its own fundamental law. First, Americans were living longer and thus generational turnover was decreasing. That reality sparked a simple realization: the longer the period between constitutional conventions, the greater the need for constitutional amendments; the greater the need for amendments, the lower the hurdle to amending the Constitution should be. Second, Jeffersonian constitutionalism obviously meant that *new* constitutional texts were to be introduced at periodic moments in America's development. New constitutions inevitably require revision because they are immature and untested. The introduction of a Bill of Rights in 1789 was the first, and still most famous, example of an omission that needed immediate correction.

Levinson took direct aim at Article VI. He stood before his fellow delegates and relayed the history of America's tussle with constitutional amendments. Then, he reminded the assembly of the critical need for an effective mechanism to both assess and reform the Constitution. "We must not revere any Constitution," Levinson continued, "for to do so is to ignore the very human—and very political—influence that always goes into its making."

He thus entered into the record a concrete proposal, a motion to dramatically change the amendment process: "An amendment may be proposed by a two-thirds vote of each house of Congress or by a three-fifths vote of both houses in two consecutive

Congresses. Upon proposal, it will be submitted for ratification by the states. Ratification occurs if and when a majority of states endorse the proposed amendment, so long as the ratifying states also contain a majority of the national population. An amendment may also be submitted by the states themselves, so long as the text is identically worded by each state, and it gains the assent of a majority of states. Upon such approval, Congress must vote on the proposed amendment within sixty days, and if two-thirds of each house assents, it shall be deemed to be ratified."[37] Levinson then went further by offering a new formula for calling constitutional conventions. "If two-thirds of the states, or half the states so long as they contain a majority of the population, petition Congress to call a new Constitutional Convention for the purpose of proposing amendments, Congress shall, within sixty days, call such a Convention and establish rules for its conduct, though any such rules will be subject to override by the Convention itself when it meets. Finally, the national electorate shall, at intervals of twenty years, be given the opportunity to vote, at the time of regularly scheduled congressional elections, to call a new Constitutional Convention for the purpose of assessing the existing Constitution and proposing useful amendments. Should a majority of the electorate vote for such a Convention, Congress shall, within sixty days, pass the requisite legislation for the operation of the Convention, including the selection of delegates by a process of random selection from the voting-eligible population of the United States."[38] This last proposal was meant to circumvent, or at least accelerate, the automatic call for generational conventions that accompanies Jeffersonian constitutionalism.

There was much to unpack in the motion. Levinson and his supporters knew going in that the first half—involving amendments—was most likely to gain support from the assembly. It was the second half—altering the process for calling constitutional conventions—that was less popular. Both components of the measure received lengthy and sustained attention from the delegates and from the Sunday morning talk shows and the op-ed pages of national newspapers. The rule that a simple majority of the states could ratify amendments so long as the aggregate population in those states amounted to greater than half the entire electorate of the United States was scrutinized especially closely. MSNBC devoted no fewer than twelve news program segments over a full week to imagining the combinations of states that could ensure an amendment's passage. Red states were paired with red states, and blue states were paired with blue. The Trump base was closely parsed to see if it, alone, could just about ensure passage of certain amendments. Regional coalitions—like the Deep South and the Mountain West states—were surveyed to see if conservative-leaning amendments could secure the necessary backing. Commentators noted that the cities along the Atlantic and Pacific coasts could practically deliver the necessary population numbers to ensure passage of any amendment. It was a fascinating debate.

And so was the debate about two consecutive Congresses supporting a proposed constitutional amendment. That provision was quite popular across partisan lines, and it seemed especially timely given the addition of a term limits clause to Article II of the draft Constitution. Compared to requiring two-thirds of each house in a session of Congress to support an amendment, it seemed more, shall we say, objective and legitimate to require consecutive Congresses (with significant turnover of members) to endorse a major change to the constitutional text. This particular part of the motion helped secure support for the entire amendment proposal. When the time came to vote on the proposed resolution, the delegation comfortably passed the set of new rules for amending the text. The call for a new process to convene constitutional conventions, however, failed to muster the necessary majority of delegates. How ironic it was that a group of convention delegates beholden to Jeffersonian constitutionalism would reject a proposal calling for more frequent conventions. Once every generation was enough, the delegation seemed to say.

Finally, Sanford Levinson addressed what in his opinion was the most glaring defect of the current Constitution.[39] For decades, he had been asking a series of fairly straightforward questions about the modern American President and the country's bend toward presidentialism. "What if the electorate turned out to be disastrously mistaken in its choice for President of the United States, he wondered?" What if we are faced with a President who is incompetent even if not a criminal? Are we stuck with that choice? For the full four years?

The 1953 Constitution extended from earlier constitutions most of the details of presidential selection and continued service, including the four-year term with the possibility of reelection. That decision perpetuated the virtual impossibility of removing a sitting President, and it made Levinson nervous, because the possibilities for presidential removal were so few. Sure, one could pinpoint a President's reelection bid as a check on presidential power, but that approach too had its downsides. What if a President was in the second term already? What if a President's incompetence was masked by certain factors that did not easily sway the average voter? An amendment had been added to the 1953 Constitution relating to a President's removal from office owing to disability, and the wording of that amendment had been added to Article III of the 2022 draft Constitution. But Levinson was asking for something different. His third and final proposal to the convention involved modifying Article III in three critical ways: first, the elimination of the Electoral College; second, the modification of the presidential term, from a one-time renewable four-year stint to a single six-year term; and third, the possibility of a congressional vote of no confidence in the President or, alternatively, a citizen-initiated recall of a President. Together, these three modifications represented a major attempt by Levinson to realize radical constitutional reform. He feared they would go nowhere, but he offered them nonetheless.

The phrasing of his motion was sharp. In place of its current wording, Levinson proposed that Article III, Section 1 should now read: "The executive power shall be vested in a President of the United States of America. The President shall be elected by a national popular vote for a single term of six years. If no candidate receives a majority of the popular vote, a runoff election shall be held, within three weeks of the certification of the first vote, between the two candidates receiving the highest number of votes."[40] Further, Levinson wanted to see changes to Article III, Section 4. That section would still include a process for impeachment, but would be expanded to include the following: "a President can be removed from office, after the first two years of the presidential term either by a two-thirds vote of the Members of Congress, assembled together, agreeing that they no longer have confidence in the President, or by a national recall election triggered by petitions signed by at least ten percent of the electorate voting in the most recent presidential election. Should the recall election be successful in removing the President, a new election for the presidency shall take place at the next scheduled congressional election."[41]

Shifting the presidential selection process to a purely popular vote represented the first significant modification. The sentiment was that the Electoral College, even as modified in 1825, was no longer working judiciously. A national popular vote and a potential runoff was one answer. Of course, several interest groups immediately opposed such a suggestion.[42] In a somewhat surprising move, a few of the television networks even sent their lobbyists to Philadelphia to put modest pressure on the delegates to oppose the measure. Why? Because networks liked the advertising revenue they received on election day, especially from those advertisers that pay a premium for commercial slots in the moments before a state closes its polls. How often do networks ramp up the drama of election night by promising to announce unit-rule electoral vote projections "right after these messages"? Viewers generally stick around, in part because of the drama of the projection. To the network managers' minds, a slow and steady tally of voting district results throughout the evening would not be nearly as compelling.

The second proposal, calling for a single six-year presidential term, had been gaining traction in elite circles across the nation. Supporters reminded skeptics that the presidential four-year term was originally a compromise between sponsors of a lifetime position and those who favored more frequent turnover. Supporters further argued that lame-duck Presidents—those who do not have to run for reelection—tend to be bolder and less self-absorbed. One opinion leader commented: "The absence of a looming reelection campaign could inspire future Presidents to be stronger leaders and more willing to make tough, unpopular decisions that could improve national well-being in the long term. And anyway, six uninterrupted years as President would be nearly the equivalent of two four-year terms—a reelection campaign invariably consumes two years of the President's valuable time and distracts the nation."[43] Levinson and his partners agreed wholeheartedly.

Levinson's other proposal, offering a mechanism for removing the President (or reconsidering the election that had placed that individual in the White House), originated from his frustration over the impeachment process, which no longer seemed an effective tool for presidential removal. It was too narrowly drawn and too far removed from the original debates in the 1787 Constitutional Convention. Indeed, the impeachment circus had become mainly a playground for attorneys to test the parameters of "high Crimes and Misdemeanors." President Clinton's 1998 impeachment, with its emphasis on obstruction of justice, perjury, and the salacious world of extramarital affairs, and Donald Trump's 2020 impeachment, with its focus on abuse of power, obstruction of Congress, and quid pro quos provided instructive examples. Attorneys like Ken Starr, who participated in both of these impeachment trials, subtly and not-so-subtly set the terms of the proceedings and in so doing removed the decision from the political arena where, Levinson argued, it belongs.

His solution was to imagine a process that allows Congress to introduce a no-confidence vote. Under Levinson's plan, a President would have two full years to demonstrate presidential abilities to the American people. If the President were unsuccessful in this, a simple no-confidence vote, much like those found in most European parliaments, could be introduced. The bar for removing the President through a no-confidence vote was appropriately high—two-thirds of the Congress, assembled together.

Three hundred and fifty-eight of the 535 Members of Congress would have to agree to the no-confidence resolution, rendering it unlikely to happen all that frequently. Still, a vote of no confidence, as dramatic and potentially destabilizing as it might be, provided a secondary path, alongside impeachment, to remove an incompetent President.

A third path, Levinson continued, should be a national recall election. Here, the idea was that the general electorate could bypass Congress altogether and trigger the mechanism for (possible) removal simply by collecting signatures. A lot of signatures! Levinson insisted on a 10 percent threshold: 10 percent of the voters who cast a ballot in the most recent presidential election must sign a petition for a national recall election. That's an extraordinarily high bar. The average voter turnout for presidential elections since the turn of the millennium has been roughly 125.5 million. Ten percent of that number is about 12.5 million.[44] At no time in American history has any organization or government body secured that many signatures. It would be difficult, to say the least, to muster that level of collective action. Still, Levinson included it in his resolution on the convention floor.

In the end, delegates were intrigued by Levinson's many proposals involving the presidency. A majority of them endorsed the single, six-year term for the President. Concerns about the rise of presidentialism in the twenty first century prevailed among the assembly. Unsurprisingly, the Electoral College in 2022 finally lost its increasingly controversial place in American politics. The delegation embraced the nation's wish to see a President chosen by popular vote. For many across the country, that outcome was long overdue. Finally, the delegates accepted the suggestion of a no-confidence vote, but they passed on the recall election. When all was said and done, then, the 2022 draft Constitution included a provision in Article II, Section 4 for Congress, assembled together, to remove a standing President by issuing a no-confidence resolution.

Of course, Levinson was not the only influencer out there. Danielle Allen, a political theorist and ethicist out of Harvard[45] issued a call to fix America's broken institutions, especially Congress. She was not present at the convention, but her ideas were well-known. Indeed, she had suggested that two structural redesigns would help. "First, increase the size of the House of Representatives by fifty" and place the additional representatives in the more populous states.[46] She pointed out that the original Framers set up a system that favored rural communities. But with the migration to urban environments over the last 200 years, representation is now out of balance. Increasing the membership of the House by fifty and carefully placing those new members in the more populous states would recalibrate the system.[47]

Second, she argued, Americans "should introduce ranked-choice voting in presidential, House and Senate voting."[48] Ranked-choice voting (RCV) works this way: rather than going to the polls to pick a *single* candidate, voters rank, in order of preference, their top three candidates. If a candidate gets a majority on the first tally, the contest is over. But if no candidate emerges with a majority, the candidate with the lowest number of "first-choice" votes is eliminated and the "second-choice" votes on that candidate's ballots are then distributed to the appropriate remaining candidates. The process continues until one candidate crosses the majority threshold. The state of Maine was the first to try RCV for the 2018 midterm elections.[49] It was controversial. Democrats, the minority party in the state, were generally supportive of RCV, while the majority GOP unsurprisingly opposed its use. Both parties understood that RCV favors moderate candidates and, perhaps more importantly, challengers to the incumbent. The process worked as planned, as a two-term Republican congressman was defeated by a relative newcomer.

Not surprisingly, the convention delegates' feelings about such proposals broke along partisan lines. Democrats advocated for the first change, insisting that an increase in congressional membership that reflected urban migration was more democratically just. Republicans balked, arguing that such an increase unfairly benefits Democrats who are concentrated in the major cities. Partisan perspectives reversed on the second proposal. Republicans favored RCV because it furthered their wish to regain majority power in the lower chamber of Congress. Democrats opposed the measure because they currently enjoyed that majority in the House of Representatives.

Neither measure would win the day, but the considerable time spent deliberating each, and the structural proposals offered by Levinson and others, said something about the mindset of this group of constitutional drafters. Those invited to Philadelphia were willing to contemplate large and small-scale structural changes to America's system of government. Ideas had their moments; some passed and others failed. In addition to debating term limits for lawmakers, revisions to the amendment process, a single presidential term, an alternative branch of Congress, national recall votes, increasing apportionment in the House, and the possibility of alternative electoral schemes, the delegates also debated, and then ultimately rejected, mostly conservative proposals to empower states to (by a three-fifths vote) "abrogate any federal law, regulation, or executive action" and to realign the scope of the Commerce Clause so as to recover its more limited and original meaning.[50] To be sure, the 2022 gathering was the most active constitutional convention since the first ever held in Philadelphia.

Individuals are not typically eager to engage in personal conflict, and most delegates to the 2022 federal Constitutional Convention (at least the 81% who were elected citizens) were not atypical. Soon, however, the deliberations turned to topics that sparked fierce partisan battles; such was the inevitable consequence of the times we were in. Issues like gun control, abortion, marriage equality, and gay rights were not debated early on, as many expected, probably because of the contested terrain surrounding them.

The country was watching closely. In fact, one major outcome of the crowdsourcing exercise in the years leading up to the federal convention was that most Americans wanted the delegates to take up these potentially explosive issues. The problem was that no clear consensus emerged from that preliminary work. Delegate opinion was just as polarized as American opinion over- all. A recent Gallup poll found that 25 percent of Americans believe abortions should be legal under any circumstances, while 21 percent believe the opposite, that abortion should be illegal under any circumstances. The largest percentage, at 53 percent, insist that abortion should be legal under certain circumstances. Slicing the data in other directions is no help either. Forty-nine percent of Americans consider themselves "pro-life," while 46 percent see themselves as "pro-choice." That same survey found that only 24 percent stated that the issue of abortion is "not a major factor" in their choice of electoral candidates.[51] That means that three out of every four Americans consider the issue of abor- tion to be a significant factor when they enter the voting booth.

These overall numbers, and the general trends associated with them, worried many delegates, especially those coming to Phila- delphia with deeply conservative religious or moral convictions. The anxiety was particularly high for those whose major work focused on restricting access to abortion. Pro-life supporters saw the constitutional convention as capable of taking the step that the Supreme Court had been reluctant to take: invoking feder- alism. The aim for most pro-life activists is always to restore the individual states as the appropriate site of decision-making au- thority. Surely, conservatives argued, a constitutional convention is the exact venue for realizing such a goal.

Abortion and the Constitution were forever linked after the landmark Supreme Court ruling in *Roe v. Wade* (1973) establish- ing "that the constitutional right of privacy is broad enough to en- compass a woman's decision to terminate her pregnancy."[52] From that moment on, the legal contest has been refracted through the prism of *Roe* and its progeny. Of course, the entire discus- sion has many tentacles. Some argue that abortion is a medical issue—a private decision between a woman and her physician— that should not be regulated by any government institution. Others claim it is within the individual states' police powers to regulate or even prohibit the procedure. Still others argue that it

is a moral decision that transcends the reach of politics or medicine. And still others say that it's a religious choice on the part
of the pregnant woman or an economic issue related to access. A
particularly disputed question that runs throughout the debate
asks about the onset of a human life. Some insist that life begins
at conception, while others claim that the fetus is not a person
in the legal or constitutional sense. The major challenge facing
participants in this debate is that on key points the sides are not
speaking a common language. Pro-life advocates rely heavily on
moral and religious language, whereas the pro-choice backers
speak exclusively in the language of autonomy and freedom.

The right of privacy, which sympathetic judges found in various parts of the Constitution's list of freedoms, is controversial
in part because the word "privacy" didn't appear in the 1953
constitutional text. For most conservatives, that right was man-
ufactured by liberal federal court judges in the 1960s and '70s.
Whether it is found in the clause of the Constitution that allows
the people to retain rights not enumerated by the Constitution
(the original Ninth Amendment) or through some penumbral
scheme articulated by Justice William O. Douglas in *Griswold v.
Connecticut* (1965), the conservative refrain is that the right of
privacy is simply a figment of judicial imagination—made up
to justify a liberal political outcome. For progressives, that argument is hollow. The right to privacy, they say, is "essential to
the concept of ordered liberty." There is no more fundamental
freedom than the "right to be left alone" to decide what to do
with one's own body.

Much had occurred in the half century since *Roe*. Federal and
State courts have regularly considered the validity of attempts
to chip away at the fundamental freedom. The Supreme Court's
thinking on the issue evolved significantly from the famous tri-
mester approach to a more conservative and restrictive "undue
burden" test. Candidates for public office have had to pass litmus
tests on their particular position. Nominated judges have as well.
Slightly out of the public eye, numerous attempts were made to
amend the 1953 Constitution in the wake of *Roe v. Wade* (1973).

These proposals now fall under the broad label of "Human Life Amendments," and all but one died in various congressional committees. As a group, the proposed amendments covered a wide swath of conservative territory. Some directly restricted the abortion procedure, while others reassigned the power to regulate and prohibit abortion back to the states. The one proposition that actually made it to the Senate floor was the 1983 Hatch-Eagleton Amendment that would have reversed the central holding in *Roe v. Wade.*[53]

Attempts to enshrine a literal right of privacy (or right to an abortion) within the Constitution have received little public fanfare. That is probably due to the fact that the current law of the land recognizes such a fundamental right. Even so, a few delegates to the 2022 gathering were keen to propose a new addition to the U.S. Constitution's Article I Declaration of Rights. As usual, they looked to the states for some guidance. Several states protect the right to personal privacy, though none explicitly refer to the right to *intimate* privacy that springs from the *Griswold* opinion or the right to *autonomous* privacy that derives from *Roe.* These state protections mostly mirror the safeguards in the federal Constitution that are more associated with criminal procedure (prohibitions against unreasonable searches and seizures, for example). But a few states, like Alaska, prefer a broad and general statement of privacy. Article I, Section 22 of the Alaskan Constitution says, simply, "the right of the people to privacy is recognized and shall not be infringed." That constitutional safeguard encompasses a lot of possible violations of privacy, from illegal searches to family-planning restrictions. The Alaska illustration would be fodder for deep debate on the convention floor. The central question was whether to transplant it into the draft federal charter.

Neither the conservatives nor the liberals were willing to concede any ground on that question or on the more general question about enshrining the right to intimate privacy in the draft text. That made things difficult. Deliberations went back and forth for days, but no real progress was ever made. Pro-life advocates wanted no such addition to the Constitution's Declaration of Rights. Pro-choice supporters were willing to bend on the particular language. Commentators from CNN and Fox both acknowledged that the left probably had the votes to ram something through the proceedings. Even so, reproductive-rights activists, dressed as Handmaids, disrupted the convention at one point by chanting, "my body, my choice." Tempers flared and voices were raised. At last, the decision was made to table any discussion about a constitutional provision banning or buttressing the right of privacy. A temporary hiatus from the intensity of the abortion debate was in order. As it turned out, the discussion about abortion was over. It would never return to the convention floor.

The same fate did not befall the debate surrounding LGBTQ+ rights. The path to the 2022 Constitutional Convention for gay rights advocates had been long, but in many ways far more successful than the journey of those seeking abortion rights. The initial steps were not promising, though. For centuries, sodomy was considered an affront to morality. Homosexuality was outlawed in most countries and in all the American colonies. The punishments were often brutal. Mutilation or even death was a common response in the sixteenth, seventeenth, and eighteenth centuries to any suspicion of homosexuality. Thomas Jefferson himself revised the Virginia law in 1777 to "make sodomy punishable by mutilation rather than death."[54]

The average person's thinking did not improve all that much in the early twentieth century, but by the 1970s there were hints of greater acceptance of different sexual orientations. The American Psychiatric Association announced in 1973 that "homosexuality is not a psychiatric disorder," while the federal government abandoned its discriminatory policy against hiring gays and lesbians two years later. By 1979, gay rights activists were bringing much-needed attention to the discriminatory policies of many industries and most state and local governments. Attacking that prejudice through the judicial system would be next up. The U.S. Supreme Court entered the gay rights arena first in 1986, when it ruled in *Bowers v. Hardwick* that the Equal Protection Clause does not protect homosexuals from state laws prohibiting sodomy.[55]

Ten years later, however, the Court showed more individual rights consciousness when it issued a landmark decision in *Romer v. Evans* (1996), a decision that essentially gutted *Bowers* and started a series of judicial victories for the gay rights movement. *Lawrence v. Texas* (2003) followed less than a decade later, at which time the Court's majority abandoned the principle of *stare decisis* and officially overruled *Bowers*.[56] In *Lawrence*, the Justices opined that any expectation of noninterference in the intimate relationships of consenting adults extends to the homosexual community. The Equal Protection Clause, they said, does not privilege certain sexual orientations, and neither does the fundamental right of privacy. A majority in the *Lawrence* case reaffirmed that fundamental right.

Relatedly, the Constitution has not always been kind to same-sex couples. Throughout American history, same-sex couples have struggled to find relief from all sorts of discriminatory policies and practices. In some ways, the most damning blow to marriage equality came with the enactment of the 1996 Defense of Marriage Act. Passed by the 104th Congress and signed by President Bill Clinton, DOMA defined marriage only in the traditional sense—between a man and a woman—and allowed states to refuse to acknowledge same-sex marriages performed in other states. Slowly, however, a few states began to defy the central provision of the Act. Beginning with Massachusetts in 2003, more than a dozen states defied DOMA's central holding by recognizing same-sex marriages performed in other states.

In the early 2000s, several conservative proposals were introduced in the House of Representatives to amend the Constitution by defining marriage as the union of a woman and a man. These proposed amendments ultimately failed to attract the 290 votes needed in the House and the 67 needed in the Senate, but they signaled a rise in congressional opposition to those states that were considering new marriage equality legislation. This sparked a greater outpouring of state laws protecting marriage equality. The trend toward greater tolerance was then accelerated in June 2013 when the Supreme Court ruled, in *U.S. v.*

Windsor (2013), that parts of DOMA were unconstitutional. The Court's majority argued that the Fifth Amendment's Due Process Clause required that the federal government recognize same-sex marriages. *Obergefell v. Hodges* (2015) then followed *Windsor* and went even further: it disallowed any *state* law prohibiting the legal recognition of same-sex marriage.[57]

Most convention delegates were familiar with the highlights of this complex history. They were also familiar with the results of the nationwide crowdsourcing project that exposed the population's general support for equal rights and marriage equality.[58] There were, of course, several delegates from states like Arkansas, Mississippi, Virginia, and Montana, which had passed state constitutional amendments barring same-sex marriage before the Court wiped them all away in *Obergefell*. These delegates could conceivably cause problems for the supporters of marriage equality. Some conservatives in those states and others were still smarting from that particular liberal Court ruling. But their opposition never amounted to much. Even if opponents of same-sex marriage wanted to return the decision about defining marriage to the states, the fire in their belly was mostly out by the time of the 2022 Convention. They would vote against any proposal to recognize marriage equality out of principle, but they would lose. The measure to include a specific provision protecting the union of all passed the assembly easily. For the first time in U.S. history, the Constitution would reference marriage; it would do so by embracing a broadly liberal, and truly tolerant, definition.

Of course, twenty-first-century constitutional conventions typically unfold in less organized ways than they once did; they are less linear than constitutional conventions of the past. The conversations are often rambling, and the topics discussed are frequently disjointed, probably as a consequence of the massive increase in the delegate pool over the years. It's simply easier for fifty-five delegates to focus on a single topic than for 535 to do so. A particularly memorable departure occurred in the 2022 Convention when deliberations about privacy, gay rights, and marriage equality were interrupted briefly by a proposal to modify Article I, Section 3 of the 1953 Constitution—the famous right to bear arms section. The section had not changed since 1791, when the Bill of Rights was added to the country's original text. That addition still read, "A well regulated Militia, being necessary to the security of a free State, the right of the people to keep and bear Arms, shall not be infringed." That section of the text was first transplanted verbatim into Article I's Declaration of Rights in the 1825 charter. It had remained, mostly without fanfare or controversy, in every Constitution since. The 2022 Convention, however, would be different.

Americans had lived through a staggering number of mass shootings since the Columbine tragedy in 1999. As a result, the country shared, and still shares, a collective fear. The source of that fear differed, though, depending on one's political and social disposition. Most Americans registered some dread that a domestic terror attack might occur in their own backyard, while others were terrified for a very different reason: that government would eventually dismantle the fundamental right to bear arms. According to Gallup, 61 percent of Americans favor stricter gun laws such as broader background checks and assault weapons bans. Only 8 percent insist that our laws are already too strict. Still, a full 71 percent of those same Americans *oppose* the banning of handguns. U.S. politicians thus face a paradox: a supermajority want stiffer restrictions on guns, but an even larger supermajority want to keep their firearms. The National Rifle Association's vast influence only adds to the aggregate confusion.

Every time a mass shooting occurs, the number of gun control advocates increases, while supporters of libertarian gun ownership fear a backlash that will restrict their freedom. The result of these competing interests and passions has been inaction, a stalemate between the power of the gun lobby and the heartbreak of a nation. The constitutional crowdsourcing exercise helped to clarify what Gallup already knew: that Americans are moving farther and farther apart on the issue. Gun rights owners and gun control activists alike dug in their heels and insisted that the Constitution's broad language was not likely to break any impasse. Americans, unfortunately, looked to the convention delegates to do just that.

Sheena Cooper, a Congresswoman from a conservative district in northeastern California, was the first to speak on the issue. Cooper was a compelling figure to lead the conversation. An advocate of gun control who had consistently received an "F" rating from the NRA, Cooper was also a strong defender of the general right of Americans to "keep and bear arms." She supported regulation, but only up to a point. She admitted to being profoundly disappointed in federal lawmakers for not passing meaningful legislation, and in the country's highest court for its decisions in *District of Columbia v. Heller* (2008) and *McDonald v. City of Chicago* (2010) affirming an individual right to keep and bear arms outside of any military service. Her record in favor of universal and comprehensive background checks for gun purchasers, as well as limitations on magazine size and a ban on military-style assault weapons, placed her squarely in the gun control camp. Moreover, she was a frequent traveler to the sites of America's horrific mass shootings, and she often positioned herself in photos with lawmakers who sponsored gun control legislation. Yet she was not willing to erase the individual right, as she saw it, to own a firearm. Shasta County—her home county—had been labeled "California's gun-buying capital."[59] She considered it political suicide to push for a complete ban.

Still, she had a plan. She proposed what to many was an unorthodox approach: to clarify the language of the constitutional clause safeguarding the right to bear arms. For too long, she insisted, the right has been interpreted as a virtual absolute, that any and all motivations for owning a gun are constitutionally protected. For her, though, the answer might be found not in the political morass of the issue but in the language of the protection. The composition of the sentence, she claimed, causes confusion. The prefatory clause—"A well regulated Militia, being necessary to the security of a free State"—is followed by the operative clause: "the right to keep and bear Arms, shall not be infringed." What if those were reversed and the operative clause preceded the prefatory wording? What if the constitutional freedom read instead, "The right of the people to keep and bear arms in order to ensure a necessary and well-regulated militia shall not be infringed"? Would that bring greater clarity to the intentions of those who originally crafted the right? Would that even matter?

The language of a "regulated militia" was anachronistic. She knew that. In fact, she wasn't convinced that retaining any of the language from the original Bill of Rights, even in the clearer form she proposed, was a useful strategy. The issue was far more complex. She understood that America's fight over gun control involved powerful organizations like the National Rifle Association, huge special interest donations, and intense feelings on both sides. She also recognized that gun rights advocates were not fools; they were not going to simply give up the fight for freedom because the language of the Constitution changed slightly.

She had to admit that many gun owners were misunderstood; she, herself, had maintained a fairly superficial grasp on their position in her early days in Congress. She knew better now what made them tick. In a recent Pew Research poll, 67 percent of gun owners cited "personal protection" as the main reason they kept a gun in the house.[60] This signaled a fear of assault and intrusion, a potential threat to the personal safety and the sacred security of the home. It also signaled a lack of faith in the law enforcement officials charged with protecting citizens. Further, she recognized that "guns aren't just a reaction to anxieties. In a way gun control advocates rarely consider, but gun owners may find obvious, they're a meaningful social asset for their owners."[61] Guns connect individuals to each other through gun shows, shooting ranges, and on-line chat rooms.[62] They link like-minded individuals together, often in protest of too much government intrusion in their lives. They build community, a community that often (with this topic at least) leans libertarian. Cooper acknowledged that the community of shared interest is, in a sense, one example of the modern bowling league.

The Congresswoman and her small band of supporters at the convention were not optimistic that any proposed change in language would generate much enthusiasm. They were right. Few were willing to fight alongside her. Debate continued for several days, but it never moved beyond mere speculation that something could be modified or added to the draft Constitution that might decrease the number of mass shootings. Short of eliminating the constitutional right to keep and bear arms, of course. The possibility of erasing the long-standing individual right was briefly considered, but it was shut down almost immediately. Even gun control advocates like Cooper recognized that such a suggestion invited constitutional bedlam and threatened the very credibility of the convention itself. Any proposal to eliminate individual rights and freedoms would be roundly rejected by a delegation that acknowledged the critical importance of personal liberty in a twenty-first-century world. Article I, Section 3 would remain unchanged.

For many, the most fascinating discussion of the 2022 Constitutional Convention came close to the end. It centered on America's struggle with its immoral past. Make no mistake, structural debates at any constitutional drafting convention are imperative and always interesting. The particular system of government adopted by any framing convention will go a long way toward determining the overall success of the regime. Indeed, protecting different convictions, lifestyles, and identities is significantly more difficult when that protection depends on a flawed governmental design. And yet it is inevitably the crucial discussions about values, beliefs, rights, and justice that generate the most intense public scrutiny. Citizens seem to care more about how a Constitution protects their worldview than they do about whether to defend a bicameral legislature or an independent judiciary. That shouldn't surprise any of us. The structural design of a polity is at least one step removed from the lived reality of individuals in a pluralist society.

The modern liberal democracy, with its multicultural, multiethnic, multiracial, multilingual, multifaith, and multiperspective footing, has to fashion a shared understanding of inclusion, equity, tolerance, discrimination, privilege, and prejudice. It must grapple with an often ugly past and a divided present, and it must decide how the constitutional form can help to heal the deepest of societal wounds.

These challenges are not just American. A post-apartheid South Africa approached its latest constitutional convention with a deep grasp of its history and its failures. So did Canada. Each was concerned that a historically marginalized population—Blacks in South Africa and French-Canadians in Canada—had been mostly shut out of the development of political society. When the time came for the countries to craft new constitutions, each attempted something revolutionary. They abandoned the traditional idea of a completely *generalized* constitution in favor of one that "recognizes a distinct group by textualizing some form of protection for that group in the nation's fundamental law."[63] In other words, they specifically singled out disempowered populations for special constitutional protection. This form of "constitutional recognition" has become popular in modern constitution-making. It involves, first, acknowledging a discriminatory past, and second, using the Constitution itself to announce a new and more inclusive set of national values and priorities. In Canada, for example, the current Constitution was significantly amended in 1982 to include a literal recognition of the country's Francophone population. Articles 16 to 22 of the 1982 Constitution "protect French as one of the official languages in Canada, granting it 'equality of status' and mandating that it, along with English, shall be used 'in all institutions of the Parliament and government of Canada.'"[64] Article 23 went even further by granting citizens the fundamental right to educate their children in their native tongue.

These are extraordinary acts of constitutional community building. In an approach that is the very definition of inclusion (and the opposite of assimilation), the framers of Canada's 1982 Constitution have essentially invited French-speaking citizens to participate *in their own way* in the collective destiny of the nation. The clauses provide special protection for a Francophone way of life. Constitutionalizing French as an official language, and then celebrating its use in French-speaking schools, immediately elevated the status of Francophone Canadians. It fortified the French linguistic community within the broader Canada; it was an exclusive invitation from the majority to be an equal player in the nation's future.

Canada's turn to specific constitutional recognition as a form of inclusion must be distinguished from the generalities of America's organic law. The closest the 1953 U.S. Constitution came to specifically recognizing particular identities was in two areas: first, the clause protecting the fundamental right to vote regardless of one's race and gender (but even there, the wording is general: "the right of citizens of the United States to vote shall not be denied or abridged by the United States or any state on account of race, color, or sex"); and second, the various mentions of Indians and Indian tribes. There is no specific mention of any specific identity beyond these broad references.

A portion of the 2022 Convention delegation was interested in enacting some form of constitutional recognition. The group consisted of several proponents of financial reparations for descendants of those who had been enslaved, and also other supporters of "truth and reconciliation" processes. What these individuals had in common was a desire to see tangible action to remedy a long history of discrimination and injustice.[65] Constitutional recognition could be part of a menu of items aimed at repairing the harm perpetrated on Black Americans and indigenous populations, they said.

It was clear that this band of restorative justice activists would fall short on any push for reparations; the convention, they were informed, was not the correct venue for such a dialogue. Even after the George Floyd murder, in May 2020, brought greater attention to the systemic racism that pervades most of America's institutions, the constitutional text would not afford historically marginalized groups a remedy. With one powerful exception: the assembly *was* intrigued by the prospect of enhancing the draft Constitution's Preamble to include some language confessing to America's racist past.[66] Such a move was not unprecedented. Several current constitutions around the world boast preambles that reference a historic struggle or injustice.[67] Eastern European Constitutions, for example, typically begin with a preamble that mentions the country's turbulent history. Most African Constitutions do too. A handful of delegates had studied the constitutions of the world, and they were familiar with the language, and the power, of preambles. They knew that preambles often serve multiple crucial functions: they locate the sovereign,[68] they tell stories of the nation's (often challenging) liberation, they articulate broad aspirations, and simultaneously, they acknowledge unhealed social wounds. They frequently use exalted words to set the nation's future course, and they regularly employ confessional language to concede a dark past. The problem for many in the convention hall in 2022 was that America's constitutional Preamble does the former, but not the latter.

A resolution was thus presented on the convention floor in the waning weeks of the assembly so that the draft Constitution's introductory statement would reflect the new trend in global preambles. The specific motion was simple: keep the core commands of the existing Preamble, but expand the scope to address the country's major historical failures. The motion incorporated possible, and somewhat provocative, language. If passed, the new Preamble would read:

> We the People of the United States, in Order to form a more perfect Union, establish Justice and acknowledge a history of injustice, insure domestic Tranquility, provide for the common defense, remedy the wounds of systemic prejudice, banish other institutional forms of discrimination, erase slavery's persistent legacy, reverse the destruction of indigenous nations and Native peoples, promote the general welfare, endeavor to achieve greater equity, and secure the blessings of liberty to all, do ordain and establish this Constitution for the United States of America.

The proposed language was bold, but it also told a far more accurate story. It was a show of regret through a constitutional portal. Delegates began debating the motion almost immediately.

Adding to the existing Preamble was simple enough. America's constitutional introduction is written in an unusual style; it does not resemble the more recently drafted preambles around the world.[69] America's constitutional Preamble is a list, pure and simple: a list of goals and aspirations—commands, even—that the new Constitution is intended to help realize. In that way, it provides critical guideposts for the constitutional experiment.[70] The singular purpose of the Preamble is to identify those ambitions that are most indispensable to America's future, ambitions such as forming a more perfect Union, securing the blessings of liberty, providing for the common defense, and so on. The concept of supplementing the extant list with additional objectives, therefore, was not particularly difficult. The problem was tone. The proposal to augment the Preamble brought out the traditionalists who feared a fresh Preamble would change the entire tenor of the draft document.

To some, the proposed Preamble felt long, perhaps even a bit clunky. To others, it felt long overdue. The entire delegation understood that America's constitutional Preamble is not legally enforceable—it cannot be used in a court of law as the basis for litigation—but that its importance reaches far beyond its limited utility. Plato understood Preambles to be the "soul" of all laws. Certain delegates pounced on that Platonic ideal to remind their fellow Americans that the country's soul has not always been pure.[71] An amended Preamble that acknowledges a discriminatory and destructive past can help to restore the nation's ailing soul, they said. Others involved in the debate were not similarly convinced. The brevity of the current Constitution's Preamble partially accounts for its elegance, they responded. The suggested new language will dim the radiance of the most important constitutional preamble ever composed. Leave the Preamble alone, these delegates argued.

Debate went back and forth until finally, after a number of proposed amendments, a majority of the convention agreed that the longer Preamble more effectively captured the will of the American public. The new language would stay. America's constitutional Preamble would receive a much-needed update. The outcome was not exactly an unconditional victory for the advocates of pure "constitutional recognition"—they still preferred direct provisions that specially protected marginalized populations, as in Canada's Charter of Rights and Freedoms— but it was an important advance in the march toward racial, and societal, reconciliation. The U.S. Constitution would have a radically new Preamble for the first time since 1787. With a new and refurbished constitutional "soul," many delegates gained a bit more confidence that the body of the text would receive a corresponding restoration.

The Convention Adjourns

The work of the 2022 federal Constitutional Convention was complete. In all, it took twenty-one weeks from commencement to adjournment. The Committee of Detail released its report with a finalized constitutional draft on October 3rd, and on October 21st, the ratification process officially began. The draft Constitution was formally released to the public on that date. Ratification would, of course, take a different form in 2022. State Ratifying Conventions were replaced by a popular voting system. The proposed text stipulated that a supermajority of citizens—60 percent, in fact—had to endorse the new Constitution in order for it to take effect. Popular ratification had arrived.

In hindsight, the convention felt slightly less political than most expected, especially given the politically charged environment the country found itself in. Slightly more temperance was probably due to the significance of the moment, the gravity of the delegates' charge, the use of state elections to populate the delegation, the natural and economic impact of the COVID-19 pandemic, and the effort to include a wide range of citizen voices. The serious work of constitution-making has always had a way of suppressing a small degree of political gamesmanship.

Perhaps the new crowdsourcing tools muffled that possibility further. But the hard work of bringing to life a new Constitution wasn't over. Not by a long shot. What remained was the arduous, and highly charged, task of securing ratification. The general show of respect among delegates in the intimate confines of Philadelphia's Convention Hall would not carry out into the dialogue over ratification. Most commentators hinted that this ratification attempt was not going to be simple. Technology and social media would allow for many voices in the process—some credible, others decidedly less so. Surveys and referenda were helpful in revealing the pulse of a country eager to see political change, but even still, those data were interpreted and manipulated in countless ways and always to fit the precise priorities of the messenger. The truth can be a tenuous prospect in these times.

Even with the most sophisticated means of measuring the thoughts, ideas, and perspectives of a ratifying population, one question nagged at the followers of American constitutional development: would this be the last federal Constitution ever produced in the United States? To this point in American history, it had been virtually inconceivable to think that Jefferson's generational cycle for constitutional formation would ever run its course. It had worked, more or less successfully, for the last two-plus centuries. The United States had undergone six constitutional conventions since the Articles of Confederation. The American public had become accustomed to the process and pageantry of crafting generational Constitutions. And yet the average life-span of an American citizen was now almost eighty and would likely top ninety at some point during the present generation. That would place the next federal constitutional convention sometime in the early twenty-*second* century.

With widespread wars, population growth, food scarcity, pandemics, and especially, global warming showing no signs of diminishing, several commentators predicted that the country would be unrecognizable in 2102. Would there be a desire, or a need, for a new Constitution at that point? Would there even be a United States to constitute a hundred years from now? A best-case scenario has the population growth leveling off in the next century. But will Americans encounter other environmental factors that might threaten the legitimacy of constitutional government? A Constitution is critical for maintaining political stability and social order, but it does not put food on the table or prevent sea levels from rising.

Even with that pall hanging over a large group of delegates, the general mood of the convention at the end was guardedly optimistic. Most delegates added their signature to the draft document, signaling their explicit endorsement of the new text. It was the best Constitution they could muster. Signatories were content with a Constitution, broader in scope and more detailed in design, that confirmed the importance of environmental protection, protected the possibility of more competitive elections, altered the term of the country's President, admitted some of the faults of the past, secured federal support for marriage equality, and on and on.

And yet many delegates couldn't shake the feeling that their work would not solve most of the wicked problems still facing a deeply divided American public. The constitutional document, like those all around the world, can only do so much. It is a notable piece of human ingenuity. It authorizes and constrains, enlightens and inspires. But so much of a Constitution's success depends on the capabilities of the institutions it empowers and the individuals who work in these institutions. Those government bodies must take the guideposts of a constitutional text and use them for good. The Constitution produced could be the noblest and best in human history, yet it will demonstrably tank if political officials ignore its rules and tenets.

Delegates emerged from the 2022 Philadelphia Convention convinced that they had drafted a solid, workable text. Yet most fretted that the product of their labors would still leave political leaders largely unchecked. They expressed concern that individual officials have power that even a new Constitution cannot contain. Some would even paraphrase Madison: men still aren't angels, they suggested, and so government remains a necessary evil. The problem is that a government made up of devils needs something to control it, and a modern Constitution is not always that faultless guardian anymore. Hence only cautious or guarded optimism was seen among the participants.

On a more positive note, the 2022 Constitutional Convention delivered a real-time civics lesson. As has been consistently reported, America's familiarity with the particulars of its constitutional history is embarrassingly shallow.[72] The constitution-making enterprise changed that, at least for a time. The public became more involved in the overall process of constitutional formation and in the particulars of America's fundamental law. The country's collective political IQ rose considerably in the years leading up to the convention and during the two-year ratification period that followed. There were other consequences as well—some positive, others just plain odd. Electoral turnout pushed noticeably higher as a result of greater public engagement with the entire political system. Ballot numbers were more robust in many electoral contests. There was an uptick in social capital and membership in the very civic organizations that Robert Putnam, in *Bowling Alone*, insisted were on the decline.[73] Schools began experimenting with mock conventions, while pundits predicted the failure or success of the new constitutional form. Vegas bookmakers even set odds on the prospects for ratification. The process of constitutional formation sparked pride and passion in every region of the country.

The convention was a success, if for no other reason than that it gave the United States a fresh start. Almost seventy years between constitutional conventions had strained the limits of Jeffersonian constitutionalism. The nation was experiencing a cultural and political division that had many heads: the legacy of slavery, the continuing presence of racial inequality, the rhetoric from a polemical White House, socioeconomic inequity, the rise of White nationalism, the lingering threat of domestic and international terror, foreign interference with America's democratic system, an inability to talk to those across the partisan aisle, and racism, sexism, and many, many other "isms." But for many, the new Constitution represented hope. It could now set out to keep the United States as the vanguard of participatory politics and the envy of all those who cherish liberty. Only time would tell if this Constitution would live up to the elegant constitutional texts of the past and successfully achieve its most ambitious goals.

EPILOGUE ────

WHEN I FIRST CONCEIVED of the idea to write a fictional account of generational Constitutions, Donald Trump was just a Manhattan real estate mogul and a part-time reality television host. The country was not facing a pandemic that threatened the physical and financial health of virtually every global citizen, and America's prosperous future was not in doubt. The President was Barack Obama, and he seemed to exude the confidence and cool swagger of a modern leader. Most Americans were content, less worried. The world—especially the political world—seemed very different then.

To be sure, the country was quite divided in the Obama years, but partisan divisions—in the halls of Congress, the state leg-islatures, town halls, our own backyards—were comparatively muted. Charlottesville hadn't happened yet; the Russians hadn't yet interfered in America's elections; Trump's impeachment trial had not yet begun. Indeed, the gap between those on the ideo-logical right and those on the left was more or less bridgeable. The same is certainly not true today. We are as politically and socially fractured as at virtually any moment in American history. Families and friends are breaking up under the stress of political division. Thomas Friedman claims we are in a new "Civil War," not as bloody as the first Civil War thankfully, but every bit as destructive. We speak of tribalism, polarization, conspiracy theories, and enemies next door. Politics in America, to put it mildly, is in a bad way.

Donald Trump has something to do with our current state of intractable division. But not all of it. He is as much a symptom of a political environment that breeds polarization as he is an accomplice. Both liberals and conservatives refuse to find common ground on almost anything nowadays, even as they publicly claim to be willing and eager to do so. Democrats and Republicans very rarely cross the aisle, preferring instead to shame their opponents with insults, insinuations, and innuendoes. Untruths are used as political ammunition to gain ground and get ahead. As Friedman writes, "In a tribal world it is rule or die, compromise is a sin, enemies must be crushed and power must be held at all costs."[1] The cut-throat game of politics has apparently reached new heights, where *compromise* and *consensus* are treated as four-letter words.

What does this gloomy assessment of America's deepening political divide have to do with constitutional renewal? A lot, actually. The Constitution has to accept some of the blame for the current state of American politics; the Constitution is partly at fault for America's tribal mentality. For better or worse, the text permits—some might say even encourages—the type of partisan entrenchment, political bickering, and functional deadlock that currently characterizes the entire American political experiment. Take checks and balances as just one obvious example. The institutions of American government are designed in such a way that they must assist each other in the advancement of shared policy aims. Each branch of the federal government has a stake in the success of the others. And yet overlapping and connected powers also means that these institutions are organized so that they can *thwart* progress. Unfortunately, that's exactly what's happening. Preventing the progress of the opposite party is now the primary goal of most politicians.

That's not all. The Constitution's staunch protection of liberty and freedom allows antagonists to say virtually anything about their opponents, civility be damned. Former President Trump can mark most of his opponents with insulting nicknames, while politicians on the left trade barbs right back.[2] Further, the fact that America's Constitution is limited to the "great outlines" of the law allows Presidents to exercise power in ways that would make George Washington cringe. Trump's various "travel bans" are but a few illustrations. Most disturbing perhaps is that a divided Congress is seemingly powerless to stop any of this. Madison wished that the Congress would always be the most crucial branch of the federal government, the one that ensured equilibrium and moderation in the republic. His wish is not currently being realized.

The answer to our present political dysfunction just may be a jolt of Jeffersonian constitutionalism. If we could hit the constitutional restart button, that might help. It's too bad we have no federal mechanism to make that happen. What is interesting, though, is that states—those laboratories of political experimentation—have dabbled in the practice of periodic constitutional renewal for centuries. Jefferson's idea has been tested on the state level. New Hampshire was the first state to include, in its governing charter, a provision for assembling periodic future constitutional conventions. The document instructs the political leaders of the state to take the pulse of the eligible citizenry every seven years on the subject of constitutional revision. Should the need arise, delegates would be sent to Concord to take up the challenge of revising or rewriting the state's fundamental law. The emergent text would then be presented to the people "of the several towns and places" for ratification.

Today, many more states have followed in New Hampshire's footsteps. Alaska, Hawaii, Iowa, and Rhode Island require mandatory ballot questions every ten years on the prospect of assembling a constitutional convention. Article VII of the Michigan Constitution insists on a similar ballot question every sixteen years. Connecticut, Illinois, Maryland, Missouri, Montana, New York,

Ohio, and Oklahoma do the same every twenty years.[3] Twenty-eight additional states have voting mechanisms for convening constitutional conventions, including simple majority votes by the population and/or the state legislatures or supermajority votes by these same bodies. Interestingly, Virginia is one of these states. Article XII of the Virginia Constitution stipulates that a constitutional convention can be called if two-thirds of both houses vote in favor of such action. That's a notoriously high threshold for such action. It seems Jefferson still has not been able to fully convince his fellow Virginians of the merits of generational constitutionalism.

Even so, I think it's clear that Jefferson lost the battle but won the war, at the state level at least. The development of state constitution-making over the past two centuries has shown that his argument was ahead of its time. The number of states that have adopted some mechanism to require a decision on the need for a constitutional convention is testament to the appeal of Jefferson's position. The trend toward mandated ballot initiatives at the state level calling for "con-cons" (as they are informally called) is part of a wave of democratization that characterizes the last fifty years. If these states' examples demonstrate anything, it is that the response to the public's skepticism of political power is to take fundamental decisions—like whether to gather in convention—away from the traditional locus of power and place them directly into the hands of the citizenry. To do the same at the federal level might just be the answer.

With that said, I feel compelled to end on a more hopeful note. It comes in the form of a scene and a challenge. First, the scene. There comes a moment in episode four of the highly acclaimed HBO miniseries on John Adams when Thomas Jefferson introduces his idea for generational constitutional change to the contemporary television audience.

The year is 1786 and the location is a garden in Paris. Jefferson, Adams, and Benjamin Franklin are there when the discussion among the three turns to rumors of an upcoming convention in Philadelphia to construct a "binding Constitution." Franklin remarks that he will be there, "if only to have an effect on the style of the Constitution's prose." The three chuckle at Franklin's self-deprecating humor. Jefferson then says something that takes his audience—both on screen and on couches the world over—by surprise. "I expect that any constitutional document that emerges from Philadelphia," he remarks, "will be as compromised as our Declaration of Independency." "I'm increasingly persuaded," he continues, "that the earth belongs exclusively to the living, and that one generation has no more right to bind another to its laws and judgments than one independent nation has the right to command another." Franklin's and Adams' subtle reactions are exquisite. They look both puzzled and somewhat concerned. After a pause, Adams is first to speak: "But surely the Constitution, as it did with the ones we wrote for our own states, is meant to establish the stability and, uh, the long-term legality essential to the continuation of civilized society." Adams, in that moment, adopts a Madisonian stance, to which Jefferson responds, "Yes, possibly. But I fear it could prove a breach in the integrity of our revolutionary ideals through which will pour the forces of reaction." Exasperated, Adams concludes the conversation by accusing Jefferson of being a "walking contradiction," to which Franklin remarks, "We're all contradictions, Mr. Adams."

In all, the scene lasts fewer than two minutes, and yet it perfectly captures the characters' personalities and their thoughts on the value of enduring Constitutions. Jefferson states his position and Adams, ever the antagonist, replies bluntly. Franklin, in contrast, lounges, says little, and takes it all in.

What I've tried to accomplish in this book is an experiment in constitutional imagination. Readers will no doubt applaud some decisions I have made and criticize others. Still, I hope we can all agree on one thing: that the exercise of constitutional contemplation, in whatever form, is a useful endeavor. Especially in our current highly polarized political environment, it is important that we commence a renewed dialogue about constitutionalism, liberty, and justice. Let us all gather in our metaphorical Parisian garden, like Jefferson, Adams, and Franklin, and explore the contemporary meaning of the U.S. Constitution. Let us replicate the conversation between these three statesmen and ask ourselves if the text fully captures the "laws and values" of the current generation. Is it still worthy of reverence? Does it deserve our continued endorsement, or has it run its course? Can it still be a beacon for a modern political age? Does it have the stuff to resurrect this fragile republic?

Which brings us back to the beginning, of this book and of America's experiment in constitution-making. How deep is our responsibility to be active constitutionalists in this era of discord and cynicism? We have managed to hold on to our current Constitution through great challenges like the Civil War and the Great Depression, but this Constitution most certainly has not protected a sizable portion of the American population; it has not been a revelation for so many. I'll repeat a bold statement here: the U.S. Constitution has changed the world, mostly for the better. But we know so much more about constitutional design and constitution-making now than at any other moment in human history that it is right for us to ask the critical questions: Should we enter Signers' Hall in the National Constitution Center and add our signature to the signatures of the many others who have ratified the document? Or should we abandon this Constitution, and meet in Philadelphia to craft an altogether new one? Important questions, to be sure, for a constitutional people in a constitutional age.

Acknowledgments

I began writing this book more than a decade ago, and had I not taken a lengthy detour into Skidmore College's administration, I would have finished well before now. But I'm not complaining. The time away from the manuscript was a godsend. Whether I knew it or not, the fictional stories in this volume were bouncing around in my head even as my attention was diverted to such non-constitutional topics as tenure decisions, accreditation requirements, and strategic planning. Imagination, it seems, is as much a qualification for administering as it is for constitution-making.

Of course, the time away also meant that I accumulated a large number of intellectual debts, debts that I will never be able to repay in full. Still, thanking the scores of people who supported and encouraged me along the way is the finest reminder of my great good fortune. It begins with the many administrative and faculty colleagues I consider to be wonderful friends: Corey Freeman-Gallant, Karen Kellogg, Paty Rubio, Crystal Moore, Ron Seyb, Philip Glotzbach, Joshua Woodfork, Mary Lou Bates, Rochelle Calhoun, Cerri Banks, Paul Calhoun, Brooke Toma, Debbie Peterson, Sue Blair, Shannon Melvin, Dan Nathan, Beck Krefting, Greg Pfitzer, Mark Youndt, Erica Bastress-Dukehart, Pat Oles, David Karp, Barbara Black, Michael Arnush, Leslie Mechem,

John Brueggemann, Sarah Sweeney, Peter von Allmen, Susannah Mintz, Kim Frederick, Pushi Prasad, Jeff Segrave, Casey Schofield, Marla Melito, Cori Filson, and Kiernan Mathews. Each of you has, in your own special way, propped me up and made me laugh. I can't ask for anything more.

Another source of delight comes from my colleagues in Skidmore's Political Science Department, particularly Natalie Taylor, Flagg Taylor, Kate Graney, Chris Mann, Barbara McDonough, Feryaz Ocakli, Yelena Biberman-Ocakli, Emmanuel Balogun, and Bob Turner. Thank you one and all.

I have also benefited from the wonderful counsel of a few members of the broader public law and constitutional theory communities: Brad Hays, George Thomas, Gary Jacobsohn, and Austin Sarat, as well as two anonymous readers procured by Stanford University Press. I will never be as intellectually gifted as the members of this club, but I am delighted that they have accepted my membership anyway. A special thanks goes to the best teacher I ever had—John Donato—who was forced to suffer through a retelling of my imaginary convention stories on our epic 2018 cross-country road trip. There is nothing like talking with a brilliant friend while experiencing the breathtaking vistas of the Badlands and the Tetons. Absent from that journey were two other great souls—Rich Maloof and Doug Edlin—though they were never far from our minds.

Kate Cavanaugh and Ben Polsky—exceptional students who have taught me more than I them—were present at the beginning. They helped me to organize the entire project, and they were especially crucial in the development of the 1825 story. My debt to them cannot be overstated. Sanford Levinson, Michael Brune, Philip Blumel, and the Reverend W. Douglas Banks generously agreed to "participate" in the imaginary 2022 Constitutional Convention. Thank you, Sandy, Mike, Philip, and Doug for your ideas, your words, and your wisdom. I hope you had fun acting as imaginary convention delegates.

The professionals at Stanford University Press deserve special recognition. Kate Wahl, SUP's Publishing Director and Editor-in-Chief, recognized the kernel of an idea so many years ago. It was she who suggested that each convention chapter could be written in a more narrative style. I can't thank her enough for steering me in this direction. Not only was the process of writing stories more enjoyable than was my two other forays into academic publishing, but I hope the product is better (or at least more accessible). Michelle Lipinski and Marcela Maxfield took Kate's idea and molded the manuscript into its final form. They are both extraordinary editors. Full stop. The book is far better (and far shorter) because they put their considerable imprint on it. Sunna Juhn shepherded the manuscript through its final stages, and Gigi Mark fashioned what I think is a most handsome product. Sincere gratitude goes to both. That same level of gratitude is extended to Stephanie Adams, SUP's marketing marvel, and to Bridget Kinsella, the press' remarkable publicist. The press' authors, including me, are so fortunate to be in their most capable hands. And finally, I would be remiss if I didn't express my profound thanks to Elspeth MacHattie, the press' extraordinarily talented copyeditor. She cleaned up my many silly errors and, in the process, delivered a manuscript I hope is worthy of her name.

Always the most satisfying part of acknowledging support for a book project is the opportunity to publicly thank family. The encouragement I continually receive from my family is inexpressible. My mother, Wendy, and my late father, Jud, along with my brothers, Dave, Matt, and Jamie, their wives, Kristen, Dorsey, and Megan, and their children, Luke, Kayleigh, Colleen, Blakeney, Patrick, Annie, and Hattie, are an endless source of inspiration and good cheer. The same is true about my in-laws: James, Mary, Larry, Tina, Ben, Jimmy, Jane, Daniel, and Luka. My second greatest blessing has been being born into the Breslin family and then marrying into the Starke clan.

My greatest blessing, of course, is right in front of me. Indeed, my life is *so* rich and *so* abundant because of two extraordinary human beings: my wife, Martha, and our daughter, Molly. They are a most magnificent and adventurous pair and, together, we are a squad. Put simply, I love them more than even the wildest imagination could comprehend. This book, as is my life, is dedicated to them.

Notes

1. The signing of the Constitution is captured most famously in Howard Chandler Christy's celebrated painting, which now hangs in the House of Representatives wing of the U.S. Capitol. Each day, Americans experience their own "Christy" moment as they too line up to sign the constitutional document.

2. Beau Breslin, "Is There a Paradox in Amending a Sacred Text?" *Maryland Law Review* 69, no. 1: 66.

3. Sanford Levinson, *Constitutional Faith* (Princeton, NJ: Princeton University Press, 1988), 180.

4. Martin Kady II, "Boehner Mixes Up Constitution and Declaration," *Politico*, November 5, 2009, https://www.politico.com/blogs/on-congress/2009/11/boehner-mixes-up-constitution-and-declaration-022622.

5. A recent survey conducted by the National Constitution Center in Philadelphia concluded that 28% of the respondents believed that the Constitution "has no impact on events today," while 23% didn't believe the text "matters much in daily life." The Center for the Constitution (an independent organization housed at James Madison's Montpelier and devoted to educating the public about the Constitution) conducted a separate national survey in 2010, and the results are most interesting. Citizens were asked questions about their attitude toward the Constitution, their familiarity with its provisions, their outlook on

voting and federalism, and perhaps most importantly, their views on constitutionalism. The juxtaposition of several findings reveals much about America's political attitude. In one question, respondents were asked if the Constitution still works today or whether it is time for a new one. A whopping 88% said that it still works, while only 12% said we need a new one. And yet in a separate set of questions about American constitutionalism—the principle that the Constitution's main role is to limit the power of government and its officials—55% of respondents believed that it badly misses the mark. More than half of these American citizens insisted that the Constitution's first principle—that government should be constrained and limited—is unrealized. And that's not all. Another survey question from this same poll revealed that 44% of respondents believed that the government is not acting for the common good, despite the aim of the constitutional text to promote that specific virtue. See National Constitution Center, *Startling Lack of Constitutional Knowledge Revealed in National Constitution Center Survey Civic Research Poll,* 1997, Press Release, September 15, 1997, https://www.heartland.org/_template-assets/documents/publications/3025.pdf; and Sharon C. Fitzgerald, "Survey: U.S. Admires, but Hasn't Read, Constitution," *Daily Progress,* September 17, 2010, updated May 15, 2019, https://dailyprogress.com/news/article_a4d58bd4-3e2d-50e3-859b-fcede87ec145.html.

6. An Annenberg Public Policy Center survey revealed that few Americans can correctly answer rudimentary questions about the Constitution, such as how many branches of government there are. See Annenberg Public Policy Center, *Is There a Constitutional Right to Own a Home or a Pet? Many Americans Don't Know,* Press Release, September 16, 2015, https://cdn.annenbergpublicpolicycenter.org/wp-content/uploads/Civic-knowledge-survey-Sept.-2015.pdf.

1787

1. Letter from Thomas Jefferson to James Madison, January 30, 1787, *Founders Online,* https://founders.archives.gov. All quotations from Jefferson's letters are from this National Archives source.

2. William Howard Adams does a marvelous job of describing the specifics of the dinner. See Adams, *The Paris Years of Thomas Jefferson* (New Haven, CT: Yale University Press, 1997), esp. chap. 1.

3. See Publius, *Federalist* 51, in *The Federalist Papers* [1787–1788], https://avalon.law.yale.edu/subject_menus/fed.asp. All quotations from the Federalist Papers are from this Avalon Project source.

4. Stephen Holmes probably captures the essence of constitution-alism best (or at least most vividly). "Citizens," he writes, "are myopic; they have little self control, are sadly undisciplined and are always prone to sacrifice enduring principles to short-run pleasures and benefits. A constitution is the institutionalized cure for this chronic myopia; it disempowers temporary majorities in the name of binding norms. A constitution is Peter sober while the electorate is Peter drunk. Citizens need a constitution, just as Ulysses needed to be bound to his mast. If voters were allowed to get what they wanted, they would inevitably ship-wreck themselves. By binding themselves to rigid rules, they can avoid tripping over their own feet." Holmes, "Precommitment and the Par-adox of Democracy," in *Constitutions and Democracy*, ed. Jon Elster and Rune Slagstad (Cambridge: Cambridge University Press, 1988), 196.

5. The Magna Carta, the British Declaration of Rights, and other premodern documents have constitutional characteristics, but they are not fully formed constitutions in the way we understand such doc-uments now. They are more akin to bills of rights than the more archi-tectonic constitutions of the last two centuries.

6. Not all countries adhere to the same type of constitution. In fact, most Middle Eastern countries have a dramatically different constitu-tional model. But the existence of written constitutions has exploded in the last two centuries. See Nathan J. Brown, *Constitutions in a Non-Constitutional World: Arab Basic Laws and the Prospects for Accountable Gov-ernment* (Albany: State University of New York Press, 2002).

7. See Publius, *Federalist* 9.

8. John R. Vile has written an interesting book in which he relays the stories of 170 various proposals to redraft the American Constitution. These stories are not fictitious; they are absolutely real. The book is a very fine, and very fun, read. See Vile, *Re-Framers: 170 Eccentric, Vision-ary, and Patriotic Proposals to Rewrite the U.S. Constitution* (Santa Barbara, CA: ABC-CLIO, 2014).

9. Zachary Elkins, Tom Ginsburg, and James Melton, *The Endur-ance of National Constitutions* (Cambridge: Cambridge University Press, 2009), 1.

10. See Beau Breslin, *From Words to Worlds: Exploring Constitutional Functionality* (Baltimore, MD: Johns Hopkins University Press, 2009).

11. Though Benjamin Franklin proposed one—the Albany Plan—that was not adopted.

12. *The Founders' Constitution*, "Continental Congress, Letter Trans-mitting Proposed Articles of Confederation" [1777], vol. 1, ch. 7, doc.

4 (Chicago: University of Chicago Press), http://press-pubs.uchicago. edu/founders/print_documents/v1ch7s4.html.

13. See Gordon Wood, *The Creation of the American Republic: 1776–1787* (Chapel Hill: University of North Carolina Press, 1969).

14. "For the *National Gazette*, 18 January 1792," *Founders Online*, https://founders.archives.gov/documents/Madison/01-14-02-0172.

15. John R. Vile, *The Constitutional Convention of 1787: A Comprehensive Encyclopedia of America's Founding* (Santa Barbara, CA: ABC-CLIO, 2005), 879.

16. "Madison Debates, Monday July 23, 1787," https://avalon.law. yale.edu/18th_century/debates_723.asp.

17. Forrest McDonald and Ellen S. McDonald, "John Dickinson, Founding Father," *Delaware History* 23, no. 1 (1988): 24–38.

18. Richard Labunski, *James Madison and the Struggle for the Bill of Rights* (New York: Oxford University Press, 2006), 110.

19. Letter from Thomas Jefferson to James Madison, December 20, 1787.

20. Letter from Thomas Jefferson to John Adams, August 1, 1816.

21. For the best treatment of the problem of precommitment, see Holmes, "Precommitment and the Paradox of Democracy."

22. See Breslin, *From Words to Worlds*.

23. Letter from Thomas Jefferson to Samuel Kercheval, July 12, 1816.

24. Letter from Thomas Jefferson to James Madison, September 6, 1789.

25. Ibid. One dinner guest in particular—Condorcet—had stimulated Jefferson's thinking. His mathematical skills deeply impressed the Virginian, especially in the areas of half-lives and actuarial tables. Jefferson was particularly influenced by Condorcet's idea that actuarial calculations could reveal the general time in which a new generation emerged. Here's how it worked: most legal contracts are binding on parties as long as those parties are alive. The contracts thus expire when one or more of the signatories die. Thus, there is always a fixed time in the future when a legally binding contract becomes null and void. That stretch of time fascinated the mathematician in Condorcet. He convinced Jefferson that after nineteen years at least one party to a contract would likely no longer be among the living. More precisely, after nineteen years, the chances were doubled that one or more signatories to a contract would be dead. And this finding applied to constitutions too. Based on these actuarial predictions, Jefferson calculated that

generations last roughly nineteen years and that a constitution—which he saw as a contract between living citizens—could last that long. But that was it. After nineteen years, more than half the individuals who had agreed to live under an existing constitution would have left the earth, and thus it was time for a new drafting convention. Consider the words of Iain McLean and Arnold Urken, who probably describe this situation best: "Jefferson's well-known letter to Madison dated September 1789, 'That the Earth belongs in usufruct to the living,' is plainly derived from Condorcet. Jefferson proposed that contracts should be repudiated after nineteen years, because by that time the probability that at least one of the contractors had died would have reached 0.5. This idea of the half-life of a contract, and the actuarial calculations needed to establish it, are both due to Condorcet." McLean and Urken, "Did Jefferson or Madison Understand Condorcet's Theory of Social Choice?" *Public Choice* 73, no. 4 (June 1992): 447.

26. Herbert Sloan understands this side of Jefferson's thinking with impressive subtlety. In reference to the Virginian's specific use of the concept of "generation" as opposed to, say, the "people" in his letter to Madison, Sloan writes:

> To speak of "the people" is to speak abstractly. . . . "The people" never dies; it has the same corporate immortality and collective right of sovereignty that is attached to the king's political body in earlier theory. A "generation," on the other hand, and certainly a "generation" as Jefferson defined it, is specific and identifiable. Unlike "the people," it has a limited duration, so that there will be a time after which it no longer has rights. That limitation is critical, for it allows Jefferson to establish with precision who can exercise rights and when. With "the people," rights are, in effect inchoate; with a "generation," we know exactly what we are dealing with.

See Sloan, "The Earth Belongs in Usufruct to the Living," in *Jeffersonian Legacies*, ed. Peter S. Onuf (Charlottesville, VA: University of Virginia Press, 1993), 297.

27. Letter from Thomas Jefferson to Samuel Kercheval, June 12, 1816.

28. Ibid. Jefferson may have softened his stance a bit in the period between corresponding with Madison and Kercheval. Specifically, in the letter to Kercheval he seems to acknowledge that along with convening an actual constitutional convention to draft a generation-specific

constitution, a detailed and extensive process of *amendment* to an existing constitution might also suffice to adequately reflect a generation's needs.

29. Lucien Jaume, "Constituent Power in France: The Revolution and Its Consequences," in *The Paradox of Constitutionalism: Constituent Power and Constitutional Form,* ed. Martin Loughlin and Neil Walker (Oxford: Oxford University Press, 2007), 70–71.

30. Nadia Urbinati, *Representative Democracy: Principles and Genealogy* (Chicago: University of Chicago Press, 2008), 185.

31. Thomas Paine, *Rights of Man* [1791], https://www.ushistory.org/paine/rights/c1-010.htm.

32. See *Federalist* 49.

33. In a sense, Madison's argument anticipates one that appears almost two centuries later, made by one of the great legal theorists of our time. Joseph Raz argues that the key to an enduring, authoritative constitutional text is the validity of its drafters. If the community perceives the drafters as legitimate, the constitution will enjoy the moral authority to carry on for long periods of time. See the chapter "On the Authority and Interpretation of Constitutions," in Raz, *Between Authority and Interpretation: On the Theory of Law and Practical Reason* (Oxford: Oxford University Press, 2009).

34. Letter from James Madison to Thomas Jefferson, February 4, 1790, *Founders Online,* https://founders.archives.gov/documents/Madison/01-13-02-0020.

35. For a detailed discussion of Madison's instinct toward preservation and, in particular, his Burkean (and Aristotelian) argument that stability requires public obedience toward a nation's fundamental law, see Elkins et al., *Endurance of National Constitutions,* esp. chap. 2.

36. See also *Federalist* 62.

37. Brutus, "Essays of Brutus: II, 1 November 1787," in *The Anti-Federalist: Writings by the Opponents of the Constitution,* ed. Herbert Storing (Chicago: University of Chicago Press, 1981), 117.

38. See Friends of the Article V Convention, www.foavc.org.

39. Frederick Douglass, "The Constitution and Slavery," *The North Star,* March 16, 1849.

40. Sanford Levinson, *Our Undemocratic Constitution: Where the Constitution Goes Wrong (And How We the People Can Correct It)* (New York; Oxford University Press, 2006), 9. (Emphasis added.)

41. National Constitution Center, *Startling Lack of Constitutional Knowledge Revealed in National Constitution Center Survey Civic Research Poll,* 1997, Press Release, September 15, 1997, https://www.heartland.org/_template-assets/documents/publications/3025.pdf.

42. National Constitution Center, *More Teens Can Name Three Stooges Than Can Name Three Branches of Government*, Press Release, September 2, 1998, https://constitutioncenter.org/media/files/survey-1999-stooges.pdf.

43. National Constitution Center, *Startling Lack of Constitutional Knowledge Revealed.*

44. Carl J. Friedrich, "The Political Theory of the New Democratic Constitutions," *Review of Politics* 12, no. 2 (April 1950): 215.

45. See Bruce Ackerman, *We the People: Transformations* (Cambridge, MA: Belknap Press, 2000).

46. Jon Elster, "Deliberation and Constitution Making," in *Deliberative Democracy*, ed. Jon Elster (Cambridge: Cambridge University Press, 1998), 117.

47. The best explanations of the value of counterfactuals come from Richard J. Evans and Niall Ferguson. See Evans, *Altered Pasts: Counterfactuals in History* (Waltham, MA: Brandeis University Press, 2013); and Ferguson, ed., *Virtual History: Alternatives and Counterfactuals* (New York: Basic Books, 1999).

48. Gary J. Kornblith, "Rethinking the Coming of the Civil War: A Counterfactual Exercise," *Journal of American History* 90, no. 1 (June 2003): 79.

49. The story goes as follows: during the founding period, indebted farmers held a majority in Rhode Island's legislature. Fearing that they would suffer the same fate as Daniel Shays, these poor, agrarian politicians hatched a clever scheme to eliminate debt by printing and circulating paper money. Their plan was to pay off their creditors with this worthless currency. Unsurprisingly, the creditors, expecting payment in the form of legitimate money, refused to accept the newly minted bills. The legislators' response? Rather than coming to their senses and realizing the transparency of their scheme to avoid debt repayment, they exercised their lawmaking power by passing legislation that mandated acceptance of the repayment. In other words, they used their power as elected representatives to shove the useless money down the throats of their creditors. The result was a standoff (in fact, some creditors simply left the state). When creditors still refused to accept payment and challenged the constitutionality of the law, and the Rhode Island Supreme Court ruled in their favor, the legislature simply passed another law dissolving the current court and replacing all of its Justices. With a few quick strokes of a pen, the Rhode Island legislature managed to accelerate a currency crisis, dry up most of the available credit, frighten away some of the most

important landowners in the entire state, and shut down the state's highest judicial body. It is probably an understatement to say that the actions of the Rhode Island legislators petrified the delegates to the Constitutional Convention, all of whom were wealthy landowners concerned about their fortunes.

50. To put that total number into context, consider that CODESA 1, the Convention for a Democratic South Africa, had 228 delegates. That gathering gave rise to South Africa's current Constitution, promulgated in 1996 and ratified in 1997.

51. It's important to acknowledge that there are many altered realities that could emerge from this exercise. Different individuals will no doubt make different choices. That is, after all, the joy of the counterfactual enterprise.

52. One illustration might suffice. The Northwest Ordinance of 1787, though renewed in 1789, continued to be in force beyond the life of the Articles of Confederation.

53. John J. Dinan, "The Political Dynamics of Mandatory State Constitutional Convention Referendums: Lessons from the 2000s Regarding Obstacles and Pathways to Their Passage," *Montana Law Review* 71, no. 2 (Summer 2010): 395–432.

54. State constitutions and state constitutional conventions are valuable source information for this project, but their value probably wanes over time. State constitutions carried more gravitas or weight during the *national* constitutional dialogue in the eighteenth and nineteenth centuries than they do in the twentieth and twenty-first centuries.

55. Now, some facts: twenty states have known only a single constitution in their entire existence. In contrast, two states—Georgia and Louisiana—have undergone ten or more constitutional conventions throughout their history. The average number of constitutions for those states that have assembled more than one constitutional convention is four. The state constitutional convention schedule was most active in the nineteenth century, with ninety-four state constitutions drafted and ratified—almost one per year—in that 100-year stretch. The pace slowed considerably in the twentieth century. Twenty-six state constitutions were forged in that period. No state has yet produced a new constitution in the twenty-first century.

56. The idea of constitutionalizing a periodic "con-con" picked up steam only in the second half of the twentieth century.

1825

1. Only the three candidates with the highest electoral vote totals were eligible in a contingent election.

2. Paul C. Nagel, "The Election of 1824: A Reconsideration Based on Newspaper Opinion," *Journal of Southern History* 26, no. 3 (August 1960): 315–329.

3. James Traub, "The Ugly Election That Birthed Modern American Politics," *History* (November/December 2016), https://www .nationalgeographic.com/history/magazine/2016/11-12/america -presidential-elections-1824-corrupt-bargain.

4. Edward Pessen, *Jacksonian America: Society, Personality, and Politics* (Homewood, IL: Dorsey Press, 1969), 211.

5. The number 131 represents one more than half the total number of members of the 19th Congress. Each state had been asked to send a number of delegates equal to half of its respective delegation in Congress. If it had three Members of Congress, the state could send two delegates to the Constitutional Convention.

6. Wiktor Osiatynski, "The Paradoxes of Constitutional Borrowing," *International Journal of Constitutional Law*, 1, no. 2 (April 2003): 244.

7. Of course, the most frenetic period of constitution-making probably occurred during the fall of the Soviet Union in the late 1980s and early 1990s. It was then that former Soviet states looked to other constitutional regimes for inspiration and ideas. The process was anything but simple; Jon Elster referred to the task of crafting post-Soviet constitutions as "rebuilding the boat in the open sea." He argued that the Eastern European experiment in constitution-making was unlike any before or since. Elster did insist that the conditions were ideal for constitutional imitation, however. The countries of Eastern Europe shared a similar tradition (Soviet rule), a similar transition from a centralized to a market economy, similar histories, even a similar quest to modernize and become, shall we say, more European. They even inspired each other to accelerate the democratization and constitutionalization of their newly independent states. These conditions, combined with the fact that Eastern European constitutional designers had dozens of constitutional texts around the world from which to borrow, made the task of forming new constitutional regimes just a tad easier. Not easy, mind you, but easier. See Elster, "Constitution-Making in Eastern Europe: Rebuilding the Boat in the Open Sea," *Public Administration* 71 (1993): 169–217.

8. Osiatynski, "Paradoxes of Constitutional Borrowing," 244. (Emphasis added.)

9. Traub, "Ugly Election That Birthed Modern American Politics."

10. Alexander Keyssar, *The Right to Vote: The Contested History of Democracy in the United States* (New York: Basic Books, 2000), 40.

11. Thomas W. Howard, "Indiana Newspapers and the Presidential Election of 1824," *Indiana Magazine of History* 63, no. 3 (September 1967): 177–206.

12. The Seventeenth Amendment, calling for the direct election of Senators, was ratified in 1913.

13. Keyssar, *Right to Vote*, 30.

14. Merrill Peterson, *Democracy, Liberty, and Property* (Indianapolis, IN: Liberty Fund, 1966), 171.

15. Keyssar, *Right to Vote*, 37.

16. Peterson, *Democracy, Liberty, and Property*, 69.

17. Ibid., 84.

18. Ibid., 86.

19. Robert V. Remini, *Daniel Webster: The Man and His Time* (New York: Norton, 1997), 175.

20. Remini, *Daniel Webster*, 181.

21. Peterson, *Democracy, Liberty, and Property*, 186.

22. Keyssar, *Right to Vote*, 45.

23. Ibid.

24. Peterson, *Democracy, Liberty, and Property*, 185.

25. William Price, *Nathaniel Macon, Planter* (Raleigh: North Carolina Office of Archives and History, 2001), 204.

26. Troy L. Kickler, *Nathaniel Macon: American Patriot and Defender of Liberty*, North Carolina History Project (Raleigh, NC: John Locke Foundation, 2016), www.northcarolinahistory.org/commentary/327/entry.

27. Letter to Thomas Jefferson from Nathaniel Macon, February 2, 1822, in the American History Collection, Founders Early Access, Papers of Thomas Jefferson (Charlottesville: University of Virginia Press), http://rotunda.upress.virginia.edu/founders/default.xqy?keys=-FOEA-print-04-02-02-2632.

28. Keyssar, *Right to Vote*, 331.

29. Peterson, *Democracy, Liberty, and Property*, 178.

30. Letter from Thomas Jefferson to Samuel Kercheval, June 12, 1816.

31. John Niven, *John C. Calhoun and the Price of the Union: A Biography* (Baton Rouge: Louisiana State University Press, 1993), 30.

32. John C. Calhoun, *A Disquisition on Government* (Indianapolis, IN: Bobbs-Merrill, 1953), 5.

33. Peterson, *Democracy, Liberty, and Property*, 175.

34. Michael Waldman, "The Right to Vote? Don't Count on It," Brennan Center for Justice, February 29, 2016, https://www.brennancenter.org/our-work/analysis-opinion/right-vote-dont-count-it.

35. Peterson, *Democracy, Liberty, and Property*, 59.

36. Letter of Thomas Jefferson to Edmund Pendleton, August 26, 1776.

37. Keyssar, *Right to Vote*, 337.

38. *Federalist* 84.

39. Donald Lutz has an interesting take on this phenomenon. He suggests that state constitutional framers might have considered the federal Bill of Rights as distinct and separate from the federal Constitution proper. See Lutz, *The Origins of American Constitutionalism* (Baton Rouge: Louisiana State University Press, 1988).

40. With one exception. The word "Posterity" was dropped from the original Preamble, because it contradicted the very essence of Jefferson's generational constitutionalism.

41. In 1786, he wrote to George Washington that "it is an axiom in my mind that our liberty can never be safe but in the hands of the people themselves, and that too of the people with a certain degree of instruction. That is the business of the state to effect, and on a general plan." See the letter from Thomas Jefferson to George Washington, January 4, 178[6]). Similarly, he wrote to John Adams that public education would eventually become the "key-stone of the arch of our government." He was adamant that universal public education was a key ingredient for a burgeoning America. See the letter from Thomas Jefferson to John Adams, October 28, 1813.

42. See "Elementary School Act" [1871], *Thomas Jefferson Encyclopedia*, https://www.monticello.org/site/research-and-collections/elementary-school-act.

43. See Thomas Jefferson, *Notes on the State of Virginia* [1781], https://docsouth.unc.edu/southlit/jefferson/jefferson.html.

44. See George Thomas, *The Founders and the Idea of a National University: Constituting the American Mind* (New York: Cambridge University Press, 2015).

45. Marbury v. Madison (1803).

46. Martin v. Hunter's Lessee (1816); and Cohens v. Virginia (1821).

47. McCulloch v. Maryland, 17 U.S. 316 (1819).

48. Gibbons v. Ogden, 22 U.S. 1 (1824).

49. Remini, *Daniel Webster*, 55.

1863

1. Alan Guelzo, "What Did Lincoln Really Think of Jefferson?" *New York Times*, July 3, 2015.

2. Charles A. Beard and Mary R. Beard, *The Rise of American Civilization* (New York: Macmillan, 1930).

3. Gary Kornblith said it best: "[T]he parallels are striking. Both the Revolution and the Civil War broke out roughly a dozen years after the formal conclusion of a war for empire on the North American continent that ended in an overwhelming triumph for Anglo-Americans. In each case, the acquisition of new territory raised critical questions about the authority structure of the empire and the limits of local autonomy." He continued, "What began as a debate over the powers of the central government developed into a full-blown constitutional crisis that resulted in a declaration of independence and military resistance by several geographically contiguous provinces (thirteen in the case of the Revolution, eleven in the case of the Civil War)." Kornblith, "Rethinking the Coming of the Civil War: A Counterfactual Exercise," *Journal of American History* 90. no. 1 (June 2003): 76.

4. Many thanks to Allen Guelzo, Director of the James Madison Program Initiative on Politics and Statesmanship and Senior Research Scholar in the Council of the Humanities at Princeton University, for his helpful assistance on this topic.

5. The Crittenden Compromise proposed six constitutional amendments and four congressional resolutions and was introduced by John J. Crittenden (Kentucky), in December 1860, to resolve the growing tension between the North and the South. The proposal did not pass.

6. This "peace conference" was held in February 1861 at a hotel in Washington, DC. The goal of the conference was to draft constitutional amendments that would prevent the outbreak of the Civil War. These amendments, too, failed.

7. Eric Foner, *Free Soil, Free Labor, Free Men: The Ideology of the Republican Party before the Civil War* (New York: Oxford University Press, 1970), 116.

8. The language of the rider itself was not novel. It mirrored the language of the Northwest Ordinance of 1787. Wilmot was tapped

to introduce the measure primarily because his northern colleagues believed he could attract some southern support. Most knew that southerners viewed Wilmot as a moderately sympathetic voice in the slavery debate, in contrast to others who backed the provision but were viewed as far too extreme in their anti-slavery positions. The latter group of men would never secure votes from southern Members of Congress because they had been so vociferous in opposition to slavery itself. Many from the South thought abolitionists would use the rider as leverage to attack the institution of slavery in the Deep South. Wilmot's name was added simply because he was an agreeable character.

9. See Martin Diamond, "Review: *The Federalist* on Federalism: Neither a National nor a Federal Constitution, but a Composition of Both," *Yale Law Journal* 86, no. 6 (May 1977), 1273–1285.

10. Paraphrased from *John Brown's Raid*, Teachinghistory.org, 2018, https://teachinghistory.org/history-content/beyond-the-textbook/25478.

11. Mark A. Graber, "The Second Freedmen's Bureau Bill's Constitution," *Texas Law Journal* 94: 1361.

12. See Jim Downs, *Sick from Freedom: African-American Illness and Suffering during the Civil War and Reconstruction* (Oxford: Oxford University Press, 2012).

13. Nicole Duncan, "5 Things to Know about the Civil Rights Act of 18[6]6," *TheGrio*, September 12, 2019, https://thegrio.com/2019/09/12/civil-rights-act-of-1886-facts.

14. Betty L. Mitchell, "Massachusetts Reacts to John Brown's Raid," *Civil War History* 19, no. 1 (March 1973): 65–79.

15. See Douglas Keith and Eric Petry, *Apportionment of State Legislatures, 1776–1920* (New York: Brennan Center for Justice, 2015).

16. See Alabama Legislature, Constitution of 1868, http://www.legislature.state.al.us/aliswww/history/constitutions/1868/1868all.html.

17. Especially given that Lincoln's son, Robert Todd Lincoln, was a student at Harvard College at the time. However, the President never visited his son in Cambridge.

1903

1. "Reconstruction vs. Redemption," National Endowment for the Humanities (February 11, 2014), https://www.neh.gov/news/reconstruction-vs-redemption.

2. The Civil Rights cases of 1883 were also part of this series.

3. Justice David Brewer did not participate.

4. Plessy v. Ferguson, 167 U.S. 537 (1896).

5. It can be said that the 1825 Constitution was also unsuccessful in overcoming the country's major troubles. It could not prevent the Civil War.

6. Segregation was a northern problem as well, though the form it would take differed from that in the South. See Thomas Sugrue, *Sweet Land of Liberty: The Forgotten Struggle for Civil Rights in the North* (New York: Random House, 2008); and Richard Rothstein, *The Color of Law: A Forgotten History of How Our Government Segregated America* (New York: Liveright, 2017).

7. See Michael Rosenthal, *Nicholas Miraculous: The Amazing Career of the Redoubtable Dr. Nicholas Murray Butler* (New York: Columbia University Press, 2015).

8. It wasn't always the smoothest period for the university—Butler was well-known for dismissing faculty members who crossed him and all but ignoring the fine arts departments—but Columbia emerged as one of the world's great havens of intellectualism during his tenure.

9. See Thomas Mallon, "An Empty Robe," *New York Times*, January 22, 2006.

10. Rosenthal goes on in *Nicholas Miraculous* to offer a devastating portrait of Butler. He argues that the Columbia president was more bluster than intellect, more narcissistic than altruistic, and generally concerned only with his own ambitions. He even describes a friendship between Butler and Mussolini.

11. Eventually, the speech would be remembered for stirring controversy because, in it, Washington took an accommodationist stance against Jim Crow and discrimination. Rather than agitate for social justice, Washington insisted that Blacks should concentrate on education and industry to improve their lot. He argued that racial tension would improve once Whites recognized that Blacks could "contribute to the marketplace of the world" and "live by the production of our hands." But that required Blacks to remain fixed in a social structure that promoted intolerance and subordination. Washington would later butt heads with more radical Black leaders like W.E.B. Du Bois, who opposed Washington's restrained and conciliatory attitude. Du Bois, in fact, accused Black accommodationists like Washington of ignoring White racial privilege—a "public and psychological wage" that benefits Whites just as wealth benefits elites—to the detriment of the entire

Black race. Du Bois would go on to split from Washington around the turn of the century.

12. Interestingly, it would be sixty-five more years before another Republican represented the state of Alabama in Congress.

13. W.E.B. Du Bois called the *Tribune* "the chief news-sheet in the city."

14. Sims, a Democrat, worried about partisan power too.

15. Four states allowed women to vote prior to 1900: Wyoming, Colorado, Utah, and Idaho. These were rugged and mountainous states with very small populations. They were logging states and trapper states: beautiful to behold, but hard to endure. The winters were long and the terrain was harsh. These mountainous states boasted famous trading posts and military bases, but little infrastructure and even less commercial activity. The discovery of gold in California brought pioneers to, and through, the Rocky Mountains, and some fell in love with the region's natural beauty. Most of those who fell in love with the area were men, and that presented its own problems. In order to attract single women to the mountain west, these four states decided to take the lead in the women's rights movement. They each included the grant of women's suffrage in their state constitutional documents. It was purely a marketing strategy: "Relocate to Wyoming, ladies, and you too can vote!" States didn't have slogans, formal marketing campaigns, or brands at the time (think "I love New York"), but they were always jockeying for ways to attract more residents. The strategy of western states was to offer women the franchise. And it worked. The brand campaign was ultimately successful because each state experienced a modest influx of female immigrants. Of course, the objective of gender migration was not as pressing elsewhere, especially east of the Mississippi where men were not hurting for female companionship. Enticing women to relocate to various parts of the country by offering the right to vote just didn't have the same allure outside of the desolate mountain west.

16. Published in 1901, the autobiography was widely scrutinized at the time, and it remains one of the best-selling African American autobiographies of all time. The work provides a glimpse into Washington's worldview. About forgiveness, the author writes: "It is now long ago that I learned this lesson . . . that I would permit no man, no matter what his color might be, to narrow and degrade my soul by making me hate him. With God's help, I believe that I have completely rid myself of any ill feeling toward the Southern White man for any wrong that he may

have inflicted upon my race." In chapter 2, he writes about resilience and perseverance: "I have learned that success is to be measured not so much by the position one has reached in life as by the obstacles which he has overcome while trying to succeed." Throughout the book, Washington tells of his struggles and triumphs. He recounts the many experiences—both good and bad—that helped to shape his character. See Booker T. Washington, *Up from Slavery: An Autobiography* (New York: Random House, 1999).

17. Washington was never a fan of organized labor, though he was an impassioned champion of the working man.

18. Kenneth Hamilton, ed., *Records of the National Negro Business League* (Bethesda, MD: University Publications of America, 1995), v.

19. Booker T. Washington, "Pragmatism," *Lapham's Quarterly* (1903).

20. Washington's position on women's rights (especially in terms of the vote) was complicated. In a *New York Times* piece in 1908, he confessed to some reluctance to extend the franchise to women, though he concluded that article by saying, "but this is a question concerning which, it seems to me, the women know better than men, and I am willing to leave it to their deliberate judgment." Washington demonstrated over and over again that women, who were educated at Tuskegee alongside men, were capable of productive labor and were deserving of dignity.

21. Booker T. Washington, "The Negro and the Labor Unions," *The Atlantic*, June 1913, https://www.theatlantic.com/magazine/archive/1913/06/the-negro-and-the-labor-unions/529524.

22. Washington's attitude toward organized labor was also complicated. Throughout much of his life, he argued that the "Negro laborer did not trust the unions" because the southern worker was "more accustomed to work for persons than for wages." He also witnessed numerous times in which Black workers were strikebusters, and he was aware that some unions maintained the belief that Blacks were stealing White jobs. Nevertheless, over time, Washington came to appreciate the unions and to recognize that they were a force for good, that they actually understood that including Blacks among the members was mutually beneficial to all races. In a famous *Atlantic* article, he wrote, "I am convinced that [labor unions] can and will become an important means of doing away with the [racial] prejudice that now exists in many parts of the country against the Negro laborer." Washington, "The Negro and the Labor Unions."

335

23. See Steven G. Calabrisi and Larissa Price, "Monopolies and the Constitution: A History of Crony Capitalism" (Faculty working papers, Paper 214, 2012), http://scholarlycommons.law.northwestern.edu/facultyworkingpapers/214.

24. United States v. E. C. Knight Company, 156 U.S. 1 (1895).

25. In re Debs, 158 U.S. 564 (1895).

26. Booker T. Washington, "Atlanta Compromise" Speech, September 18, 1895, https://www.loc.gov/exhibits/civil-rights-act/multimedia/booker-t-washington.html.

27. Interestingly, some contemporary conservatives claim the current debate about the constitutional right of privacy exposes Hamilton's general fear.

28. Progressives were particularly skeptical of the substantive due process cases, like *Allgeyer v. Louisiana,* 165 U.S. 578 (1897) and *Lochner v. New York,* 198 U.S. 45 (1905).

29. Frank Pommersheim, *Broken Landscapes: Indians, Indian Tribes, and the Constitution* (Oxford: Oxford University Press, 2009), 128. Teller had intimate knowledge too. He had been appointed Secretary of the Interior by President Chester Arthur in 1882 and served three years in Arthur's cabinet. The Bureau of Indian Affairs reported directly to Teller's Interior Department. While Secretary of the Interior, Teller approved the Code of Indian Offenses, a set of rules that punished Native peoples for such activities as performing ritual healings, participating in tribal ceremonies, engaging in polygamy, and following traditional burial practices. The judge and jury for these "offenses" were Indian appointees working for the federal government. They were often unsympathetic to arguments made by their fellow tribesmen. The system was stacked against American Indians who fought to save their cultural traditions.

30. Federal citizenship for American Indians would not be granted until the passage of the Indian Citizenship Act in 1924.

31. Teller was born in the Finger Lakes region of upstate New York, and moved west to Colorado after he began practicing law. He was familiar with New York's 1821 law because of stories he'd heard of a time when his father was prevented from leasing land from a White landlord in nearby Seneca County, New York. It was Cayuga country, his father was told. The elder Teller could not lay claim to the land because it was protected under the 1821 law. He was forever bitter about that squandered opportunity.

32. Theodore Roosevelt, First Annual Message—December 3, 1901,

https://millercenter.org/the-presidency/presidential-speeches/december-3-1901-first-annual-message.

33. See Josiah Strong, *Our Country: Its Possible Future and Its Present Crisis* (Astor Place, NY: American Home Missionary Society, 1885).

34. Hundreds of thousands of Cubans were forced into concentration camps where conditions were horrific.

35. The previous declaration of war occurred in 1848, beginning the Mexican-American War.

36. The biggest headache associated with the selection process was that state legislatures often could not decide between two or more candidates. Some "campaigns" ended in a legislative tie, while others paralyzed the state legislatures. Frequently, a Senate seat would remain unoccupied for long periods of time because of these highly political challenges. Delaware, for example, could not decide on a Senator for four full years (1899–1903). Oregon's entire legislative agenda was held up for twelve months when the state House refused to select a U.S. Senator.

In a few cases, U.S. Senators were accused of buying their seats, a relatively simple transaction when you consider that the selection committee is just the small number of state legislators in the state capital. Some might even argue that the simple process of selecting Senators even *encouraged* bribery. The scandal that most highlighted the problem of selection occurred when the Senate refused to seat William A. Clark, the Senator-elect from the state of Montana. Evidence surfaced that Clark had bribed state legislators in Helena to "win" the seat. The Senate, trying to take the ethical high road, and perhaps trying to shed its reputation as a corruptible institution, rebuffed Clark altogether. They refused to let him take the oath of office. The cost to Clark's bank account was probably modest, but that to his dream of representing Montana in the U.S. Senate was considerable. At least for a while. As it turns out, Clark's story had a certain redemptive ending. He was elected a year later to fill the other open Montana Senate seat. This one he apparently earned fair and square.

1953

1. The 1787 Constitution's word count amounts to a mere 4,440 words, measuring in length somewhere between the average *People* magazine cover story and a fiction piece in the *New Yorker.*

2. McCulloch v. Maryland, 17 U.S. 316 (1819).

3. Edmund Randolph was just as direct. Randolph was a member of the 1787 Convention's Committee of Detail, the group responsible for taking all the resolutions passed by the delegates and assembling them

into a draft constitution. The committee's report included a preamble, or introduction, penned by Randolph himself, which articulated the following constitution-making rules: "1. "To insert essential principles only; lest the operations of government should be clogged by rendering those provisions permanent and unalterable, which ought to be accommodated to times and events: and 2. To use simple and precise language, and general propositions, according to the example of the constitutions of several states." His sentiments were a clear precursor to Marshall's famous interpretation of a "living" constitution.

4. In some ways, civil liberties were under attack to a degree unmatched since the fall of slavery. Unless, of course, you were an African American in this country. Then your civil liberties were continually under attack in the nine decades that separated the ends of the Civil War and the Korean War. Enslavement did not end during the Civil War. It just evolved and took different forms.

5. See Robert Bellah et al., *Habits of the Heart: Individualism and Commitment in American Life* (Berkeley: University of California Press, 1985); and Robert D. Putnam, *Bowling Alone: The Collapse and Revival of American Community* (New York: Simon and Schuster, 2000).

6. There were eleven state constitutional conventions in that period. Louisiana underwent two constitutional changes.

7. John Joseph Wallis, NBER/University of Maryland State Constitutions Project, http://www.stateconstitutions.umd.edu/index.aspx.

8. His enduring popularity is so huge that a bust of Percival Baxter—a one-term Governor who presided almost a century ago—still greets all visitors to the Maine statehouse.

9. It is interesting: periodic or generational constitutional conventions have a way of focusing people's attention on those issues, practices, customs, and policies that generate strong feelings on both sides. Even if years have passed and the spokespeople who promoted the controversial policies have retreated from the spotlight, opponents and skeptics still want to re-litigate them on the constitutional convention floor.

10. FDR's frustration was so palpable that he even proposed a court-packing plan, a fundamental reconfiguration of the U.S. Supreme Court, in an attempt to appoint sympathetic jurists. The plan was unsuccessful.

11. Donald Lutz, Foreword, in *The Constitutionalism of American States*, ed. George Conor and Christopher Hammond (Columbia: University of Missouri Press, 2008), xvi–xvii.

12. During the six-year period in which the Texan led the House,

he managed to pass a number of measures, including funding for the Manhattan Project, a secret initiative to develop atomic weapons.

13. Another story confirms this tale. Along with 142 Democrats, 50 Republicans contributed to a fund to purchase a car for Rayburn when he first stepped down from the speakership. You see, the Speaker of the House is entitled to a car while in office. Rayburn was left without wheels when the Democrats lost the majority in 1946, so his friends, on both sides of the aisle, pooled their money to buy him a vehicle. A Cadillac, in fact. Rayburn was genuinely touched by the gesture, especially because it came in large part from his political opponents. Ultimately, he returned the dollars donated by his Republican colleagues because he did not want to create the illusion of a conflict of interest, but he never forgot their generosity.

14. Ford attributes Nixon's decision to appoint him as Vice President, at least in part, to the friendship they forged during the Chowder and Marching Club days.

15. Juan Williams, "The Many Masks of Thurgood Marshall: Behind the Justice's Curmudgeonly Persona a Special Kind of Torment," *Washington Post*, January 31, 1993, https://www.washingtonpost.com/archive/opinions/1993/01/31/the-many-masks-of-thurgood-marshall/049c3d2f-b7b9-4120-8fde-e418cecb9d45.

16. America's experience in generational constitutional renewal added yet another wrinkle to the practice of constitutional interpretation. The concept of "originalist" interpretation takes on a different meaning when there are a number of texts vying for attention. Does an originalist interpret the words as they were commonly understood at the time of the most recent constitutional convention or as they were understood at the time when the particular clause was first introduced into the U.S. Constitution?

17. One can only wonder how states' rights advocates like Baxter and Holt would have reacted to FDR's power if the President had simply followed convention and retired after two terms in office.

18. Ulysses S. Grant and Theodore Roosevelt both sought third terms after stepping away from the presidency for a while. Neither was successful in his third-term bid.

19. David Jordan, *FDR, Dewey, and the Election of* 1944 (Bloomington: Indiana University Press, 2011), 290.

20. Youngstown Sheet and Tube Company v. Sawyer, 343 U.S. 579 (1952).

21. The mention of "Indians not taxed" in the civil rights clauses

introduced into the 1863 Constitution was removed in the 1903 federal Constitution.

22. Cynthia Levinson and Sanford Levinson. *Fault Lines in the Constitution: The Framers, Their Fights, and the Flaws That Affect Us Today* (Atlanta: Peachtree, 2017), 7.

23. Mark A. Graber, "Why Nine Meant Thirteen," National Constitution Center, n.d., https://constitutioncenter.org/interactive-constitution /interpretation/article-vii/interps/24#why-nine-meant-thirteen-by -mark-graber.

24. New Hampshire was the ninth state to ratify. It did so on June 21, 1788.

25. Graber, "Why Nine Meant Thirteen."

26. The most earnest discussion came in 1863, but the unusual circumstances of that convention probably prevented a full discussion about the proper process going forward.

27. Pew Research Center, "Trust in Government: 1958–2015," in *Beyond Distrust: How Americans View Their Government*, November 23, 2015, https://www.people-press.org/2015/11/23/1-trust-in-government -1958-2015.

28. David O. Stewart, *The Summer of 1787: The Men Who Invented the Constitution* (New York: Simon and Schuster, 2007), 166.

29. Ibid.

30. They also erased the mention of "Ourselves," which seemed redundant and unnecessary without the reference to "our Posterity." The entire Preamble thus read, "We the People of the United States, in Order to form a more perfect Union, establish Justice, insure domestic Tranquility, provide for the common defense, promote the general Welfare, and secure the blessings of Liberty, do ordain and establish this Constitution for the United States of America."

31. See Zachary Elkins, Tom Ginsberg, and James Melton, *The Endurance of National Constitutions* (Cambridge: Cambridge University Press, 2009).

2022

1. The recent COVID-19 pandemic is certainly another disrupter.

2. Todd Wasserman, "Iceland Unveils Crowdsourced Constitution," *Mashable*, July 29, 2011, https://mashable.com/2011/07/29/ iceland-crowdsourced-constitution/?utm_source=feedburner&utm_ medium=feed&utm_campaign=Feed%3A+Mashable+%28Mashable %29.

3. Some experts insist that this was the worst financial collapse in the world's economic history.

4. Over 500 Icelandic men and women stood for the 25 open spots. Those who were eventually elected represented a wide variety of professions and backgrounds, from pastor to journalist to teacher to mathematician. There were farmers and filmmakers, students and architects. The physicians outnumbered the lawyers 3 to 2.

5. It is clear from the Amendment Article (Article V in the original 1787 Constitution) that Congress, when pushed by two-thirds of the states, retains the authority to call a constitutional convention.

6. Christopher Phillips, *Constitutional Café: Jefferson's Brew for a True Revolution* (New York: Norton, 2012).

7. Larry J. Sabato, *A More Perfect Constitution: Why the Constitution Must Be Revised: Ideas to Inspire a New Generation* (New York: Walker, 2007), 226.

8. Ibid., 227.

9. Ibid., 228.

10. Ibid., 228–229.

11. American Bar Association, Special Constitutional Convention Study Committee, *Amendment of the Constitution by the Convention Method under Article V* (Chicago: American Bar Association, 1974).

12. Sabato, *More Perfect Constitution*, p. 211.

13. Ibid., 212.

14. Jamiles Lartey, "Conservatives Call for Constitutional Intervention Last Seen 230 Years Ago," *Guardian*, August 11, 2018, https://www.theguardian.com/us-news/2018/aug/11/conservatives-call-for-constitutional-convention-alec.

15. Partisanship has always been part of the American political landscape, but the entrenchment of party representatives (in Congress and elsewhere) over the last two decades has been particularly noticeable.

16. W. Douglas Banks, "We Are All in the Room," *HuffPost*, July 11, 2017, https://www.huffpost.com/author/rev-w-douglas-banks.

17. That's a historically high number. The news isn't any better when we dig down and examine the specific institutions of American government. Seventy-six percent of American voters—including 70% of Republicans and 83% of Democrats—believe it is "too risky" to give the President any more power. More unsettling perhaps is the intractability of the American people. Fewer than half of all Americans (44%) prefer politicians to "compromise" to get things done; 54% would prefer their elected officials to simply walk away from the table rather than budge on any agenda item. See Carroll Doherty, "Key Findings on

Americans' Views of the U.S. Political System and Democracy," Pew Research Center, April 26, 2018, https://www.pewresearch.org/fact-tank/2018/04/26/key-findings-on-americans-views-of-the-u-s-political-system-and-democracy.

18. Congress' approval rating is at a historic low. The numbers are alarming. At no point in the entire calendar year of 2018 did Gallup's "favorability" rating for federal lawmakers eclipse the 25% mark. Think about that. The Gallup organization tracks this particular measurement every two weeks, and never did more than one in four Americans approve of Congress' performance. Relatedly, Gallup traced Congress' "disapproval" rating, and it never dipped below a whopping 73%. Three out of every four voters in the United States believe that the country's federal legislative branch is ineffective and dysfunctional. And those numbers did not improve much in 2019. The highest congressional approval rating that year was 26%. Moreover, the perception among a vast majority of Americans is that a whole new slate of lawmakers would reverse those pitiful survey results. A recent Rasmussen report found that 74% of likely voters "favor establishing term limits for all members of Congress." Just 13% oppose that measure. See Gallup, *Congress and the Public*, 2020, https://news.gallup.com/poll/1600/congress-public.aspx; and "More Voters Than Ever Want Term Limits for Congress," *Rasmussen Reports*, October 26, 2016, https://www.rasmussenreports.com/public_content/politics/general_politics/october_2016/more_voters_than_ever_want_term_limits_for_congress.

19. Constitution of Virginia, 1776, Article V.

20. This rule may have been partially responsible for the ineffectiveness of the Articles of Confederation and the federal legislature that document created.

21. Casey Burgat, "Five Reasons to Oppose Congressional Term Limits," Brookings Institution, January 18, 2018, https://www.brookings.edu/blog/fixgov/2018/01/18/five-reasons-to-oppose-congressional-term-limits.

22. "How Many States Have Term Limits on Their Legislatures?" U.S. Term Limits, June 8, 2018, https://www.termlimits.com/state-legislative-term-limits.

23. Burgat, "Five Reasons to Oppose Congressional Term Limits."

24. A 2013 Gallup survey found that 75% of Americans "would vote for congressional term limits" and only 21% would not. Lydia Saad, "Americans Call for Term Limits, End to Electoral College," Gallup, January 18, 2013, https://news.gallup.com/poll/159881/americans-call-term-limits-end-electoral-college.aspx.

25. Since 1950, the average incumbency rate for candidates in House elections has been 94%. See Tom Murse, "Do Members of Congress Ever Lose Re-Election?" *ThoughtCo*, July 13, 2019, https://www.thoughtco .com/do-congressmen-ever-lose-re-election-3367511.

26. *Federalist* 52.

27. A. E. Dick Howard, "State Constitutions and the Environment," *Virginia Law Review* 58, 2 (February 1972): 193.

28. See Dan L. Gildor, "Preserving the Priceless: A Constitutional Amendment to Empower Congress to Preserve, Protect, and Promote the Environment," *Ecology Law Quarterly* 32, no. 4 (2005): 821.

29. See Howard, "State Constitutions and the Environment."

30. The New York State Constitution, for instance, references the Raquette Lake surface reservoir, the solar power farm in St. Lawrence County, a Long Lake forest preserve, and mineral sampling by NYCO Minerals, Inc., among dozens of other initiatives and resources.

31. See Emily Zackin, *Looking for Rights in All the Wrong Places: Why State Constitutions Contain America's Positive Rights* (Princeton, NJ: Princeton University Press, 2013).

32. Email exchange with Michael Brune, August–September 2019. All quotations from Brune are from this exchange.

33. Adams was, of course, not at the 1787 Philadelphia Convention; I am drawing here on his reputation, mainly forged as a delegate to the Continental Congress, of speaking his mind and challenging his colleagues.

34. Sanford Levinson, *Our Undemocratic Constitution: Where the Constitution Goes Wrong (And How We the People Can Correct It)* (New York: Oxford University Press, 2006), 50.

35. Author's interview with Sanford Levinson, September 4, 2019.

36. Levinson. *Our Undemocratic Constitution*, 160.

37. Author's interview with Sanford Levinson. See also Sanford Levinson, *Framed: America's 51 Constitutions and the Crisis of Governance* (New York: Oxford University Press, 2012); and Cynthia Levinson and Sanford Levinson, *Fault Lines in the Constitution: The Framers, Their Fights, and the Flaws That Affect Us Today* (Atlanta: Peachtree, 2017).

38. Author's interview with Sanford Levinson.

39. It was, for him, especially critical in light of the Trump presidency.

40. Author's interview with Sanford Levinson, September 4, 2019.

41. Ibid.

42. Among these groups was National Popular Vote, Inc., a nonprofit organization pushing for the National Popular Vote Interstate

Compact, an agreement by states that they would commit their electoral votes to the winner of the *national* popular vote, not their individual state vote. Thus far, fifteen states and the District of Columbia, possessing 196 electoral votes altogether, have signed the compact.

43. Myra Adams, "Why One Six-Year Presidential Term Would Be Good for America," *Daily Beast,* July 11, 2017, https://www.thedailybeast.com/why-one-six-year-presidential-term-would-be-good-for-america.

44. To put that figure into perspective, consider that all but the four most populous states in the Union, and all but ten of the forty-eight independent European nations, have fewer than 12.5 million inhabitants.

45. Allen is one of the few academics whose thoughts regularly cross over to mainstream America. In addition to her teaching, she is a frequent contributor on the *Washington Post* editorial pages, writing about everything from the founding to the current state of America's civil rights movement.

46. Danielle Allen, "We Are in Our Articles of Confederation Moment," *Washington Post*, July 25, 2019, https://www.washingtonpost.com/opinions/we-are-in-our-articles-of-confederation-moment/2019/07/25/93bd43c4-ae4e-11e9-8e77-03b30bc29f64_story.html?utm_term=.9d50cb2ee39f.

47. Allen reminds us of the history of congressional apportionment. Article I, Section 2 of the original 1787 Constitution required that "the number of Representatives [in the House] not exceed one for every thirty-thousand [citizens]." How times have changed. Each congressional representative in the twenty-first century represents approximately 750,000 citizens. Even James Madison's failed proposal to include an amendment requiring that congressional districts not exceed 50,000 citizens is distantly in the rearview mirror. See Allen, "We Are in Our Articles of Confederation Moment."

48. Allen, "We Are in Our Articles of Confederation Moment."

49. Robert W. Glover and Amy Fried, "Maine's Ranked-Choice Voting Experiment Continues," *American Prospect*, November 20, 2018, https://prospect.org/article/maine's-ranked-choice-voting-experiment-continues.

50. See Convention of States, "Historic Simulation," 2016, https://conventionofstates.com/cos-simulation.

51. Gallup, *Abortion,*" 2020, https://news.gallup.com/poll/1576/abortion.aspx.

52. Roe v. Wade, 410 U.S. 113 (1973).

53. The Senate Judiciary Committee at the time was charged with the responsibility of reviewing the Hatch-Eagleton proposal. After

considerable debate, the committee sent the measure to the full Senate without an official endorsement. The committee vote was 9 to 9, in part because two staunchly pro-life Senators—Joe Biden (D-DE) and Alan Simpson (R-WY)—decided at the last minute to oppose the draft amendment. For the co-sponsors, however, holding debate in the full Senate was the prize. Senators Hatch (R-UT) and Eagleton (D-MO) were aware that the odds of passage were slim. They wanted the debate. In the end, the Senate rejected the amendment 50 to 49, far short of the 67 votes it takes to move any proposed constitutional alteration to the states. But it was the closest the country has ever come to a constitutional amendment banning abortion.

54. *A Timeline of Lesbian, Gay, Bisexual, and Transgender History in the United States*, https://www.gsafewi.org/wp-content/uploads/US-LGBT -Timeline-UPDATED.pdf.

55. See Bowers v. Hardwick, 478 U.S. 186 (1986).

56. See Romer v. Evans, 517 U.S. 620 (1996); and Lawrence v. Texas, 539 U.S. 558 (2003).

57. See U.S. v. Windsor, 570 U.S. 744 (2013); and Obergefell v. Hodges (2015).

58. Today, survey data points in favor of LGBTQ+ rights. Seventy-three percent of Americans believe that "gay or lesbian relations among consenting adults should be legal," while 26% believe they should not. Similarly, 63% of Americans prefer that the law recognize same-sex marriage, while 36% do not. That number is a dramatic improvement from 2005 when 68% of Americans argued that same-sex marriages should *not* be valid. Gallup, *Gay and Lesbian Rights*, 2020, https://news. gallup.com/poll/1651/gay-lesbian-rights.aspx.

59. Josh Richman, "Welcome to Shasta County, California's Gun-Buying Capital," *Mercury News*, March 21, 2013, updated August 12, 2016, https://www.mercurynews.com/2013/03/21/welcome-to-shasta -county-californias-gun-buying-capital.

60. Kim Parker, Juliana Menasce Horowitz, Ruth Igielnik, J. Baxter Oliphant, and Anna Brown, "America's Complex Relationship with Guns," Pew Research Center, June 22, 2017, https://www.pewsocialtrends .org/2017/06/22/americas-complex-relationship-with-guns.

61. Austin Sarat and Jonathan Obert, "What Both Sides Don't Get about American Gun Culture," *Politico*, August 4, 2019, https://www .politico.com/magazine/story/2019/08/04/mass-shooting-gun-culture -227502.

62. Ibid.

63. Beau Breslin, *From Words to Worlds: Exploring Constitutional*

Functionality (Baltimore, MD: Johns Hopkins University Press, 2009), 115.

64. Ibid., 128.

65. Attempts at African American reparations date back to the Civil War, when Union General William Tecumseh Sherman called for each slave family to receive 40 acres and the loan of a mule. Later, during Reconstruction, Andrew Johnson vetoed legislation that would have distributed the land (and the mule) to former slaves. For the past 160 years, several attempts have been made to extend reparations to the descendants of former slaves. At various times, the push for reparations has been more intense, especially after other groups—American Indians and Japanese Americans, in particular—have successfully secured some form of reparations. See Constitutional Rights Foundation, *Reparations for Slavery Reading*, n.d., https://www.crf-usa.org/brown-v-board -50th-anniversary/reparations-for-slavery-reading.html.

66. For a thorough treatment of constitutional preambles, see Sanford Levinson, *Framed*, 55–74.

67. South Africa has the most obvious example. Its Constitution begins:

> We, the people of South Africa
> Recognize the injustices of our past;
> Honour those who suffered for justice and freedom in our land;
> Respect those who have worked to build and develop our country; and
> Believe that South Africa belongs to all who live in it, united in our
> diversity.
> We therefore, through our freely elected representatives, adopt this
> Constitution as the supreme law of the Republic, so as to–
> Heal the divisions of the past and establish a society based on
> democratic values, social justice and fundamental human rights;
> Lay the foundation for a democratic and open society in which
> government is based on the will of the people and every citizen
> is equally protected by law;
> Improve the quality of life of all citizens and free the potential of
> each person; and
> Build a united and democratic South Africa able to take its rightful
> place as a sovereign state in the family of nations.

68. For example, "We the People of the United States . . ."

69. See Liav Orgad, "The Preamble in Constitutional Interpretation," *International Journal of Constitutional Law* 8, no. 4 (October 2010), 714–738.

70. Levinson is even more direct. He writes of America's Preamble: "it is the *single most important part* of the Constitution. The reason is simple: it announces the *point* of the entire enterprise." Levinson, *Our Undemocratic Constitution*, 13.

71. See Plato, *The Laws*, ed. Trevor Saunders (New York; Penguin Classics, 2005), 137–145, 424–429.

72. Gallup conducted a simple survey to measure the population's understanding of basic constitutional and political facts. The results weren't impressive. Only 17% of American could identify the current Chief Justice of the United States. Around half of all Americans couldn't even identify the judiciary as the third branch of the federal government, while a meager 59% knew that each state retains two Senate seats. Only one in three citizens recognized the name of the Vice President. That sobering survey, combined with those from the Constitution Center and other venues, reveals a certain American ignorance about the political and constitutional landscape. Basic concepts about their Republic and the structure of its government elude many Americans. Indeed, Madison, who insisted that a free nation is possible only with an educated populace, would be frustrated by the widespread lack of awareness. George H. Gallup Jr., "How Many Americans Know U.S. History? Part I," October 21, 2003, https://news.gallup.com/poll/9526/how-many-americans-know-us-history-part.aspx.

73. Robert D. Putnam, *Bowling Alone: The Collapse and Revival of American Community* (New York: Simon and Schuster, 2000).

EPILOGUE

1. Thomas Friedman, "The American Civil War—Part II," *Seattle Times*, October 2, 2018, https://www.seattletimes.com/opinion/the-american-civil-war-part-ii.

2. Michael Bloomberg's reference to Trump as a "barking clown" is a case in point. See, e.g., Eileen Sullivan, "'Mass of Dead Energy' vs. 'Barking Clown,'" *New York Times*, February 13, 2020.

3. Surely, Jefferson would be particularly pleased with these states because he maintained that a generation lasts roughly nineteen years.

Index